☀ CYCLE	☾ SHADOW	◉ TASK	...TION
Roots & Foundations	Addictions →	Practicing Self-Care (Core Values) →	Abundance
Gifts from the Inner Child	Neglecting Needs	Claiming Inner Validation (Emotional Fluency)	Pleasure, Belonging
Nurturing Empowerment	Defenses	Fealty to Self (Boundaries)	Independence
Union & Partnerships	Core Issues	Living with Heart (The Inner Nurturers)	Unconditional Love
Shining Truth & Creativity	Subpersonalities	Reflecting Archetypes Within (Choice)	Truth
Visioning Self	Core Negative Beliefs	Crafting Personal Mandate (Resilience)	Reality
Effects of Gratitude	Key Lesson	Surrender to Inner Growth (Service)	Wisdom
Healing from Loss	Ungrieved Losses	Finding the Meaning (Remembering)	Universality

D1160990

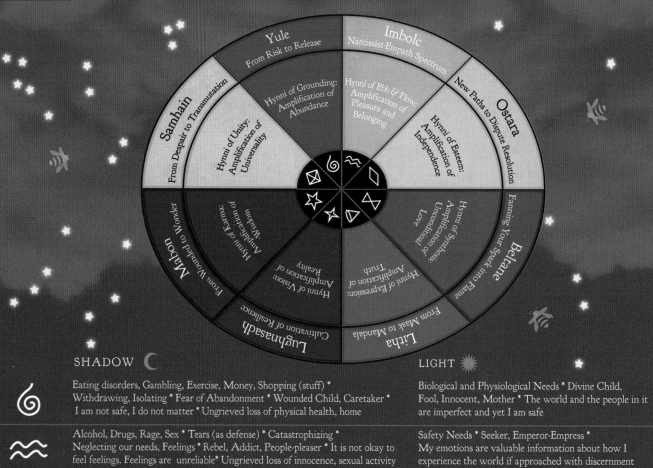

Wheel diagram contents (from top, clockwise):

- Yule — From Risk to Release
- Imbolc — Narcissist-Empath Spectrum
- Ostara — New Paths to Dispute Resolution
- Beltane — Fanning Your Spark into Flame
- Litha — From Mask to Mandala
- Lughnasadh — Cultivation of Resilience
- Mabon — From Wounded to Wonder
- Samhain — From Despair to Transmutation

Inner ring:
- Hynni of Grounding: Amplification of Abundance
- Hynni of Ebb & Flow: Amplification of Pleasure and Belonging
- Hynni of Esteem: Amplification of Independence
- Hynni of Synthesis: Amplification of Unconditional Love
- Hynni of Expression: Amplification of Truth
- Hynni of Vision: Amplification of Reality
- Hynni of Karma: Amplification of Wisdom
- Hynni of Unity: Amplification of Universality

	SHADOW ☾	LIGHT ☀
୬	Eating disorders, Gambling, Exercise, Money, Shopping (stuff) * Withdrawing, Isolating * Fear of Abandonment * Wounded Child, Caretaker * I am not safe, I do not matter * Ungrieved loss of physical health, home	Biological and Physiological Needs * Divine Child, Fool, Innocent, Mother * The world and the people in it are imperfect and yet I am safe
≈	Alcohol, Drugs, Rage, Sex * Tears (as defense) * Catastrophizing * Neglecting our needs, Feelings * Rebel, Addict, People-pleaser * It is not okay to feel feelings. Feelings are unreliable* Ungrieved loss of innocence, sexual activity	Safety Needs * Seeker, Emperor-Empress * My emotions are valuable information about how I experience the world if approached with discernment
◇	Work, Power, Shopping (status) * Anger (as defense) * Difficulty resolving conflict, Low self-esteem * Victim, Bully, Pillar of Strength * I am unworthy, I am powerless * Ungrieved loss of job, freedom	Esteem Needs * Warrior * I am valuable. My worth is non-negotiable
⧖	Love, Relationship, Healing * Blame* Over-responsible, Difficulty giving or receiving * Rescuer, Fixer, Martyr * My pain is my fault. I am unlovable * Ungrieved loss of relationship (divorce or separation)	Love Needs * Love, Healer, Servant * I am loved, loveable, and loving. I embrace both my strengths and my flaws
◁	Smoking, Talking * Humor, Sarcasm * Being real, Seen and heard * Saboteur, Judge * What I say and do does not matter * Ungrieved loss of culture	Aesthetic Needs * Communicator, Ruler * My voice has an impact whether I see the results or not
✦	Gaming, Computers, Social media, Entertainment * Justifying, Rationalizing, Intellectualizing, Minimizing, Denial * All-or-nothing thinking * Perfectionist, Critic * I am a failure * Ungrieved loss of career (retirement)	Cognitive Needs * Visionary, Magician * I am capable
☆	Meditation, Prayer, Spiritual bypass * Forgiving * High tolerance for inappropriate behavior * Guru * Spirit has deserted me. There is no meaning to the chaos and pain. * Ungrieved loss through death (including suicide, miscarriage, abortion, accident)	Self-actualization Needs * Sage * I am always guided whether I make the connection or not
◈	Guides, Angels, Psychics * Dissociating * Not grieving ungrieved losses, hurts, and traumas * Alien * I don't belong here * Ungrieved loss of traditions	Transcendence Needs * Destroyer, Creatrix * I am already home

Praise for *The Noble Art*

"A well-crafted, powerful combination of ritual, energy work, meditative journeying, and deep psychological insight. Author Tiffany Lazic guides the seeker through a multilayered path of nature's cycles with practical and spiritual techniques for real transformation and growth. This book is a must-have for anyone truly interested in achieving inner alchemy: transmutation of the shadows into the light."

—Michael Furie, author of *Spellcasting: Beyond the Basics*

"A complex and comprehensive guide, map, and compass for the inner and outer journey through the great seasonal rounds of our lives. Tiffany Lazic offers a wealth of history, lore, meditation, and ritual—tools accessible to all readers and of great benefit to practitioners working with clients. Best of all, as I read, I felt the presence of the author as a compassionate witness who knows her terrain intimately and understands the courage it takes to face and embrace our whole selves."

—Elizabeth Cunningham, author of *The Maeve Chronicles*

"This is an exceptional book, written with a great depth of passion and drawn from years of experience… For those of us with more experience, she also provides guidance on how to pass on that insight and healing energy to our clients, with great effect… Delivered with a joy in her subject that is felt on every page, this powerful work is not only nourishment for the spirit but a joy to read as well."

—Danu Forest, Celtic scholar, magical teacher, and
traditional wisewoman; author of
Wild Magic and *Celtic Tree Magic*

"Combining elements of psychology, alchemy, druidic principles, and good common sense, *The Noble Art* is a profound guide to and through our challenges and joys… Altogether, *The Noble Art* is a master stroke from a masterful teacher. Highly recommended."

—Jenya T. Beachy, author of *The Secret Country of Yourself*

"Tiffany Lazic has crafted a psychospiritual masterpiece of personal practice in *The Noble Art*… Well-organized and richly detailed, *The Noble Art* provides the seeker with abundant tools to catalyze self-transformation, including prompts for reflection, meditative practices, guided journeys, and ritual experiences."

—Jhenah Telyndru, MA, author of *Avalon Within* and *The Mythic Moons of Avalon*

"A remarkable collection of rituals, exercises, and techniques to use the power of the eight holidays as an integrative framework for the Great Work. This is not a book that you simply read, it is one that you think about and work through to become more fully and truly yourself."

—Ivo Dominguez Jr., author of *Four Elements of the Wise*

"Backed by years of practice and decorated with pearls of infinite wisdom, Lazic's latest offering is a profoundly transformational journey into the self that is simultaneously challenging, magical, and cathartic all at the same time… After reading this book and employing its exercises, a brighter and wiser 'you' will rise, noble and transformed."

—Kristoffer Hughes, head of the Anglesey Druid Order, author of *Cerridwen: Celtic Goddess of Inspiration*

"Lazic has deftly woven the threads of transpersonal psychology with experiential practices, exercises, and rituals to create a truly unique psychospiritual healing journey that is rooted in the cycles of the Wheel of the Year. At once empowering, cathartic, and illuminating, *The Noble Art* is an indispensable and comforting guide on the path to greater self-understanding. As a registered counselor, I enthusiastically recommend this book to both practitioners and clients alike."

—Danielle Blackwood, author of *A Lantern in the Dark*

"A readable, hands-on manual and guidebook for living a satisfying, rich, and joyful life… It is an essential and valuable resource for anyone seriously interested in exploring and facing the challenge of shadow work."

—Dodie Graham McKay, author of *Earth Magic*

The
NOBLE ART

About the Author

Tiffany Lazic (RP, BAA) is a Registered Psychotherapist and Spiritual Director with a private practice in individual, couples, and group therapy in Kitchener (Canada) and internationally online. She completed training in Spiritual Psychotherapy and Spiritual Direction at the Transformational Arts College of Spiritual and Holistic Training in Toronto (Canada), where she also taught in the college's Discovering the Total Self Program, Spiritual Psychotherapy Training Program, Spiritual Directorship Program, and the Esoteric Studies Program. She served as a staff psychotherapist in the college's counseling clinic and as a case supervisor to intern psychotherapists. She continues to teach at the college as a guest facilitator.

An international presenter, retreat facilitator, and keynote speaker, Tiffany has conducted workshops and retreats for many conferences and organizations in Canada, the US, Mexico, the UK, and India. She was one of the co-creators and co-organizers of Kitchener's SPARKS (Seeking Passion, Adventure, Renewal, Knowledge & Spirit) Symposium, which ran from 2010–2012.

Tiffany is the founder and owner of the Hive and Grove Centre for Holistic Wellness (Kitchener), through which she created two self-development courses, The Great Work: Patterns of Conscious Living and Spiritual Language of the Divine, and an immersive meditation collage inner landscape journey course, Drawing Down Divine. Tiffany offers private Hynni sessions as well as classes in Hynni practice for self-development and training for practitioners. For more information on Tiffany or The Hive and Grove, visit www.hiveandgrove.ca.

TIFFANY LAZIC

the NOBLE ART

From Shadow to Essence Through the Wheel of the Year

Llewellyn Publications • Woodbury, Minnesota

FIRST EDITION
First Printing, 2021

Cover design by Shira Atakpu
Editing by Holly Vanderhaar
Interior art on pages 88, 160, and 383–388 by Wen Hsu; all other interior art by the Llewellyn Art
    Department

Llewellyn Publications is a registered trademark of Llewellyn Worldwide Ltd.

Library of Congress Cataloging-in-Publication Data
Names: Lazic, Tiffany, author.
Title: The noble art : from shadow to essence through the wheel of the year
    / Tiffany Lazic.
Description: FIRST EDITION | Woodbury, Minnesota : Llewellyn Publicatios,
    2021. | Includes bibliographical references.
Identifiers: LCCN 2021022391 (print) | LCCN 2021022392 (ebook) | ISBN
    9780738764931 (paperback) | ISBN 9780738765051 (ebook)
Subjects: LCSH: Religious calendars—Neopaganism. | Hermetism. | Occultism.
    | Spiritual life. | Psychology—Miscellanea.
Classification: LCC BF1999 .L3245 2021 (print) | LCC BF1999 (ebook) | DDC
    203/.6—dc23
LC record available at https://lccn.loc.gov/2021022391
LC ebook record available at https://lccn.loc.gov/2021022392

Llewellyn Publications
A Division of Llewellyn Worldwide Ltd.
2143 Wooddale Drive
Woodbury, MN 55125-2989
www.llewellyn.com

Printed in the United States of America

Other Books by Tiffany Lazic

The Great Work

Disclaimer

The meditative and energy healing approaches in this book are not a substitute for psychotherapy or counseling, nor are they a substitute for medical treatment. They are intended to provide clients with information about their inner workings that can add another helpful dimension to treatment with a trained medical or mental health professional, as their circumstances may warrant.

Contents

Acknowledgments   xiii

*Introduction: From Shadow to Essence Through
    the Wheel of the Year   1*

PART ONE: Cycle One (December 21–January 31)
From Risk to Release

ONE: Yule and the Divine Child   23

TWO: The Shadow Trap of Addiction   27

THREE: The Light of True Essence   35

FOUR: Journey to Encounter the Dragon Meditation   41

FIVE: The Hermetic Concept of Universal Law Contemplation   45

SIX: Welcome the Divine Child Ritual   49

SEVEN: Be Excellent to Yourself   55

PART TWO: Cycle Two (February 1–March 14)
The Narcissist/Empath Spectrum

EIGHT: Imbolc and the Inner Child   59

NINE: The New Shadow Face of Codependency   63

TEN: The Light of Non-Duality   71

ELEVEN: Journey to Meet Grandfather Sun and
    Grandmother Moon Meditation   77

TWELVE: The Hermetic Principle of Gender Contemplation   81

THIRTEEN: Cleansing and Purification Ritual   85

FOURTEEN: Love Is the Highest Law   91

PART THREE: Cycle Three (March 22–May 2)
New Paths to Dispute Resolution

FIFTEEN: Ostara and Celebration of Life   95

SIXTEEN: The Shadow of the Enemy at the Gate   99

SEVENTEEN: The Light of Boundaries   107

EIGHTEEN: Journey to Encounter Your Personal Power Animals Meditation   115

NINETEEN: The Hermetic Principle of Cause and Effect Contemplation   119

TWENTY: Planting the Seed of Intention Ritual   123

TWENTY-ONE: You Are Whole Within   127

PART FOUR: Cycle Four (May 3–June 13)
Fanning Your Spark into Flame

TWENTY-TWO: Beltane and the Passion for Life   133

TWENTY-THREE: The Wounded Heart's Shadow   137

TWENTY-FOUR: The Light Heart's Gift   143

TWENTY-FIVE: Journey to Honor the World Tree Meditation   149

TWENTY-SIX: The Hermetic Principle of Rhythm Contemplation   153

TWENTY-SEVEN: Weaving Passion Ritual   157

TWENTY-EIGHT: Honor Diversity   163

PART FIVE: Cycle Five (June 21–August 1)
From Mask to Mandala

TWENTY-NINE: Litha and the Inner Adult   167

THIRTY: The Shadow Mask of Subpersonalities   171

THIRTY-ONE: The Light of Archetypes   177

THIRTY-TWO: Creating a Mandala Prayer Bundle Meditation   183

THIRTY-THREE: The Hermetic Principle of Polarity Contemplation   187

Thirty-four: Honoring Self Ritual   193

Thirty-five: Walk Your Talk   199

Part Six: Cycle Six (August 2–September 12)
The Cultivation of Resilience

Thirty-six: Lughnasadh and Life's Harvest   205

Thirty-seven: The Shadow of Soul Debris   209

Thirty-eight: The Lightness of Soul Decluttering   215

Thirty-nine: Wyrdwalking Meditation   221

Forty: The Hermetic Principle of Vibration Contemplation   225

Forty-one: Illumined Vision Ritual   229

Forty-two: Gaze Upon Earth with Clarity of Light   235

Part Seven: Cycle Seven (September 20–October 31)
From Wounded to Wonder

Forty-three: Mabon and the Higher Self   239

Forty-four: The Shadow of the Wounded Healer   243

Forty-five: The Light of the Wonder Healer   249

Forty-six: The Bridge Between the Worlds Meditation   255

Forty-seven: The Hermetic Principle of Correspondence Contemplation   259

Forty-eight: The Golden Gratitude Ritual   265

Forty-nine: Practice Gratitude and Acts of Thankful Appreciation   269

Part Eight: Cycle Eight (November 1–December 12)
From Despair to Transmutation

Fifty: Samhain and the Zero Point   275

Fifty-one: The Shadow Fear of the Dark Specter   279

Fifty-two: The Lightness of Being   285

Fifty-three: Resting in the Cosmic Egg Meditation   289

Fifty-four: The Hermetic Principle of Mentalism Contemplation   293

Fifty-five: Embraced by the Dark Ritual   297

Fifty-six: We Are All Part of the All   301

Part Nine: The Noble Art in Practice
Hynni Energy Healing for Practitioners

Fifty-seven: Session Considerations and Ethics   305

Fifty-eight: Pre-Session Assessment   311

Fifty-nine: Scripts for Hynni Energy Healing Sessions   321

Sixty: Hynni Harmonics   361

Conclusion: The Sweet Song of the Self   369

Appendix A: Chart of Cycle Correspondences   371

Appendix B: Cheat Sheets for Hynni Energy Healing Sessions   373

Appendix C: Sample Hynni Practitioner Session Notes Sheet   379

Appendix D: Ritual Preparation   381

Appendix E: Steps for a Three-Armed Brigid's Cross (Cycle Two Ritual)   383

Appendix F: Steps for Branch Weaving (Cycle Four Ritual)   385

Appendix G: Steps for God's Eye Weaving (Cycle Six Ritual)   387

Bibliography   389

Acknowledgments

As any author knows, writing a book is such a paradoxical endeavor. It is, at its heart, a completely solitary act, requiring hour upon hour of one's own company, being in one's own head, following odd nudges down rabbit holes that may prove to be fruitless ventures or abundant motherlodes. It feels very much like existing between the worlds, with one foot in a reality shared by others and the other foot in a wisp of a world that is being coaxed into being. Solitary as it may be, it is an endeavor which certainly benefits enormously by having supports and champions along the way, not only to help one stay tethered to solid ground throughout the process, but also to help sustain the spirit through what is always a far longer process than anticipated.

I am so grateful to my book family. I am grateful to Elysia Gallo, Lauryn Heineman, Holly Vanderhaar, and Donna Burch-Brown for the incredible vision they bring to the work. The grace of their insight and feedback is undeniably invaluable. The work they do, to me, is a wonder and they are absolutely brilliant at it. I am grateful to my bookish colleagues, most especially Jhenah Telyndru and Kristoffer Hughes, who always had the time for an encouraging word and a supportive nudge, even being half lost in their own wispy worlds and rabbit holes.

I am grateful to my own family, both of blood and of heart, who not only encouraged along the way, but held up a light for me to follow in the particularly dark moments. Now, as always, they have guided with impeccable example and courageous experience. To Linda, Wendy, Cecilie, Adrianna, Emily, Sue, and Elinor.

I am grateful for a tribe of Sisters who nourished and nurtured in countless ways. There is almost nothing like stumbling upon a full pannier of goodies to feed the soul when one is lost on the twisting, turning paths. To Nicole, Sara, Karen, Alexa, Sydney, Kate, Lori, Diana, Kelly, Sharone, Elisa, and many, many more too countless to name.

I am grateful to my wise, wild at heart colleague, Carrie Lee, for being a willing and insightful guinea pig. Her reflections every step of the way, chapter by chapter, word by word, through the lens of her astute eyes were so vital to the process—and very often they were the impetus needed to dive ever onward. And to my discerning, soul-seeker colleague, Ben Stimpson, for providing those razor-sharp reflections that helped the honing process.

I am grateful to my son, Connor, who carries the very spirit of this book indelibly with him at all times, for being its guiding star. It is not always those who know how they are supporting who offer the brightest illumination. And I am ever grateful to my husband, George, for being the solid rock beneath my feet. When I needed another knot in the tether line, he was there. When I needed a puff of air under my wings, he was there. There has been no greater or more constant companion on this—and so many other—adventures.

In my first book, I thanked my teachers, all those who have paved the way and dropped the kernels of wisdom that lead me along this path. Their lessons and teachings have unquestionably shaped the course of my life and my gratitude for that never wanes. To those I add those teachers who come to me a different way: my clients, my students, and all those I have met in so many ways, who have struggled and still do struggle with their own Shadows. They have been with me, in my heart, every step of the way.

My eyes may have faced forward toward the words as I wrote, but my heart was always filled with those who stood behind me as I did.

I dedicate this book to my beloved brother,
Hugh Lacey.

Who knew well how to sit in the place
where Awen, Matter, and Magic meet
and always did so with such great
humor, compassion, and curiosity.

Introduction:
From Shadow to Essence
Through the Wheel of the Year

There is an indescribable sense of relief that comes when one finishes a herculean undertaking. I imagine it is much like running a marathon with the culmination of persistent effort resulting in the exquisite intertwining of depletion and elation. I certainly felt that upon the completion of writing *The Great Work: Self-Knowledge and Healing Through the Wheel of the Year*: such a wave of release, surrender, and gratitude. If I recall correctly, when the work was done and toddling off on its foal-like newborn legs, my overriding sense was "I am grateful for that experience *and* I am grateful it is behind me." I felt blessed for the opportunity to share some of what was in my mind, heart, and soul and I was fairly certain that I had said absolutely everything that I wanted or needed to say.

As is also usually the case in moments of relieved certainty, it was not long after that that I began to feel the tentative little knock at the back of my mind. A little murmur that said "You haven't said everything yet. There is more that needs to be shared." It was easy enough to ignore for the moment, but, after a time, the tentative little knock became a full-on sharp RAP. There was a goddess who wanted in.

I have always felt that *The Great Work* is Arianrhod's book. As the Celtic goddess of the celestial cycles, she was with me through the entire writing. On those quavery occasions when I felt not equal to the task of the writing and I turned to my "mega-goddess oracle" (five separate goddess oracle decks combined in one massive bowl totaling more than two hundred cards), the goddess who showed up was always Arianrhod. It was unnerving, actually. In those moments, I always heard her message to be "Take a breath, stop your lollygagging, and write my book." I would take a deep breath and head back to the computer.

I knew, before I even knew the general shape of the second book, that it is Cerridwen's book. That sharp rap at the door in my mind had a distinctly Cerridwen feel to it. I was very happy with *The Great Work*, presenting as it does the different facets and reflections of the Wheel of the Year. I was happy to be able to capture the energy of each "spoke" and present how it is reflected within each of us personally and the arc of a life's journey universally. And yet, I felt that *The Great Work* was akin to lining up a slew of tasty ingredients on the counter in preparation of a sumptuous dish. Each ingredient was fabulous on its own, but the acquisition of all the ingredients does not equate to the dish itself. Something else needs to happen. The ingredients need to be acted upon. The steeping, the simmering, the stewing of the ingredients in a huge pot—a cauldron—needed to happen. The work of crafting ingredients into a "healing brew," a "nourishing stew," or a "soothing soup" requires techniques for application. It requires recipes. Cerridwen wanted her book as well.

For those unfamiliar with her tale, Cerridwen comes to us from Welsh tradition. There is much depth to her—far more than can be shared here—but one well-known story is of how she tried to accommodate for her son's physical shortcomings by crafting a brew, a year and a day in the making, that would bestow the blessings of Awen (Divine wisdom and inspiration) upon him. In this she enlisted the aid of an old blind man to stoke the fire, and a young boy, Gwion Bach, to stir the cauldron. At the very moment of the culmination of all the work that was intended for her son, whether by accident or design (stories differ), the three potent drops containing the gift of Awen fell to Gwion Bach. This event sparks a whole other chapter to the tale, but ultimately, it is this newly enlightened boy who undergoes transformation and rebirth to become Taliesin, the greatest of all bards.

To me, *The Great Work* and *The Noble Art* work together, very much in reflection of the Hermetic axiom "as above, so below." As Arianrhod's book, *The Great Work* focuses on the cycles themselves, the archetypal energies of the eight spokes that make up the annual seasonal pattern. It is "as above," following the sun on its own waxing and waning journey, presenting the *theory* or foundation for a seasonal experience of the self through a multitude of reflections. Each of the eight spokes is seen through the lens of eight Reflections, which together allow for a deeper entry into the archetypal energies at play within each individual Cycle. The *Mythological Reflection* presents the general theme and overarching guiding qualities. The *Elemental Reflection*, aligned with the physical realm, presents the vibrational range of the building blocks of existence from the solidity of earth to the all-permeating essence of Energy. The *Active Reflection*, also aligned with the physical realm, presents the activities that open us to the Cycle's archetypal themes on an experiential level. The *Developmental Reflection*, aligned with the emotional realm, presents each Cycle through the lens of Eric Erikson's Human Development model. The *Psychological Reflection*, also aligned with the emotional realm, presents the core Cycle theme through the inner lens of key emotional issues. The *Alchemical Reflection*, aligned with the mental realm, presents the progression through the alchemical stages of healing from "dark night of the soul" to attainment of the Philosopher's Stone. The *Energetic Reflection*, also aligned with the mental realm, presents each of the cycles through an association with the chakras, including the eighth Transpersonal Point or soul star chakra. The *Guidance Reflection*, aligned with the spiritual realm, presents different types of guides that may show up to support the journey to self-knowledge. The *Intuitive Reflection*, aligned with the spiritual realm, introduces the various tools for accessing insight that resonate with each of the Cycle themes.

Physical Realm	Elemental Reflection	Building blocks of manifest existence
	Active Reflection	Activities to access experientially
Emotional Realm	Developmental Reflection	Stages in development from child to adult
	Psychological Reflection	Core themes in emotional healing
Mental Realm	Alchemical Reflection	Stages of alchemical healing
	Energetic Reflection	Primary chakra system
Spiritual Realm	Guidance Reflection	Guides that introduce wisdom
	Intuitive Reflection	Tools for accessing insight

The Noble Art takes all those individual cycles of the spokes on the Wheel of the Year and drops them into the cauldron of experience. It is "as below," presenting the <u>application</u> or the craft of a seasonal experience of self. As Cerridwen's book, it introduces each Cycle as a mini transformation, inviting us to work more deeply with the material on a far more introspective and experiential level. It invites the journey from Shadow to Essence within each individual Cycle as one moves through the greater seasonal journey from Dark to Light and back again. It allows the bubbling and the simmering within each of the cycles through various techniques and exercises to turn all the separate ingredients into her wondrous brew.

My entire career has revolved around this relationship between Shadow and Essence. As a spiritual psychotherapist, my work has involved holding space for those who have found themselves lost in the dark of anxiety, depression, despair, confusion, resignation, and addiction. I have years of training behind me and a pouchful of techniques on my belt, but the truth is, over the years I have found the heart of my work truly lies in the ability to be comfortable standing with someone in their darkest places, holding the space and reassurance for them to explore without fear, holding up a beacon to invite a few steps toward a different space, if they choose to step in that direction. That is not to say that the training and techniques are not of great value in and of themselves, but there is a variable that is not inherent in either of those. Holding space for one who feels lost, empty, and bereft without trying to dive in with the answers requires an unwavering belief in the innate wisdom of the psyche. It requires trusting in the other person's own process, as challenging as it can be to observe; and being a mirror to the brilliance seen shining forth, as delicately or as strongly as it appears. It requires a fearless and faithful hand to steady the cauldron while witnessing another stirring themselves into authenticity.

Over the span of many years, in the course of much witnessing, I came to recognize that there were certain themes that seemed to show up at the same times of the year. Being "client-centered" in approach meant following the client's lead in terms of issue or topic being addressed in each session, but I found it absolutely fascinating that most clients seemed to land in very similar places, despite widely varied backgrounds, circumstances, and personalities. There was a fairly consistent presentation of grief around October, or renewed enthusiasm for a project in the spring, or a yearning for partnership (or addressing relationship issues) in May. As the universality of theme at certain times of the year became clear, I started to work more actively with those themes. It was this that culminated in *The Great Work: Self-Knowledge and Healing Through the Wheel of the Year.* Though *The Great Work* presents the main archetypal themes and key reflections that can guide the healing process through the cycle of the seasons, it also introduces the synthesis of these themes and reflections into a cohesive energy healing modality that I call Hynni. Pronounced "honey," *hynni* is the Welsh word for "energy." In the context of the eight Reflections, Hynni is the Active Reflection of Cycle Eight. It is an approach to energy healing that actively weaves the Earth cycles into relationship with higher vibrational energies, thus accommodating the full range of personal vibration from physical to energetic. *The Noble Art* takes this introduction to Hynni much further, illustrating the craft of this energy healing approach. It presents how blocked energy, held pain, or Shadow can show up in each of the seasonal cycles and offers several solid techniques for each cycle that invite the transmutation of Shadow to Essence. To draw upon another alchemical axiom, not only does *The Noble Art* drop the conceptual structure of the "above" (knowledge) into the cauldron of the "below" (experience), it stirs the personal "within" until there is insight into how that affects and is affected by that which lies "without" (wisdom).

Experience + Knowledge = Wisdom

Wisdom is the unerring awareness that comes from knowing that the truth is not "I think therefore I am," but "I feel therefore I am": the potential for the dramatic shift in perspective that comes from acknowledging the inherent wisdom of the emotional response to our experience as informed by a higher perspective. It is this shift that opens us to transformation, becoming the Self[1] we were always meant to be, the potent drops that are the completion of the brew. And it is this, the container of transformation, the ingredients to be transformed, and the resulting drops, that are represented in the healing approach of Hynni.

In exploring the movement from Dark to Light or Shadow to Essence that is presented for each cycle, *The Noble Art* invites the crafting of a new, solid bridge between

....

1. Carl Jung distinguished between the adapted self (mask or persona) and the individuated Self (autonomous and self-determined) by the use of the small or capital "s."

the "above" and the "below," the Earth and the Stars, as well as the "within" and the "without." As is clear in the ancient and familiar image of the taijitu (or as we tend to know it "the yin-yang symbol"), there is a bridge between the dark half and the light half, the line that snakes up the middle. There is a truth that lies between the two poles that invites the exploration of transformation, the sloughing off of the too-tight skin that the snake does so well.

Dark	Transformed	Light
Shadow	True Self	Spirit
Core Issue	Lesson/Learning	Higher Purpose
Unconscious	Conscious	Superconscious

If the taijitu reflects the relationship between Dark and Light from an Eastern perspective, the (arguably) modern Druidic Awen symbol reflects that same relationship through a slightly different lens. Purported to have been invented by Iolo Morganwg, an eighteenth-/nineteenth- century stonemason and collector of ancient manuscripts, this symbol represents the three Divine rays of Light that shine down to the below from the above. These individual rays carry three different energetics that have been interpreted in multiple ways, including the three Druidic grades of Bard, Ovate, and Druid; qualities of masculine, feminine, and neutral such as presented in Hermetic wisdom; or qualities such as are named in the Celtic triad "Three candles that illuminate every darkness: Truth, Nature, and Knowledge." In a slightly different manner than seen in the symbol of the taijitu, the central ray of the Awen serves as the bridge between those energies on either side, creating a powerful trinity that can also be reflective of our psycho-spiritual experience.

Land	Sea	Sky
Nature	Truth	Knowledge
Experience	Wisdom	Enlightenment
Physical	Emotional	Spiritual

Each in their own way, the central line of the taijitu and the center ray of the Awen serve as a bridge between the chthonic energies of the earthy, embodied, human experience and the higher vibrational essence of spiritual enlightenment. The sense of two opposing energies informing each other and finding synthesis around a central, anchoring energy is represented in a familiar image that has its roots all the way back to the time of the ancient Greeks. Associated with Hermes (Greek) and Hermes Trismegistus (Greco-Egyptian), the caduceus represents alchemical transmutation by showing these three energies in direct, engaged relationship with each other.

The Earth	The Bridge	The Stars
Chthonic	Psychospiritual	Cosmic
"As Below"	Synthesis	"As Above"
Transformation	Transmutation	Transcendence

The Noble Art presents each of these three perspectives—the Earth, the Stars, and the Bridge—as a key aspect on the path to healing and wholeness. With Hermes Trismegistus and his noble art of alchemy as the guide, the intertwining of "the Below" with "the Above" offers the potential to experience such profound healing that what is experienced goes beyond transformation into transmutation, change so profound that it affects one at the deepest core level.

Shadow/Shame → The Earth/As Below → The Stars/As Above → The Bridge/Synthesis

Stasis → Transformation → Transcendence → Transmutation

We experience *Stasis* when we are so afraid of the pain that lies in the Dark of the Shadow that we are terrified to change. We hold tight to old modes of behavior and interrelationship because we feel we do not have the strength or the wherewithal to be able to change. We crouch in the corner of the Shadow, trapped in the Dark, slowly experiencing an agonizing soul death as the possibilities for our lives become smaller, tighter, and more and more out of reach.

There are a lot of different challenges that can bring us to a place where we feel lost in the dark. The one absolute that I know of in my work as a psychotherapist is the common underlying foundation to all these different challenges: the internalized experience of shame. Shame is not the same as conscience. The admonition "Have you no shame?" is a cumbersome and inelegant call to conscience. It is a reminder that there is always a part of us that knows which course of action is going to keep us aligned to Higher Self or higher principles. That is not the same as the shame that drives a wedge between us and our Higher Self; that tells us that we are worthless and flawed and unlovable; that badgers and harangues us to hide our true face from the world. There is not a single one of us who has not—or does not—have an experience of <u>this</u> shame. It is divisive. It is isolating. It is rampant in epidemic proportions in the world, and it is something we rarely talk about.

This is the shame that sits in the belly as a low-grade nausea, intensifying to an urge to vomit when we feel exposed or called out or rejected.

This is the shame that sits on our shoulder calling out a laundry list of our wrongs twenty-four hours a day and giving us direction on the very narrow path we need to walk if anyone is ever going to see us as worthy of love and attention.

This is the shame that causes us to proceed ever so tentatively, ever so slowly through our lives, expecting it to jump out from behind every bush or wall to berate us with our inadequacies, even on those days when we feel that we have finally—finally!—given it the slip.

This is the shame that settles in our bowels like a dark, swirling poison, telling us to fear exposure and vulnerability because to be known is to guarantee rejection.

This is the shame that swoops us into a dizzying terrifying roller coaster in our stomachs when we are caught off guard by a situation that feels like a lightning-fast curveball thrown at our heads.

This is the shame that weighs on our heart, slowly petrifying it into stone, whispering to us that it is protecting us from being hurt when in reality it is preventing us from feeling loved.

This is the shame that fuels anxiety, seeing every situation as a potential threat to our delicate sense of self and compelling us to run even farther, jump even higher, dance even faster.

This is the shame that slams us into depression, taking the wind out of our sails and dropping us into solitary desolation and inertia.

This is the shame that tells us we will never be good enough, we will never be loved if people actually get to know us, that we are not safe in the world, and that, if we really want to get to the heart of the matter, we have no value, and our lives have no meaning.

Absolutely devastating. All of it. And absolute rubbish. All of it.

In the movement from Shadow to Essence, shame is the shackle that keeps us trapped in the Dark. Those trapped in this endless circle of pain and shame deserve so much compassion. It is a terrible way to live, and it does require a degree of solid ego strength to begin the process of challenging the Dark. We need to know that there is some chance of defeating the beast that guards the prison if we are going to attempt to break out of it.

Transformation comes when we are able to draw upon our inner resources and outer tools to challenge the Dark, release the shackles of shame, and embrace the Light of our Essence. It is this process that allows us to throw off the ill-fitting cloaks that have been placed upon us by others, claiming our empowerment back from the expectations of others. This, in and of itself, is victory. To live from this place is truly life-changing. It is the full experience of Transformation that gives us the experience of the efficacy of our tools such that we are able to confront and defeat the Dark again and again. Transformation is all about living from a place of self-determination, knowing that we alone have the power to choose the course of our own lives.

But, in the long process of the Soul's journey in life, there can come a time of realization that there is yet a further refinement in the experience of Self. When we are able to come to a place where we focus so completely on our Light that the Dark no longer has <u>any</u> power over us, we step into the experience of *Transcendence*. This path rises above the Dark to offer detached perspective and enlightened experience. It is not touched by the Dark. At times it may not even see the Dark. This is a beautiful expansive way to walk through the world, but it can potentially be problematic if one arrives at this stage without having fully experienced the challenges and growth offered by the process of Transformation.

Spiritual bypass is the result of "rising above" before one has truly "descended below." It has a strong tendency to deny the pain and discomfort, sometimes even the existence of the Shadow. It has a strong urge to box up certain emotions as "not spiritual" and refuse their guidance. It has an impulse to move from the discomfort of Shadow straight to the bliss of Enlightenment without the first step of anchoring Empowerment, which is necessary in order to develop a healthy ego. Spiritual bypass is as full of shame as if we were back in the prison of Stasis. It just offers a prettier cell. We need to face the Dark before we can transcend the Dark; otherwise, as Carl Jung presented, it will make itself known to us in unexpected and often calamitous ways. History is full of devastating harm done in spiritual circles or institutions that have not been able to face their own Shadow. Exploring the unhealthy, shame-based ego through Transformation before embracing the Light of Transcendence is the best way to ensure the devastation of spiritual bypass does not happen.

The movement from Stasis to Transformation is the monumental shift from being entrapped in our own negative self-perceptions to the inner experience of Empowerment. In challenging the Shadow and releasing our shame, we come to claim the truth of who we are. This is to live from a solid, centered solar plexus chakra, confident in our identity and our ability. This is "the Earth" snake of the caduceus, urging us to heal the pain of our human experiences.

The movement from Transformation to Transcendence expands the strength of Empowerment into the solid guidance of Enlightenment. In acknowledging our hard-won strengths and seeing them from the higher perspective of gift, lesson, and higher purpose, we shift to "the Stars" snake of the caduceus, seeing the whole of who we are and knowing how to skirt the dangers and pitfalls of shame. It is a beautiful place to land, and yet, from an alchemical perspective, it is not the final place to land. Though currently, there is a trend to focus on the attainment of Enlightenment, Alchemy offers yet another stage. In the healing journey, there is one more emanation to explore. There is the central column of the caduceus, that of synthesis.

Transmutation is the fusion of Transformation and Transcendence that results in such radical inner shifts that the Dark can never hold power over us again. It is an inner shift so complete that there is no possibility of going back to a way of being that you were before. The movement from Transcendence to Transmutation is reflected in a shift past Enlightenment into the embodiment of Engagement. Engagement does not "rise above." It courageously enters into the fray of life. With Transmutation, we know unquestionably that we are not defined by circumstances, and thus can open to life without fear. Engagement brings the process of alchemical Transmutation full circle as is illustrated in the stage of the "hero's journey" named "Return to the Ordinary World." And it holds an eternal gift: the wisdom to know that who you are is not a destination; that life is not a problem to be solved; that detachment is not necessarily the ultimate response; and that the sooner one releases the concept of "healed" as a final goal to be achieved, the better off one will be. It recognizes the profound gift that is this human life, even if it does contain pain, challenge, and muckiness. It is this experience of Engagement with the whole of life's experience, and the potential for a heart-centered, compassionate experience of self within that life that is the force behind *The Noble Art*.

How to Approach *The Noble Art*

As with *The Great Work*, this book is intended to be highly interactive and to serve as a guide for the inner journey as you cycle through the annual Grand Cycle from the dark days of Yule through the height of summer and harvest back through to the dark once again, ending with Samhain. Each cycle provides an opportunity to explore the dark Shadow of the season and to shift that Shadow into a reconnection with Essence.

The first chapter for each cycle presents an overview of the archetypal energies of that particular "spoke" on the Wheel of the Year, including some examples of how that festival was or is celebrated around the world.

The next two chapters of each section introduce the cycle theme as reflected through the dark lens of Shadow and the reclaimed lens of Essence. When we are informed by the sludge of shame, how is that reflected in the particular archetypal energies of that cycle? And then, if shame is released and Essence is able to shine through instead, what would that look like? These two chapters work almost like a taijitu: How does the energy present if blocked or stuck, and how does it look instead if the energy flowing through it is clear and unimpeded?

Having explored the Shadow and the Light, the next three chapters introduce exercises and practices that reflect the particular healing approach of each of the three aspects of the caduceus. Starting with the Earth, or that which represents "As Below," a guided meditation invites you to drop into the inner landscape of your Unconscious, engaging in the soul adventure of reclaiming your Light and your Essence. The next chapter reflects the wisdom of the Stars, or that which represents "As Above," through the contemplation of the Hermetic Principles, allowing insight into how these eternal and universal structures have given shape to your life's experiences and how they can be utilized in the future to reflect your highest potential. The last of these chapters presents the outline of a ritual that invites the blending of the "As Above" and the "As Below," allowing for synthesis into the engaged and embodied activation of the cycle's archetypal themes. If you are familiar with ritual, particularly in a Pagan context, these rituals may appear very different from expected. The focus of these rituals is to create a direct conscious line of communication between the Unconscious and the Superconscious from a psycho-spiritual perspective. Joseph Campbell said that the "dream is the personalized myth, myth the depersonalized dream"[2] and ritual invites us to step into the myth, to embody it and personalize it so that we are changed by it. It is this synthesis of personal and transpersonal which allows for the possibility of Transmutation. It allows for the possibility of forever changing the way in which you experience yourself.

Each cycle section ends with the key axiom that serves as the distilled message from all that has been explored through the work of the cycle, and a chart of the key aspects to remember about the cycle, both from a Shadow and an Essence perspective. Most of the key aspects in the chart are presented in depth in *The Great Work* which can serve as a secondary resource, if desired.

Though there is a natural progression that occurs as one moves from Cycle One through to Cycle Eight, it is not necessary to go through the book starting from the beginning and following it through until the end. If it feels more impactful to start the book in the cycle that relates to the time of year in which it came into your hands, start there. If it feels more aligned to find the cycle that is reflective of how you are feeling within at the moment, start there. Chapter 58 outlines assessment approaches for Hynni energy healing sessions that can be used by practitioners to determine which cycle to focus on with clients. You can also use these methods, particularly the "Self-Actualization Survey as Hynni Indicator" approach, to determine the best cycle with which to begin for you. Most of the cycle sections flow easily one to the next, no matter when you start. The only sections that follow a progression to a certain degree

....
2. Joseph Campbell, *The Hero with a Thousand Faces*, 14.

are the guided visualization meditations. These chapters present a loose story that builds one cycle to the next, but it is a cyclical story which you will fall into rhythm with soon enough, no matter when you start. Disregard the statement "find yourself in the place you were before" at the start of the meditation and simply allow yourself to be in the place that you are.

At relevant points throughout the chapters, you will find additional elements that are an invitation for you to dive even deeper into the material.

Further Explorations

Found at the end of several chapters, this section offers some suggestions of other books that focus solely or primarily on the topic at hand. It is highly recommended, especially for those resources dealing with the Shadow reflection of each cycle, to seek more deeply into the material than is presented in the chapter itself. Each of these topics is extensive and there are many wonderful resources available. Even picking one book from each of these Shadow chapter "Further Explorations" sections would bring much clarity to your work.

Inner Workings

Found at the end of the Essence chapters, these exercises are intended to anchor a personal experience of the healthy, transformed, or reclaimed sense of Self presented in the chapter through tangible application.

Enhancements to Experience

For both meditative and contemplative chapters, there are additional elements suggested that can enhance either the understanding of the material in the chapter or deepen the experiential component. For the meditations drawing upon the Earth alignment of "As Below" that informs these chapters, several high-vibration "stones of the new consciousness" are recommended. If you are able to source them, these powerful stones—many of them newly discovered—can open your energies to quite profound inner journeying. Most are readily available, although a few are quite rare. If there are stones and crystals you are already familiar with and enjoy working with, think about holding them while meditating. For the contemplations, which draw upon the Stars alignment of "As Above," there is a reiteration of the chakra associated with the cycle as presented in *The Great Work* along with expanded material on the energy of the back of the chakra and the higher vibration of the associated "fourth dimension" chakra. These are aspects of chakra work not often utilized, but in seeking to clear heavy energies from one's causal body and to access higher knowledge, expanding your experience of the chakra associated with the cycle in these ways will bring heightened insight to your contemplation.

Recommendations

Each ritual section ends with recommendations for intuitive tools that can be incorporated into the ritual itself. Using the intuitive tool itself is optional, but it always seems to bring that final revelation that helps to put the entire ritual experience into clear context. It allows for the voice of the Divine to be a part of the ritual itself. If there is a favorite that you already have, of course that would be the one to use, as it can be quite an investment to try to attain one specific tool for each one of eight cycles.

Engaging in the Craft of *The Noble Art*

As Arianrhod held the arc of the cosmos through the journey to self-knowledge in *The Great Work*, so Cerridwen holds the sacred container during the process of reclaiming Essence in *The Noble Art*. If Arianrhod set out the course of destiny, the karmic path, it is Cerridwen who sets the challenges that invite us to step into that destiny. It is she who steadies the container of transmutation, the cauldron that reflects the pattern of the cosmos above in its iron depths. It is she who stirs us through the cycles. It is she who crafts the healing brew. It is she who directs the distillation and in the moment of attainment, when the brew coagulates into those three perfect golden drops, it is she who, in *The Noble Art*, bestows them on us.

In Cerridwen's tale, at the culmination of all her work, the moment when those drops touch Gwion Bach, the cauldron cracks and all that remains of the brew, the toxic sludge that no longer serves any purpose to the magic at hand, drains away. As *The Great Work* presents the "ingredients" required to craft the healing brew, *The Noble Art* offers the techniques that can potentially bring us to a place of being able to crack the cauldron itself. It is my hope that the pages of this book will provide the information, the tools, and the practices that can facilitate the transmutation of shame into the immutable drops of Self, Soul, and Spirit. In other words, release the karma. Let the sludge of shame and the heaviness of all the past pain and trauma drain away. Get off Arianrhod's wheel. Achieve the Shining Brow. Be the actualization of Spirit in Matter.

In a talk he gave on Cerridwen, Kristoffer Hughes of the Anglesey Druid Order ended with these words: "Cerridwen sits in that space where Awen, Matter, and Magic meet." From the perspective of *The Noble Art*, in the space where the Matter of the Earth, the Awen from the Stars, and the Magic that occurs with the alchemy of Synthesis meet, Cerridwen sits. What she introduces us to is nothing less than the transmutation of Self, inviting us to sing our exquisite souls into a waiting world and to sing a succulent world into being.

The Great Work is guided by the axioms "Know Thyself" and "Carpe Diem." Coming from the ancient Greek and Latin, respectively, these two axioms urge us to name ourselves, claim our strengths, and step fully into the life of our choosing—an appropriate invitation for Arianrhod's book. *The Noble Art* is guided by words that come to us from modern Greece. A precious memory I have from many years ago is a trip to Greece with my parents after I had graduated from film school. I recall standing with my father outside of Heraklion on Crete at the unmarked grave of Nikos Kazantzakis. A prolific writer, author of *The Last Temptation of Christ* and *Zorba the Greek*, who had been nominated for the Nobel Prize in Literature nine times, much of Kazantzakis' philosophy centered around the idea that we need to move beyond being motivated by either hope or fear, being drawn toward heaven or running from thoughts of hell. Along that road lies the potential to get lost in either the "above" or the "below." As we will see again and again in the pages of this book, a long-standing Greek concept is that of the Golden Mean, the truth that lies in the middle. "Balance, balance," my father used to say all the time. For Kazantzakis, the only truth we can hold on to, the truth that lies in the center of fear and hope (or Shadow and Light) is the meaning that we must find the courage to imbue into every moment. Claiming our Essence. To be engaged regardless of "best" or "worst" outcomes, that is the trick. On Kazantzakis' grave is carved the epitaph:

Δεν ελπίζω τίποτα. Δε φοβούμαι τίποτα. Είμαι λέφτερος
I hope for nothing. I fear nothing. I am free.

This is not the height of discouragement and despair. It is the exact opposite. It is the claiming of each and every moment as the fullness of engaged life: not to be continually shaped by the fears of that which has already been, nor continually grasping at the potential of that which has not yet manifested, but allowing the heart to settle into the fullness of this moment. And this moment. And every moment that follows.

The three epitaph lines act like the three drops of illuminated wisdom offered by Cerridwen's brew. They guide the course of the Noble Art that is the crafting of that brew.

I ended the Introduction to *The Great Work* with the words: "As you engage in your own Magnum Opus, know that you are *The Great Work*." And that is truth. You are a magnificent spark of the Divine made manifest on Earth to engage in the wondrous process of discovering your magnificence. However, in the reflection of Cerridwen's book, *The Noble Art*, you, the reader, are Gwion Bach: the young lad who, in the process of attending to the work, is destined to receive the drops of transmuting illumination. There is an art to that process that requires patience, dedication, compassion, and the openness to take some courageous steps. In seeking the transmutation of Shadow to Essence that is at the heart of this noblest of arts, know that you are not alone and know, without question, that you are far, far more than the work. You are *The Noble Art*.

Ye blessèd creatures, I have heard the call

Ye to each other make; I see

The heavens laugh with you in your jubilee;

My heart is at your festival,

My head hath its coronal,

The fulness of your bliss, I feel—I feel it all.

~ William Wordsworth

(from "Ode: Intimations of Immortality

from Recollections of Early Childhood")

Through these pages, may you revive ...

Part One

Cycle One
December 21–January 31

From Risk to Release

The Solid Hynni of Grounding

As Below
Risk
Alchemical
Calcination
Abandonment
Addiction

As Above
Release
Prima Materia
Birth of the Divine
Child
Core values

Synthesis
Place within tribe
Victory of order over chaos
Rebirth of the Light

One

Yule and the Divine Child

The Winter Solstice marks the "birth of the sun," the astronomical moment when the days begin once more to lengthen, bringing more light day by growing day into our lives. It marks the turn from the time of darkness toward the Light and the sigh of relief that the rigid back of the winter's hardship has been breached. It is hope springing eternal in the most delicate rays of a still-weak sun. *Rebirth of the Light* is the main archetypal theme of this festival. In a similar vein, the archetypal theme of the *Victory of Order over Chaos* reflects that we have survived the most dangerous time. We are not wholly out of the woods as of yet, but there is certainly more brightness to our days as we continue to wind our way through the dark forest and that in itself is cause for celebration.

The third main archetypal theme of Yule, highlighting the metaphoric and mythological birth of the Divine Child, is that of knowing our *Place Within Tribe*. Nowhere is it more clear that we are dependent on our community than when we are in the midst of hardship. In the recent global pandemic, this was brought starkly and devastatingly to light. Not only do our actions have an impact on the safety of others, but our security also lies in their hands. In times of crisis, certainly, it becomes abundantly clear how codependent we are. When we are confident of our place within our tribe, secure in our belonging, and cognizant of the significance of our input, this is a wonderful experience. But the Shadow reflection of this theme is abandonment. The dark pain that stems from the inability to fully embrace or experience this archetypal theme is the core issue of abandonment.

There are as many myths that tell of the lost child as there are of the Divine birth: infants lost to supernatural forces, children left by dying parents to deal with horrid stepparents, abandoned royal babies raised by unsuspecting shepherds or fishermen. These lost tales do as much to reflect the importance of a sense of place within tribe as those that speak of inclusion within the community. They tell us that as much as we carry that spark of the Divine Child within, we also experience the sense of isolation in the world. Birth to life may on some level be experienced as the shock of leaving our Divine home, the "otherworld": a profound experience of disconnection that creates a core of abandonment which shapes our journey back to wholeness.

In human terms, any neglecting of our needs is a form of abandonment. The spectrum of abandonment can run from unintentional neglect all the way to abuse. It can take the form of inattention, distracting us away from our needs, or be overbearing and smothering. What we require—what the Divine Child within requires—is to be celebrated unconditionally and to know that we are safe in all the ways we need to be safe: physically, emotionally, mentally, energetically, and spiritually. We need to know that we are seen to be the precious beings that we know ourselves innately to be, and that those who are responsible for our care and feeding will do so in ways that meet our needs, but also allow us the space to grow naturally and organically. When that is our experience of the world in which we live and the community that surrounds us, only then are we able to truly connect with the sense of Divine within, feeling held and cherished, and able to engage with the world from a place of trust.

The celebration of the Return of the Light has been recognized for thousands of years and still takes many forms around the world today. In ancient times, the Romans recognized the interplay of order and chaos in their festival of *Saturnalia*, which ran from December 17 to 23. Later Romans (circa third century CE) celebrated *Dies Natalis Solis Invicti*, which translates as the Birthday of the Unconquerable Sun, on December 25. Christians, starting around the same time frame, celebrate *Christmas* on December 25 as the birth of Christ. *Diwali* (India) comes the earliest in the year. This Festival of Light can fall from October to November, depending on the cycle of the moon. However, Hindus also celebrate *Pacha Ganapati* from December 21 to 25. This holiday honors Ganesh, the Divine son of Shiva and Parvati, who endured a terrible accident at the hand of his father and became the "remover of obstacles." *Hanukkah* (Jewish) can occur anytime between late November and early January as its date is determined by the Jewish rather than Gregorian calendar. *St. Lucia Day* (Scandinavia) is celebrated on December 13. *Dong Zhi* (China), meaning "Winter's extreme," is one of the most important Asian festivals, and is celebrated at the time of the Winter Solstice. It is celebrated in Japan as *Toji*, and in Vietnam as *Dong Chi*. It is also a time for honoring the ancestors. *Alban Arthan* is a more modern name for the Celtic Druids' celebration of the Winter Solstice, and of course *Yule* is the Norse name for the same. *Shabe Yalda* (Iran) means "birth" and it is celebrated at the time of the Winter Solstice. For the Hopi of North America, the Winter Solstice celebration was called *Soyal*. *Los Posados* (South and Central America), which commemorates the journey of Mary and Joseph to Jerusalem in search of lodgings, is celebrated from December 16 to 24. The most modern of the festivals celebrated during this time is that of *Kwanzaa*, which was created in the United States in 1966 and is held from December 26 to January 1. *Koliada* (Slavic) is one of the latest festivals, falling on the Orthodox Christmas of January 6.

At this time of the Winter Solstice, no matter what has transpired in the year before, we have the opportunity to begin anew. We have the opportunity to rejoice in the reconnection to the Divine Child within, and to recommit to nurturing that precious spark into a fully realized and actualized Self.

 Further Exploration on Yule

Mankey, Jason. *Llewellyn's Little Book of Yule*. Woodbury, MN: Llewellyn, 2020.

Pesznecker, Susan. *Yule: Rituals, Recipes & Lore for the Winter Solstice*. Woodbury, MN: Llewellyn, 2015.

Raedisch, Linda. *The Old Magic of Christmas: Yuletide Traditions for the Darkest Days of the Year*. Woodbury, MN: Llewellyn, 2013.

Two

The Shadow Trap of Addiction

All the archetypal energies of Yule seen through the lens of Shadow result in the triggering of feelings of loss and abandonment. It is the sense of the Divine Child forgotten on the outskirts of tribe, place, and community. From this place, winter does not inspire with crisp, clean beauty. Rather, it leaves us frozen, dropping us into the cold, bleak inner landscape of emptiness. When the Child Within is constantly and consistently bombarded by the message that they are not good enough (or smart enough or attractive enough), or that what they feel (or think or dream) is not important enough to warrant consideration, or that they are inherently unlovable, that is the baseline for a shame-based and fear-based life. It is the perennial, eternal inner winter.

Addiction is the way we try to compensate for the loss of connection with Source (or self) by trying to fill the empty hole in the pit of our bellies with substance or activity from the material world. But that doesn't work. It can't work. It is looking for connection and wholeness in the wrong place and so we never feel nourished. We keep trying to get more and more in a devastating, self-destructive, potentially dangerous never-ending circle.

The Onion Model adopted for psychological purposes presents the loved and nurtured Child Within at the core. Essence is the Divine Child, the one that brings the light of hope and joy to the world. It is that sense of self that needs to be at the very core of our being, and yet that is rarely our experience. When we are informed by security and trust and we know that all is well in our world, even as we go through challenges and obstacles, the experience we have when we plumb the depths of our inner life is connection to that Essence. We see that light within, even if all around is still in darkness. However, if, when we plumb our inner depths, we instead encounter the dense, painful tar of shame that gives us the false message that we are inherently flawed, and that if anyone really found out the truth of who we are, we would be utterly and absolutely rejected, that triggers the creation of layers and layers of unhealthy coping tactics that strive to shield us from that inner pain.

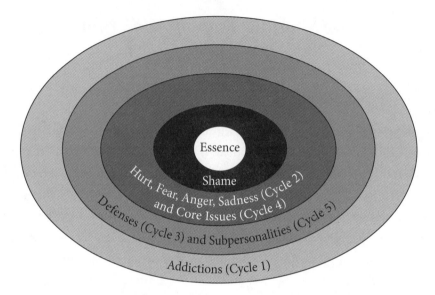

The first layer of protection reflects the inner calibration to the overriding experience of shame. It is reflected in the way in which we view our emotions, marginalizing those that are uncomfortable or unpleasant to experience. This will be dealt with in detail in Cycle 2. This layer also relates to the core beliefs we carry about ourselves and the world, whether we see the world as safe and accepting or whether we are reacting to a fear-based and fear-run society. This will be explored in Cycle 4.

The next layer of protection reflects more of an outer calibration with the unconscious implementation of methods to keep us safe and ensure no one gets too close. There are the wide range of defenses we employ, which is presented in Cycle 3, and there are all the masks we wear, also referred to as subpersonalities or the Persona. The wide variety of these "false selves" are presented in depth in Cycle 5.

The Addict is one such "false self." It is one of the masks we can wear to keep ourselves safe, as problematic a mask as it ends up being. Addiction is the last place we go to in the unconscious attempt to protect the most valued and precious aspect of self, which we perceive on some level to be in danger. The truth of our Essence, the light of the Child Within, has gone so far into hiding that when we seek inside all we feel is that empty gaping hole of shame. The depth of that emptiness brings us to the painful emotions of fear or anger or hurt, all of which slide us into the pit of shame that tells us it is our own fault, the reason we feel so terrible inside is because we are unworthy and unlovable.

When we cannot fill ourselves with the Light of self-love, we will fill ourselves with a substance or activity. Addiction is the last place we turn to in order to alleviate the pain of disconnection with self, that Wonder Child within. As such, it is often the first place we can turn to start the healing process. In addressing the healing needs of a fear-based and fear-run society, we invite the birth of the Inner Sun that starts the gradual movement into full summer strength and the soul harvest in the months and years to come.

The topic of addiction is a massive subject, one that has so many layers and aspects itself. A shame-based approach to understanding addiction, such as is presented here, does not detract from nor negate work being done to understand the genetic or neurological aspects of addiction. There is much excellent research being done in the study of addictions. In fact, the determination of what constitutes an addiction has changed dramatically over the decades. Psychiatrists, psychologists, psychotherapists and other mental health professionals use the *Diagnostic and Statistical Manual of Mental Disorders* (DSM) as a standard and standardized professional resource. First published in 1952, it is now in its fifth revision, which is referred to as the DSM-V (published in 2013). Along with alcohol, opioids, and other substance-related addictions, the DSM-V has expanded to include both Gambling Disorder and Gaming Disorder, neither of which were addressed in previous editions. It is important to note, however, that there are issues with the DSM that cause some to regard its contents with caution. It is worth noting that homosexuality was removed from the DSM in 1973. In initial editions, homosexuality had been listed as a "sociopathic personality disturbance." Additionally, there has been criticism of the DSM-V for potential conflict of interest through the connection of the majority of its advisory panel with "big pharma."[3]

As a different approach to the clinical diagnosis of addiction, the Onion Model presents addiction as the final place the psyche turns to try to ease the pain of soul disconnection before falling into the abyss of despair and numbness. It gives us another lens through which to understand and appreciate what is going on in the psyche, and it provides a map to the first steps we can take in the journey to healing. When we are able to recognize the way in which we have lost ourselves to a substance or a process or an activity, it crashes us into the Dark Night of the Soul. Calcination, the first alchemical stage of healing, is the catastrophe that opens the potential pathway back to the Light of our Essence. It forces us to face the cold, harsh fact that the ways in which we have been trying to distract ourselves from our inner pain are not working for us. It drops us into the irrefutable knowing that we have been living in the depth of winter, but that there is the glimmer of the light of hope on the horizon. It starts us on the path to true inner reconnection, allowing for the tender embracing of the Inner Infant, who needs to engage with the world from a place of trust, and the loving encouragement of the Inner Toddler, who needs to explore the world confident in its safety and acceptance.

Even for those who are not struggling with the devastation wrought by an active addition, we all know what it is to hand over our autonomy to something other than our own free choice. More and more, we are living in a society that promotes the addictive impulse. Even outside of the over sixty thousand deaths due to opioid addiction in the US in 2018,[4] there are more and more invitations, specifically through

3. Moisse, Katie. "DSM-5 Criticized for Financial Conflicts of Interest." ABC News. ABC News Network, March 13, 2012. https://abcnews.go.com/Health/MindMoodNews/dsm-fire-financial -conflicts/story?id=15909673.

4. National Institute on Drug Abuse. "Overdose Death Rates." NIDA. National Institute of Drug Abuse, March 10, 2020. https://www.drugabuse.gov/related-topics/trends-statistics/overdose-death-rates.

technology, to relinquish our freedom of choice and slip into unconsciousness and distraction. When it comes to healthy caring for the toddler child, distraction may keep the child from harm, but new approaches to child psychology are indicating that not only does distraction thwart a child's ability to learn how to make a more positive choice, it can also give the message that feelings are not okay, and that bypassing, spiritual or otherwise, is okay. Taken to the nth degree, distraction becomes compulsion or addiction that serves the purpose of trying to take our mind off that which is causing us discomfort or pain.

We are familiar with the far-reaching effects of substance addiction such as nicotine, alcohol, or drugs. Looking at a physiological dependence on sugar or caffeine would also arguably fall into the category of substance abuse. Loosely speaking, to be defined as an addiction, there is the absence of impulse control. If I think about the substance, I must have it. Seen through the lens of the Inner Infant, addiction becomes a way of self-soothing, like trying to rock ourselves to sleep with a bottle. For the Inner Toddler, being told "no," particularly with regard to using the substance or engaging in the behavior, may lead to a temper tantrum with all the inner stomping and screaming that is done in the hopes that the adult will cave to demands. This reflects another criterion in being able to identify the possibility of an addiction: that there is the change in personality if one does not have the substance.

Harder to determine than substance addiction is the phenomenon of process addiction. These are the things we do (rather than the things we ingest) that serve the same function. They distract. They numb. They soothe. But they do not support us in sitting with our feelings, nor do they empower us to determine the best course of action for ourselves in challenging times. Shopping has long been identified as a process addiction. How do we know when we are not shopping because we need to shop, or we are shopping because there is a level of enjoyment involved, but rather we are shopping because we are addicted to shopping? The same way we know when we are eating not to nourish ourselves or because we are enjoying a lovely meal, but because there is an ache deep inside that we are trying to soothe away by doing the thing that always seems to cover the pain.

What informs us forms us. What we carry inside has the power to shape us. If we succumb to the overriding message of fear and resulting sense of isolation that are the programming of a shame-based society, then addiction will show its face in our lives in some form or another. What is required of us is the courage to address the pain within, and the development of adequate and functional coping mechanisms, so that we are spiritually *trans*formed, not emotionally *de*formed.

Shadow of Cycle One: Addictions

All addictions fall within the Shadow work of Cycle One; however, a further delineation shows how different addictions can align with the energies found on the Wheel of the Year.

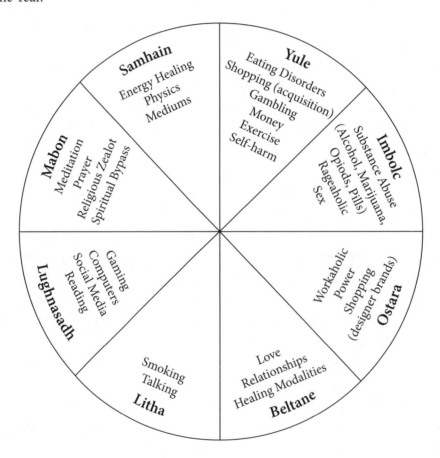

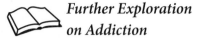 *Further Exploration*
on Addiction

Foote, Jeffrey, Carrie Wilkens, Nicole Kosanke, and Stephanie Higgs. *Beyond Addiction: How Science and Kindness Help People Change.* Reprint edition. New York: Scribner, 2014.

Maté, Gabor. *In the Realm of Hungry Ghosts: Close Encounters with Addiction.* Berkeley, CA: North Atlantic Books, 2010.

May, Gerald, MD. *Addiction and Grace: Love and Spirituality in the Healing of Addictions.* San, Francisco: HarperOne, 1988.

Three

· ·

The Light of True Essence

When draped in the dark shadow of shame, Cycle One lays an unstable foundation in our lives. Rather than be the light of hope and the triumph of order over chaos, it <u>is</u> the chaos. Shame invites the inner chaos of anxiety, depression, panic, and fear to overlay all experiences, creating the perfect ground for the intensified chaos of addiction. The roots and foundations that are laid from a source of shame are twisted and rotting, incapable of drawing up the nutrients we need to in order to survive and thrive.

To truly acknowledge the healthy, positive archetypal energy of Cycle One, we must embrace the Child Within as a pure reflection of the Divine, embodied and manifest in human form. At birth, when we enter into the beginning of the fulfillment of our contract in this life at this time, we bring with us, embedded within us, those Divine qualities that are our charge to activate in the world during our lifetime. We arrive in a tiny perfect package and, in those first moments of our lives, we know ourselves to be the reflection of Divine perfection. We are the emanation of Essence and often we are welcomed, embraced, and celebrated as the wondrous miracle that we indeed are.

It is true the experience as outlined above is not always the case. There are those infants who are born into rejection, or even incubated in terror. But the circumstances of our arrival do not detract from the miracle of our Being. The unconscious experience of the separation from our Essence through the activation of shame can begin the moment we take our first breath, but there was a moment, somewhere in the depths of our souls, that we knew ourselves to be whole and holy.

The journey from shame to Essence, from separation to wholeness, from disconnection to integration, starts here. The work of healing from a Cycle One perspective is the act of identifying all those places that we have given our power, our sense of self, the identification of our innate value, over to something that lies outside of ourselves. It is the act of reclaiming the truth of our Essence and finally, finally celebrating the triumph of inner peace and order over the chaos of shame. Carl Jung wrote in his *Red Book*, "If you marry the ordered to the chaos you produce the divine child, the supreme meaning beyond meaning and meaninglessness."[5] The gift of looking at the barren landscape around us is that there is the clarity of sightline to reveal what is, at its heart, vitally important to remember and reclaim. In alchemical terms, when all else has been leveled to the ground or set into flame by Calcination, we are able to retrieve the Prima Materia and actually begin the arduous and richly rewarding work of transmutation. In seeking the attainment of the Philosopher's Stone, the ultimate goal of the alchemical process, the true alchemist knows it is one and the same as the Prima Materia. It has just been changed, almost unrecognizable, by all the processes that have been enacted upon it. But a lump of coal holds the potential of the diamond it can become through enough heat and pressure. As reflected in the symbol of the ouroboros, where we begin and where we end are not so far from each other, but the shift from Prima Materia to Philosopher's Stone makes an immense difference in the experience of our lives. Addiction (or compulsion) can be seen as the indicator of the Prima Materia that points us toward the very path that will lead us back to what we lost. When we can garner the courage to trek through the dark forest of shame and recognize how it shadowed every aspect of our lives, we have the opportunity to come through the other side to the light of Essence and have that shine brightly upon all aspects of our lives.

If addictions are indicative of acting from the Shadow perspective of Cycle One, the recognition of core values and the realization of their importance in our lives indicates that we have broken through the dark forest into the Light. It is an indication of our reconnection to Essence.

....

5. Jung, C. G., and Sonu Shamdasani. *The Red Book = Liber Novus*, 139.

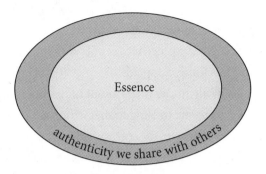

A core value is defined as a quality, principle, or standard of behavior that is held to be valuable, imperative, or non-negotiable in our lives. A core value acts as a compass pointing us along our most authentic path. Values are not the same as the choices we make. They are not our work or our relationships, but they <u>inform</u> the choices we make regarding the work we do or the relationships into which we enter. If I hold a core value of "Family," that could impact on the career I choose (i.e., summer vacations and holidays), where I live with respect to where I work (i.e., distance from home), how I approach finances (i.e., squirreling away for emergencies), the company I keep (i.e., befriending playdate parents).

Taking the time to assess our core values and determine for ourselves the shape of our Essence energy is a necessary step in the process of individuation. There is no right or wrong when it comes to values, nor is there a hierarchy. It is no better to hold Adventure as your highest ideal than it is to hold Wisdom, but it is going to urge a different approach and shape to your life and choices. What becomes highly problematic is if we allow the pursuit of Wisdom to act as our compass when we actually hold Adventure as our foundational core value. When we deny our core values, we cut ourselves off from the deep truth of our being and that causes such a deep soul pain that we turn to any means we have to numb that pain. Tragically, so very often people adopt the values of their parents, or communities, or institutions (educational, governmental, religious) without the discernment to assess how closely these values align with their own inner barometer. This is completely understandable. The sense of place in tribe and the need to be secure in that place is a strong motivator. In many ways, the traditions we practice contain the essence of our communal or societal values. These are beautiful to have as part of our lives. If we have no traditions, often we feel ungrounded and untethered, without a connection to a sense of meaning and depth in our lives. But the time comes when we are prompted to metamorphize into our True Self and that requires the reassessment of what was unconsciously adopted.

Calcination pushes us firmly in the direction of individuation and the claiming of authentic autonomy. If we continue to cling to that which is not reflective of our inner truth, the lightning *will* strike the tower and we will be compelled to start building from the ground up once again. This time, however, we are invited to turn to the solid ground of our core values and honor the guiding energy they bring to our lives.

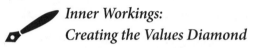 *Inner Workings:*
Creating the Values Diamond

With the following Core Values chart, take some uninterrupted time in a quiet place to breathe into your root chakra with the intention of opening yourself to gaining clarity on your personal Core Values. For each cycle, take a moment to rest mentally and energetically with each of the Core Values listed in the cycle and determine which one holds the strongest charge or pull for you. Which one from each cycle would you hold as a core aspect of your own Essence? At the end of the exercise, you will have a list of eight values, each of which reflects a different energetic. In essence, you will have created definition to each of eight facets of a three-dimensional diamond. This is integral information to remember as you move through each of the cycles, especially when you come to the work of Cycle Eight and the Integrating Hynni of Unity.

Light of Cycle One: Values

All values fall within the Essence work of Cycle One; however, a further delineation shows how different values can align with the energies found on the Wheel of the Year.

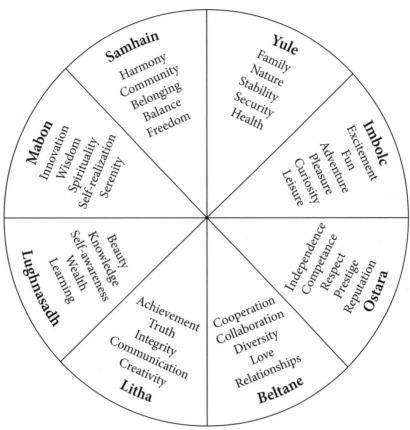

Four

··

Journey to Encounter the Dragon Meditation

The painful work of challenging an addiction (or compulsion or unhealthy habit) in our lives has often been referred to as "facing the dragon." Pictured like Smaug in *The Hobbit*, this Western dragon represents all that is the scourge of the destructive shame-based ego that is compelled by materialism and has lost all connection with the higher attributes of Spirit.

> In the West, historically we have regarded the dragon as a representation of the unhealthy ego, driven by greed and nursing a hoarding heart. St. George slays the dragon, releasing our soul from hostage and allowing it to come back to God. But if we journey back further than the separation of body and spirit, we find the dragon as the guardian of the treasure within.[6]

Similar to the healing path of addiction recovery, if we allow ourselves the courage to face the darkness and all the destructive shaming messages that seek to destroy our connection with self and keep us small and afraid, we open ourselves to the possibility of attaining the treasure that lies within. Not because our value is determined by the treasure—it is not; our value is non-negotiable—but because the treasure is beautiful and it deserves to be brought out into the light for all to see. In the darkness of the cave that houses the dragon that guards the treasure of our Soul, there are two possible fires we might encounter: the destroying fire of the dragon's breath, which is

·································

6. C. Matthews and J. Matthews, *Walkers Between the Worlds*, 58.

akin to the all-consuming fire of Calcination; or the warm embers of the hearth fire, which is the guiding light of Essence.

This meditation takes you into the inner landscape of Cycle One to face the dragon that guards the treasure within. As you journey in this landscape, know that the metaphor it reflects does indeed connect to a larger truth in your waking consciousness and lived experience. Allow yourself the gift of naming your dragon, braving the cave, and claiming your Light.

Meditation

Close your eyes. Focus on your breath. Allow your breath to drop you into a deep place within yourself. Each inhale connects you to those places within that may hold tension, discomfort, or unease. Each exhale invites you to release those tensions into the cosmos, bringing you to the balance place in the center of the Above and the Below that connects Spirit and human: the place between where magic happens.

See yourself in a stark winter landscape. This can be a place you know in the world or a place you know in your soul. Looking across the land, your eyes take in the monochromatic template of whites and browns and grays. It is the depth of the winter and you see your beloved land stripped of brilliant color and lush foliage. Everywhere you gaze, you see skeleton silhouettes of majestic trees sprouting from a snow-covered earth. Very little is hidden in this exposed vista. That which wishes to be hidden must seek secret spots with dedication.

How do you feel in the landscape of this vision? Vulnerable? Safe? Threatened? Anticipatory?

You feel a pull to walk in a certain direction. A sound or a sense draws you to further explore in this place. From deep within yourself you have a niggling impulse that there is something more than seemingly meets the eye. Challenge or treasure, it must be sought out and explored. In short order, you find you have come to a mountainous terrain. A sheer rock face filled with nooks, crannies, and caves blocks your passage further. As you scan the rocky expanse, your eye is drawn to a glint of gold that flashes in the weak light of the newly born solstice sun. A flash of brilliance in a sea of stark. As you approach the place from which the flash emanated, you feel a cloak of trepidation drop upon your shoulders. There is something in this place that stands between you and the gold. It is no small thing. And yet, you are drawn by the enticing radiance to move closer.

As you come to the gold-filled cave and peer into the dark, the sight that fills your eyes fills your heart with dread. You face the dragon that stands between you and the golden treasure. You realize that the only way to access the precious hoard is to find the courage to challenge this creature. That is the only way to harness the wealth of the soul that dwells in the dark cave. And it is the first necessary step along the path to wholeness that every true seeker must take.

What is the energy and character of your dragon? What fearful, limiting, thwarting perspective does your dragon hold for you? What fulfilling, enriching, enlivening potential does your dragon keep you from? How do you face your dragon?

Give yourself the gift of defeating or banishing your dragon, experiencing the rush of joy and the flush of success that grants you access to the treasure within the cave. As you grasp the warm, glowing gold in your hands, you see that it is not cold metal that you hold, but seeds. These small, precious golden nuggets burst with the hope of the abundant harvest of all the things to come. Things that could never be, so long as they are trapped in a cold cave behind the vicious girth of an ego-driven dragon. But, having accessed your deep inner strength for a courageous battle and banishment, you hold these hard-won seeds in your hands and look out from the mouth of the cave, beholding the white, brown, and gray landscape. And what you see across the expanse is the glorious abundance that will be.

Allow yourself to take this in, to feel it in your blood and bones. Know that you hold the seeds of your own future in your hands, the potential for an abundant harvest that will enrich more lives than yours alone.

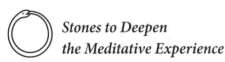 ### Stones to Deepen
the Meditative Experience

Black Moonstone eases emotional instability as we move through deep Shadow work.

Goethite helps us be gentle in our process, particularly in experiencing deep grief.

Shungite is highly protective, having the ability to neutralize almost anything of harm.

Vatican Stone activates personal power and self-control, bringing a sense of peace and calm as we address seemingly insurmountable obstacles.

Vesuvianite helps to bring old, outmoded patterns to the surface, allowing us to slowly release deep-seated fears.

Five

The Hermetic Concept of
Universal Law Contemplation

Just as there are laws in the physical world that govern the way in which all in manifest reality operate, there are Universal Laws that speak to the interrelationship between manifest and nonmanifest reality. Most of us are familiar with the laws of the physical world: if not from high school physics, then from our experiences in the world itself. Anyone who has suffered the heartbreak of losing a scoop of ice cream from one's cone to a sidewalk splat knows very well that gravity is immutable. The Law of Universal Gravitation as well as the three Laws of Motion were laid out by Sir Isaac Newton in his book *Mathematical Principles of Natural Philosophy*, which was first published in 1687. In doing so, he arguably became the father of modern science and laid the foundation for the scientific revolution. As influential as Sir Isaac Newton was to the realm of science, mathematics, and physics, what is not as widely known is that he was also a dedicated alchemist at a time in history when it was decidedly dangerous to be one. These were indeed still "the burning times" and having ideas that were contrary to the Church was worth one's life. When his alchemical papers were brought up for auction at Sotheby's in London in 1936, it was evident he had written about a million words on this esoteric subject and had spent a good part of thirty years of his life seeking the Philosopher's Stone. As there are the laws of the physical world, there are the Universal Laws. Alchemy and the Hermetic sciences establish a template for accessing the relationship between the "above" and the "below," the seen and the unseen, the manifest and the unmanifest. It is fascinating that the geniuses of the physical sciences, most notably perhaps in Newton, were drawn to explore this esoteric relationship.

Just as we may not be consciously aware of the physical laws, though we feel the impact of them upon our lives, so it is with the Universal Laws. Perhaps better known, certainly in some circles, as the Hermetic Principles, these laws inform of the cohesive structure that binds all of reality in place and of the interaction between the manifest and unmanifest worlds. The first modern presentation of the Principles was in a book published by the Yogi Publication Society in Chicago in 1908. *The Kybalion* was written by the Three Initiates who have never been named, though there has been much speculation as to their identity or identities. This slim volume has been republished in different forms many times over the last century and the Principles contained therein have found different iterations, particularly in the New Age focus of manifestation and the Law of Attraction.

The core Hermetic Principles are as follows:

The Principle of Mentalism	This Law states that all in the Universe is One. It is the force that creates everything , defined as the "One Mind." Akin to Star Wars' "The Force."
The Principle of Correspondence	As everything is a reflection of everything else, the Inner World reflects the Outer World and the macrocosm (the Universe) reflects the microcosm (ourselves).
The Principle of Vibration	Nothing in the Universe can be destroyed. Energy simply shifts to a different vibrational level.
The Principle of Polarity	All things exist in dynamic relationship to an opposing element. For example, hot and cold are not different concepts. They are polarities on a spectrum of "Heat."
The Principle of Rhythm	A principle of movement like Vibration that indicates there is an "ebb and flow" to all things and experiences in Existence.
The Principle of Cause and Effect	A principle of relationship like Correspondence that indicates the accountability of one action in regard to another.
The Principle of Gender	A principle of dynamics like Polarity that indicates the necessity of dualism. Akin to Yin and Yang, masculine (active) and feminine (receptive) support each other.

Hermetics teach us that these seven principles are what are at work in the world to transform energy to matter and back again. At this time of year when we celebrate the birth of the Divine Child, we are acknowledging the miracle of the unmanifest becoming manifest, reflecting the pure energy of the Divine even as it comes into being. And out of this one thing comes all things because, as the Emerald Tablet tells us, "this is the pattern."

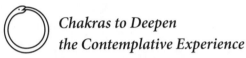

Contemplation

Contemplate how the Solid Hynni of Grounding reflects the concept of Universal Law: the labyrinthine path that opens us to the central truths that are universal and timeless.

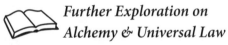

Chakras to Deepen
the Contemplative Experience

Connect with the **root chakra** to open yourself to grounded earth energies. Even as you reach up with your awareness to expand your consciousness to that beyond your physical, limited self in order to access the interconnected pattern of Universal Law, feel yourself as connected to the solid and foundational support of the Earth.

The higher-vibration chakra that sits in the base of the spine is the **Ninth Chakra of Joy and Satisfaction.**[7] It is the higher reflection of the energy that sits at the base of the spine when we have done much work to clear the negative overlay of shame. It deepens the experience of groundedness from the survival focus of safety and security to an expressed focus of joy and satisfaction.

Further Exploration on
Alchemy & Universal Law

Chambers, John. *The Metaphysical World of Isaac Newton.* Destiny Books, 2018.

D'Aoust, Maja and Adam Parfrey. *The Secret Source: The Law of Attraction is One of Seven Ancient Hermetic Laws—Here are the Other Six.* Port Townsend, WA: Process Media, 2007.

Three Initiates, The. *The Kybalion.* New York: TarcherPerigee, 2008.

....

7. Stone, *Soul Psychology: How to Clear Negative Emotions and Spiritualize Your Life.*

Six

Welcome the Divine Child Ritual

At the time of the Winter Solstice, when the "sun is born anew" and readying for its own journey into increased strength, vitality, potency, and impact, this is an opportunity to connect with that part of yourself that holds innocence and optimism. No matter what we have experienced in our lives, we came into this world with openness and trust. Even if there were some past-life trails, in-utero experiences, or birth trauma, our little Spirits held the energy of hope.

This ritual is an invitation to reconnect to the pure Essence of the Inner Infant, our personal experience of the Divine Child. In alchemical terms, the Inner Infant is the Prima Materia, that which precipitates the entire process of crafting the Philosopher's Stone. Through the symbolic enactment of this first alchemical stage of Calcination, in which matter is reduced to ash to burn off that which is not essential, this ritual serves to remind you of the beautiful Essence that lies within. It is the celebration of the birth of the Wonder Child that was and is you!

Symbols to help connect to ritual focus	• Items that help connect to the Inner Infant or Toddler, including photographs of self at those ages; greenery from evergreens (loose boughs or wreaths); mistletoe; holly; solar disk, star • Statues or photos of those deities that reflect the Child of Light or the Divine Mother of the Child of Light • An image of the Solid Hynni of Grounding
Optional: Stones from *Journey to Encounter the Dragon* Meditation	• Black Moonstone • Goethite • Shungite • Vatican Stone • Vesuvianite
Items needed for ritual activity	• A fresh unused candle (red, if you want to align with Hynni) • A lighter • A cauldron or other fire-safe container • Tealight • Some small strips of paper • A pen • Container of water (always have on hand for ritual that involves fire) • Optional: Candle snuffer • Optional: Runes

Creating the Altar

Whether on your existing altar or on a surface that can act as altar for this ritual, take some time to set up an homage to your Inner Infant. If you have a photo of yourself as a baby or a young child, place it on your altar. If there are items that remind you of this child that will help you to connect more deeply, include them as well. It may be that you are not able to have the item itself, but you may be able to have something that will twig your unconscious. For example, there is a photo of me on my first birthday with the biggest pink stuffed rabbit imaginable beside me. Of course, I no longer have this rabbit, nor do I want to find an enormous bunny for the purpose of the ritual. But I do have small stuffed bunnies that can hold a similar energy. In a pinch, photos are always useful. They bring the thing to mind, thus bringing it into our conscious awareness, and are easy enough to attain, particularly with a Google search.

You may also choose to decorate your space and your altar with those elements, including deity statues, that bring hope, optimism, and the remembrance of life everlasting to mind. It is helpful to incorporate symbols that have been associated with the different Yule, Midwinter, or Light festivals and holidays throughout the ages. In their individual ways, each of these symbols speaks to the theme of rebirth and the hope for the future that is the light of the Divine Child. Each serves to be a guide through the dark. This could include an image of the Solid Hynni of Grounding, which reminds the psyche that there is a pure dot of hope right in the center of our Being that spirals from our core out into the world.

The last things to have on hand are those items that will be used in the ritual working itself. Place these items front and center on the altar so you have ease of access to them. Place the strips of paper and pen to your left. Place the cauldron with tealight to your right. A small cast iron cauldron is recommended, big enough to hold the tealight. You will be burning paper in it, so be sure to have something small enough to fit nicely on your altar but big enough to allow for safe burning of small strips of paper. Place the unlit candle in front of you in the center of the altar. It is important that the candle is one that has not been used before, especially if this is the first time doing this ritual. You may find, if you do this ritual year after year, that you have a candle that is designated for this purpose, and the relighting of it in ritual each year as the remembrance of True Self could be powerfully moving. If you are planning to reuse your candle year after year, a candle snuffer is recommended. Blowing out a flame can dissipate its potency. Snuffing it out instead contains the energies within the candle so that when it is relit, those energies are reactivated.

When you are done preparing your space, take a moment to feel how the energy you have created affects you. You will want to ensure that there are elements that speak to the general theme of the ritual or the festival itself. This reflects the "Above," the realm of the transpersonal or mythic. You will also want to ensure that there are elements that represent you on the altar. This reflects the "Below," the realm of the personal. If it feels complete, take some time to prepare yourself for ritual (see Appendix D).

The Ritual

Lighting the tealight in the cauldron or container to your right, begin to focus on that sense of the you that is traveling through this material plane, having a human experience. If you have a picture of yourself as a child on the altar, bring your attention to that child. Look into the eyes of that child, allowing a sense of the Essence of your child self to touch you. Find the place within that responds to that wonder, knowing how precious and sacred it is.

Allow yourself to drop deep within, each time connecting to some negative message or energetic sludge that has somehow held the potential to dim the Essence of that beautifully innocent child you see before you. Each time you grasp hold of a message, write it down on one of the pieces of paper that lies to your left and then place it in front of the unlit candle in front of you. You may find that there is just a message or two. You may find that there are many that come up. It may feel like the negative messages will never stop coming up. Do not worry. Allow the dive, retrieval, and noting on paper to continue until there are no more messages that come up, or until it feels that that is enough for this ritual.

When you have placed the last piece of paper with the negative message on it before the unlit candle, take a moment to consider what lies before you. There is all that glorious potential and light just waiting to be activated, but there is this pile of negativity that must be addressed first.

Shift your attention to the cauldron on your right. Within it burns the flame of the tealight. Within it burns the means of your release from the burden of negative messaging. In your own time, pick up one of the slips of paper in front of your unlit candle. Read what is written on it. Allow the awareness of how that message shaped you to land in your consciousness. Allow the desire to release the heavy sting of that message to build within, and when you feel that desire sing through all your cells, release the paper to the flame and watch it disintegrate. Repeat this process until there is nothing that lies between you and the unlit candle.

In the space that has been freed from the dark, negative messages, find the Divine Child that resides within, and when you feel the pulse of your own unique Essence, light the candle before you. Let that flame shine like a strong beacon in the dark as you sit with the reflection that you are a gift to the world and what you bring with your presence is precious.

Take all the time you want or need to gaze upon the light that is reflective of your Light. Take this time to become clear on that sense of who you are, what is precious about you, what your values are, what is important to you. If you choose, you can pull a rune at this time, receiving a message from the Divine about the way in which you are a gift to the world.

Closure of Ritual

When you are ready to leave this liminal space, bring your conscious awareness back to your breath. Taking one last moment to anchor the connection to your sense of your Essence, using either your breath or a candle snuffer, release the flame of the candle before you. What has been experienced in ritual lives forever in your cells. It need only be called forth from within when you choose.

Take some time to move through the directions once more, thanking the elements for helping to hold space and keep you safe through the ritual. Start again in the North with earth, then move through the East with air, the South with fire (put out the tealight in the cauldron at this point), the West with water, ending with the Below of the material plane and the Above of the cosmic plane. Thank and bid farewell to the deities who have been a part of this ritual with you and know that the Wheel may turn around you, but you are—as they are—ever at the center.

Clearing Ritual Space

If you have been using an existing altar, you may decide to keep some items on your altar over the course of the cycle as a way to continue to hold the energy of what you have experienced and embodied in the ritual. That said, if there are any extra pieces of paper, you will want to remove those. It is also important to empty the cauldron of any ash or bits of unburned paper. I have a special place in my yard that I put those elements from ritual that need to be respectfully discarded, rather than putting them unceremoniously into the trash. Find a safe place to store items that you may want to keep for future rituals, such as the Essence candle, until next time.

 ### *Rune Deck Recommendations*

Lo Scarabeo. *Runes Oracle Cards*. Woodbury, MN: Llewellyn, 2013.

Tartara, Paola. *Runes of the Northern Lights*. Woodbury, MN: Llewellyn, 2017.

Voenix. *Power of the Runes Deck*. Stamford, CT: US Games, 1998.

Seven

Be Excellent to Yourself

The power of Cycle One is the healing that comes when we know in every cell that we are safe, secure, and supported.

Yule is the rebirth of hope and if there is one thing that we need to know with every fiber of our being, it is that there is always hope in every situation, no matter how dire, because we carry the energy of that hope within our very bones and cells. The human Spirit is miraculously resilient, if we give it the space and support it needs to be able to move into its natural wonder.

No matter how buffeted we are by circumstances, no matter how mistrustful we may become, no matter how crusty and hardened we may act, somewhere deep inside there is that open and curious Child of Light who wants to engage with the world. This inner being is connected to their tribe, knowing that regardless if there are good or bumpy days, they are loved and cherished.

When we know without a doubt that our value and worth is innate and that we are precious in the world, we are able to follow the axiom, inspired by the ever child-like Bill and Ted: Be excellent to yourself.[8]

There are going to be tough times. There are going to be hurtful people. There are going to be epic fails and dark days and storms within. Life is not a controlled

---

8. *Bill & Ted's Excellent Adventure* (De Laurentiis Entertainment Group, 1989).

experiment. It is messy. But within that, we can protect the part of us—the innocent Infant and the adventurous Toddler—who makes all the challenges worth the effort. We can celebrate the gift of that Light.

Key Aspects of Cycle One [9]

Archetypal Themes	Healing Themes	Indication of Crisis	Healing Practices
Birth of the Wonder Child Place within tribe; victory of Order over Chaos; rebirth of the Light	Family of origin; Infant, Toddler; trust, safe exploration; roles of survival; addiction; core shame	A sudden, unexpected loss or change of life circumstance; feeling disconnected or isolated from the world or other people; fear around new directions in life; a persistent sense of being "ungrounded"; being triggered by spending time with family	Clarification of Core Values; contemplation of Universal Law; activation of Solid Hynni of Grounding
Elemental Reflection	**Intuitive Guidance and Tool**	**Alchemical Reflection**	**Affirmations**
Earth	Animal guides; runes	*Calcination* The shock that activates the Dark Night of the Soul and healing journey	I am safe and secure; I am safe in the world with others; I honor and meet the needs of my body; I know how to take care of myself; I am grounded

9. More information on Key Aspects can be found in *The Great Work: Self-Knowledge and Healing Through the Wheel of the Year* by the author (Llewellyn, 2015).

Part Two

Cycle Two
February 1–March 14

The Narcissist/Empath Spectrum

The Loving Hynni of Ebb and Flow

As Below
Narcissist/empath
Alchemical
Dissolution
Frozen feelings/
flooding
Neglecting needs

As Above
Experiential
spectrum
Surrender
Gifts from the Inner
Child
Emotional fluency

Synthesis
Love
Purification
New beginnings

Eight

. . . .

Imbolc and the Inner Child

As the sun starts to slowly and gradually increase both in the number of hours in the day it is present and in the delicately growing strength of its rays, the land starts to experience its first hints of the thaw to come. Though we tend to perceive spring as arriving with the balancing energies of Ostara and the Vernal Equinox, in many parts of the Western world this time brought warmth enough to be able to venture outdoors for some stretches of time. The waters of the springs and rivers may be starting to trickle. There may be another freeze or two or twelve, but in between the still-icy moments, there is promise in the murmur of the cleansing waters—all signals that winter has released her grip.

Purification—in all the many ways that it shows up—is one of the main archetypal themes reflected in this festival. Being cleansed in healing waters, using those waters to bring freshness to our environment, or anointing our sacred places are all ways that the water, to which we now have ease of access, can be used to bring cleanliness of place and purity of space. Though life is still germinating beneath the surface, the moments of thaw also enable life-giving waters to saturate the Earth, encouraging the first courageous tendrils of sprouting seeds to reach for the light. *New beginnings* reflect the hope that was born at the Winter Solstice, putting down more tangible roots, starting to manifest into something than can be seen.

The third key archetypal theme of Imbolc is that of *Love*. It is present in the healing waters. There is a healers' saying that "there is no healing without love." It is present in the secular holiday of Valentine's Day celebrated in some quarters at this time. Along with the rising waters of desire and the gentle waters of beauty, love is the current that opens us to expanding connection with life and with others, and most importantly, to ourselves. There is joy to be found in the experience of allowing these emotions to flow, a joy that acknowledges the vibrant enthusiasm of the Child Within.

When we do not honor this exuberant, emotional child with the love they deserve and instead allow the permafrost of cold-hearted judgment to freeze the natural, engaged flow, we create the foundation for codependency. Codependency is defined as the ways in which one looks to the "other" for validation, a sense of worth, or approval. We become more attentive to the feelings of another than to those we are experiencing within ourselves. We create blocks to experiencing our emotions because to feel what we feel is too painful. We cut ourselves off from our needs because we despair that they will never be met. We prioritize another's experience of life, or goals for life, or perception of life in order to feel loved. But in the drowning of our own Inner Child's voice, we create a landscape of perennial winter within.

As there are moments of thaw in nature at this time, so can there be cracks in the ice of codependency that can result in a tsunami of emotion that is as challenging, and as scary, to try to manage as the deep freeze. We may find ourselves drifting in the waters of another. At first it feels so wonderful just to feel that buoyancy, until the realization comes that one is being swept down the river, unable to find a foothold on the riverbed.

Imbolc sees the Divine Child who was born at the Winter Solstice grow to a curious, spontaneous, exploratory, communicative, *emotional* being. The infant who brought hope becomes the child of wonder who sees the world through fresh eyes. There is healing and purification in allowing this experience of the world to flow through us, if we are able to embrace this new energy.

To a large degree, Imbolc is considered to be Brigid's Day. The *Feast of St. Brigid* (Christian) is celebrated on February 1. The ancient Celts celebrated the goddess Brigit (also known as Bride, Brigantia, or Brigandu) as people prepared their homes on Imbolc Eve in anticipation of a night-time visit. In Welsh, the festival was known as *Gwyl Mair Dechrau'r Gwanwyn* which basically translates as the "Early Spring Mary Festival." *Candlemas* (Christian), also known as the Feast of the Presentation of Jesus Christ and the Feast of the Purification of the Blessed Virgin Mary, is celebrated on February 2 with the blessings of the household candles. February 2 is celebrated in more secular circles as *Groundhog Day* (USA). Though said to have its roots in Germany, its modern iteration was started in Pennsylvania in 1887. Falling a little later in the month, though still in alignment with Imbolc energies, the ancient Romans celebrated *Lupercalia* between February 13 and 15. Named for Lupercus, the Roman God of flocks, this purification festival was held with the intention of warding off evil spirits and ensuring fertility for fields and flocks. And, of course, there is *Valentine's Day* (Christian), which was originally called the Feast Day of Saint Valentine and was intended to recognize two early Christian martyrs.

Another name for this festival was Oímealg, Gaelic for "ewe's milk" in reference to the lactating sheep who have birthed the early spring lambs. The meaning gives a sense of the ongoing sustenance and nurturance that is required by the young as they begin to explore their worlds. It is this care and comfort that we need to envelop ourselves in as we begin to frolic from the enfolding arms of tribe into the wider berth of interpersonal dynamics. In order to feel buoyed by the emotions that move through us in the exploration and discovery of the greater world around us, rather than overwhelmed by them, we need to bathe in the love that serves as a foundation to our sense of self.

 Further Exploration on Imbolc

Neal, Carl F. *Imbolc: Rituals, Recipes & Lore for Brigid's Day*. Woodbury, MN: Llewellyn, 2015.

Weatherstone, Lunaea. *Tending Brigid's Flame: Awaken to the Celtic Goddess of Hearth, Temple, and Forge*. Woodbury, MN: Llewellyn, 2015.

Weber, Courtney. *Brigid: History, Mystery, and Magick of the Celtic Goddess*. Weiser Books, 2015.

Nine

The New Shadow Face of Codependency

The thawing energies of Imbolc drop us into the chill waters that beckon us to address that which has been locked under ice for a very long time. Without the thaw, we are stuck in an unending deep freeze that will undoubtedly lead to the frostbite of emotional numbness. As with healing frostbite, bringing warmth and care to the places that have become as ice can be extremely, sometimes excruciatingly, painful. But as much as the thaw aches and smarts, it is far, far preferable to the alternative. To not thaw is death. That which succumbs to frostbite is dead to the life that could have flowed through it. A life of frozen emotions feels empty and numb. So it is vitally important to address those cold, hard places and slowly bring back the movement of ebb and flow.

Codependency is the dynamic that results when one prioritizes one's valuation from the other's perspective as more important than one's self-valuation. When I care more about what you think of me than what I know about myself to be true, I am locked in a codependent pattern that has enormous and far-reaching implications. If the inner relationship is defined by the experience of shame ("If you knew the real me, you would reject me"), we tend to focus outwardly to try to control the flow of relationships to ensure that we will not be hurt, we will not be left, we will not be judged. This is the inner experience of emotional numbness that creates an enormous array of potential "control dramas" that play out again and again until we are able to bring the warmth of love to our precious Child Within, feel the thaw of our emotional waters, and allow for our own natural ebb and flow to become the current we follow.

What lies under the surface, in the undertow of emotional pain, is a lack of clarity around needs: what they are, what they address, how to get them met. In 1943, American psychologist Abraham Maslow wrote a paper entitled "A Theory of Human Motivation,"[10] which outlined his now widely cited concept of the Hierarchy of Needs. This theory states that we all have innate needs. These are not options or possibilities. They are immutable and universal. Additionally, there is a hierarchy to these needs. If I am not able to meet my basic physiological needs, like the food I need to keep me alive, I am certainly not going to be concerned with aesthetic needs, like how beautiful something looks. If I am starving, I am going to eat the sandwich I am handed as quickly as I can. I am not going to take time to appreciate how artfully it is decorated with parsley on the plate. In moving into a place of emotional health, it is imperative for us to be familiar with our needs, to know it is okay for us to have them, to know it is okay for us to ask for them to be met, and perhaps most importantly, to know how to meet our needs ourselves. I need to know that there is absolutely nothing wrong with my need to feel safe in my own home. And I need to know that I can reach out to my partner to help me to feel safe and, if my partner is unable to do so—or worse, if my partner contributes to me feeling unsafe—that I know I have within me the power to create safety for myself. As with our experience of our own self-worth, needs are non-negotiable.

In my work as a psychotherapist, I have found that a surprising number of clients I encounter are taken aback when asked to identify their needs. If an understanding of and appreciation for the value of knowing our needs has been shown to be central to our development and health, why is it still so hard for us to identify what these needs are, let alone begin the process of getting them met? Needs are like the banks of the river. They are the necessary edges that show us what is required in order for us to thrive. Emotions are like the water that flows along those banks, informing us of where the edges are. In what sometimes feels like a growing epidemic of mental illness and mental health issues, it is significant to note that the language of emotions is still unwelcome in so many quarters of our lives. Not only are we not able to freely express difficult or unpleasant emotions in a healthy way, but the painful emotions

....

10. A. H. Maslow, "A Theory of Human Motivation," *Psychological Review 50*, no. 4 (1943): 370–96, https://doi.org/10.1037/h0054346.

we carry from our past with respect to unmet needs from unhealthy, dysfunctional, neglectful, or traumatic environments are pushed aside as irrelevant or inconsequential. Research shows that there are quite literally millions of children and adolescents who "have been diagnosed with having various forms of other 'mental illness,' from 'depression' to 'bipolar' to 'psychosis'"[11] who have experienced trauma that has not been recognized. Most childhood trauma (or Adverse Childhood Experiences) can be distilled down to a violation of needs: safety needs, security needs, comfort needs, esteem needs, respect needs. When one eliminates the relatively small percentage of psychiatric disorders linked to neurological and chemical imbalance, what remains is a massive body of mental illness that actually has emotional disturbance as a major factor.

In this dark Shadow of frozen emotions and unrecognized needs, the constricting cloak of codependency is donned. In the loss of the vibrant inner landscape of Essence, where we have dimmed the light on our own needs and feelings, the only safe alternative is to ramp up the light on the needs and feelings of the other. This is particularly true of the Empath, who has a gift for not only intuiting the feelings of others, but in taking them on as their own. This boundary distortion that we originally employed to keep ourselves safe is one of many codependent control dramas. It speaks to a lack of differentiation between self and other, the waters of self, overflowing the banks into the riverbed of another. This nourishes neither. The other end of this particular control drama spectrum is that of the Narcissist, whose modus operandi is to be hypervigilant and attentive to their own needs to the exclusion of the other. This is a different sort of boundary distortion. It creates an absolute hard line between self and other, completely prioritizing self. Here, the waters are so rigidly controlled it runs the risk of being a drought. But the Narcissist control drama smacks of "methinks the lady doth protest too much." The truth is, if you scratch a Narcissist, you uncover an Empath: someone who had already read the room, found it unsafe, and pulled up all the drawbridges. Narcissists have already determined that no one else will value them so they will make good and sure that they appear to be valued by themselves. Tragically, it is just a façade. By the same token, scratch an Empath and you reveal a Narcissist. Empaths can home in on what they perceive others are feeling,

....
11. Whitfield, Charles L. *Not Crazy: You May Not Be Mentally Ill*, 117.

but often that is filtered through the lens of their own past trauma, or a tendency to mind-read. In taking someone else's emotions on as their own, Empaths often lose themselves in their own inner experience. It doesn't matter that the emotions weren't theirs to begin with.

This Empath-Narcissist spectrum is the new language of codependency. Each of them is lost in the perceived experience of the other. Each experiences the deep soul pain of being lost to the inner connection to self. When we feel pain, very often the first place we go is to blame the other. "He hurt me." "It's her fault I feel this way." Though, of course, it is true that we live in relation to other people, our feelings are our own and are meant to be the emotional droplets that water our own inner seeds. When we lay the blame outside of ourselves, we start to swim in someone else's waters and are solidly in the pond of codependency. The Blame Game never has any winners. The controlling Narcissist has an over-active solar plexus chakra and needs to balance that torrential flow with some emotionally fluent sacral chakra energy. The boundary-challenged Empath has an over-active sacral chakra and needs to place some clear guidelines informed by the solar plexus chakra. As long as the focus remains on what the other needs to do, the freeze will keep everything at a wintery standstill.

Ultimately, if we are to address the Shadow of this cycle, we need to develop authenticity around our emotions. But we must start by being very clear on what healthy needs look like. We need to establish the banks of the river before we dip a toe in the water. Maslow outlined his Hierarchy of Needs in a progression from biological and physiological needs, which centered around our ability to survive physically in the world, through to self-actualization needs, which start to edge toward a sense of the soul and the fulfillment of our innate sense of potential.

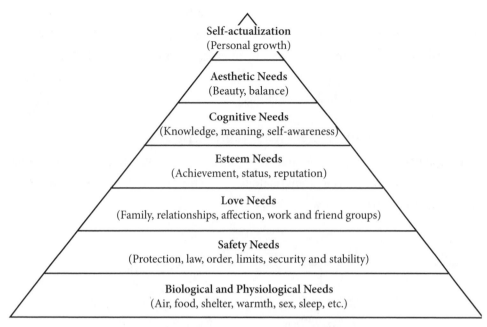

Maslow's Hierarchy of Needs[12]

This comprehensive map of human needs is a valuable resource in helping us to understand what gives context not only to our own lives, but to those of every other human being. These are not just your needs. They are everyone's needs. Interestingly, at the end of his own life, Maslow identified another level at the very top of the pyramid: that of Transcendence Needs. As he described it, "Transcendence refers to the very highest and most inclusive or holistic levels of human consciousness, behaving and relating, as ends rather than means, to oneself, to significant others, to human beings in general, to other species, to nature, and to the cosmos."[13] This pinnacle need speaks to the need to experience ourselves as part of something greater than the individual and personal; to open ourselves to experience the mystical; and to put our hard-won wisdom to the task of being of service to others. As such, it becomes fascinating to map the eight levels of Maslow's Hierarchy of Needs onto the eight-fold Wheel of the Year. It is evident that we need to plant before we harvest. No one

....

12. Adapted from *Motivation and Personality*, Abraham H. Maslow.

13. Abraham Maslow, *The Farther Reaches of Human Nature*.

is going to question that. By extension, we can see that we need to own our Esteem Needs before we can fully address our Cognitive or Self-Actualization Needs. And ultimately, true fulfillment comes when we can embrace our Spiritual or Self-Transcendent Needs. The ability to champion all our needs is a basic life skill we need to develop in order to live a healthy, fulfilled, flowing life.

Shadow of Cycle Two: Neglecting Innate Needs

Neglecting needs is a Core Issue that shows up in Cycle Four; however, an appreciation for the different needs as they relate to the Wheel of the Year can be helpful in developing Emotional Fluency.

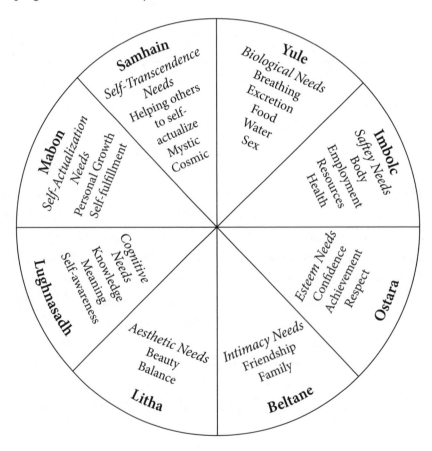

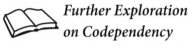 *Further Exploration*
on Codependency

Malkin, Craig. *Rethinking Narcissism: The Bad—and Surprisingly Good—About Feeling Special.* New York: Harper, 2015.

Small, Jacquelyn. *Awakening in Time: The Journey from Codependence to Co-Creation.* Eupsychian Press, 2000.

Whitfield, Charles. *Co-Dependence: Healing the Human Condition.* Health Communications, 1991.

Ten

······························

The Light of Non-Duality

In Cycle Two, as the waters that have been frozen begin to flow once more, we celebrate the Gifts from the Inner Child. The Child Within is a metaphor for our inner emotional life. As such it is our emotions, our ability to connect with and be informed by our feelings, that are the gifts from the Inner Child. The Child Within engages with the world from a purely emotional perspective, bounding through life, experiencing what they experience and sending feedback on those experiences back to us without filter. These emotions are not good or bad. They are not right or wrong. They just flow through us. Emotions are the current through which information about our experiences and beliefs about what should or should not be is transmitted. Some emotions are not very comfortable. Some can move very forcefully and that can overwhelm us. But if we are able to let them be and run their course, they actually bring enormous insight into our lives. Some emotions are light and expansive and we tend to be very drawn to those, sometimes to the exclusion of the more challenging ones.

The real issue with emotions does not stem from the emotions themselves. It stems from the tributary that can lead us to a dark, scary place. The unpleasant emotions can have a propensity to slide us into the muck of shame. It is not my hurt that the relationship ended that is the issue. It is how that hurt leads me to think that I deserved to be left, that if I had done something differently, I would not be alone, and that ultimately no one is ever going to love me because, really, how could anyone love me. That is not the message of hurt. That is the message of shame. But it is not just the unpleasant emotions that can take us there. The emotional charge of my sexual attraction to someone may feel exciting, expansive, energizing, and pleasant, but it can also slide me into shame. The heavy pit in my stomach tells me that my attraction would never be reciprocated or that I am shameful for even feeling this way. Shame is the core negative toxic emotion that <u>never</u> needs to be given the time of day. It will lead us to the Shadow of codependency and loss of self in any relationship dynamic: romantic, platonic, or professional. In the transformation of Shadow to Light, we have the opportunity to open ourselves to the depth and breadth of emotional fluency, but we have to challenge and release the stranglehold of shame in order to fully benefit from this invitation. If we can do this, there is so much the full spectrum of emotions has to communicate to us.

There are many differing views on the number of basic human emotions. The traditional approach favors "camps" of feelings. Frustration, irritation, and annoyance all have different flavors to them, but they can all fall within the general range of "anger." In this approach, there are six main categories of feeling: happiness, sadness, anger, surprise, fear, and disgust. Emotion wheels are good examples of this approach. A recent study out of the University of California, Berkeley identified twenty-seven distinct categories of emotions: admiration, adoration, aesthetic appreciation, amusement, anxiety, awe, awkwardness, boredom, calmness, confusion, craving, disgust, empathetic pain, entrancement, envy, excitement, fear, horror, interest, joy, nostalgia, romance, sadness, satisfaction, sexual desire, sympathy, and triumph.[14]

The Emotion Hive illustrated below presents six camps of emotions (three that we tend to strive toward or want to experience, and three of the more challenging emotional areas) with love as the central anchoring emotion. Spiritual teachings tell us that love is the core motivating energy of the Universe and that where there is love, shame cannot live.

14. Y. Anwar, "Emoji fans take heart: Scientists pinpoint 27 states of emotion." September 13, 2017; retrieved May 1, 2020, from https://news.berkeley.edu/2017/09/06/27-emotions/.

ANGER
Jealous • Irritated
Frustrated • Hostile
Resentful • Disgusted
Repulsed • Aggressive
Hurt • Fury

FEAR
Confused • Helpless
Insecure • Unsafe
Anxious • Rejected
Overwhelmed • Timid
Panicked • Terrified
Apprehensive

JOY
Excited • Cheerful
Playful • Amused
Hopeful • Energetic
Creative • Daring

LOVE
is letting go of the
shadow of shame.
When we can embrace
anger, fear, and sadness
as information, we can
move into the light of
joy, peace, and
empowerment.

SAD
Bored • Apathetic
Lonely • Uninspired
Ineffective • Gloomy
Isolated • Guilty
Disillusioned

EMPOWERED
Proud • Valuable
Confident • Successful
Appreciated • Respected
Discerning

PEACE
Content • Trusting
Relaxed • Serene
Grateful • Nurturing
Thoughtful

Joy tells us that life is good. It is a high-vibration emotion that expands and energizes us. It opens us to connection with others and allows us to drop fully into the experience of being alive.

Empowered tells us that we are capable, competent, and strong. It is a solid vibration that centers and grounds us in the acceptance and validation of our own experience and perception.

Peace tells us that all is well with our world. It is a soft, high-vibration emotion that tells us we are safe, all is well, and we can settle into allowing a gentle movement through our days.

Anger tells us that our boundaries have been crossed. It is a particularly kinetic emotion that needs to move. Anger that sits stagnant in the body without expression becomes tainted with the toxic emotion of shame and runs a high risk of turning into depression. But this also gives us a valuable key. If you feel yourself sinking into the sludge of depression, ask yourself: Is there something that I am angry about that I am not allowing myself to acknowledge or express?

Fear tells us that there is something in our environment or circumstance that demands a cautious approach. When it is rooted in a healthy "early warning system" or supported by the validation of our intuition, fear is a necessary centering emotion that invites us to slow down, gather more information, or choose a different direction. Fear that is disconnected from clarity concerning circumstances and instead becomes injected with the toxic emotion of shame carries a high risk of becoming anxiety. Anxiety has less to do with fear about something outside of ourselves than it does with a devastating fear that we will be "found out" and rejected.

Sad tells us that we have experienced a loss and that our hearts require some tenderness. It is a particularly delicate emotion that runs the risk of becoming the "wound that never heals" if we do not allow it the time it needs. If handled in a healthy way, we can move through anger very quickly and fear fairly quickly. But sadness needs the space to be held and rocked until it naturally ebbs into the grace of acceptance. If sadness is overlaid by shame, it can turn into despair that gives us the erroneous message that we will never feel joy again and worse, that we are isolated and alone in our sadness.

These provide a solid core of emotions to start to work with and build upon. In order to have a healthy, nurturing relationship with self, we need to be comfortable with the flow through and between all these emotions, developing emotional fluidity and emotional fluency, accepting the entire range of the emotional spectrum as providing different aspects of helpful and revealing information. The most important thing to remember with this is that there is no situation that we will face that will push our emotions to an unmanageable degree *as long as* they are not informed by shame and as long as we have done the work to heal the wounds of the past. If an emotion (usually one of the challenging ones, like anger) feels too big to be contained or verging on being out of control, that is an indication of being **triggered**. You are no longer responding solely to the current situation but rather have been dropped into the massive pool of all the other times you encountered a similar situation but did not have the language or the tools to address it. It is reactive and often explosive. Being triggered is an absolute clear message to *step away from* the current situation and deal with the past before coming back to address the current situation.

Emotional fluency is the ability to speak the language of emotions, inviting eloquence in describing what we are experiencing or how we are experiencing the world around us.

Emotional nuance is the ability to detect the subtle differences in the degrees of an emotion along a spectrum, allowing for precision and accuracy in the naming of what we feel.

Emotional complexity recognizes that often we can experience a range of opposing or contradictory emotions with respect to a single event or circumstance. If we are not comfortable with our emotional life, we may try to negate one or more of the presenting emotions in an attempt to simplify our experience, instead of allowing that humans are complex beings and that our emotions reflect that as well.

The more that we are able to foster and encourage openness in our attitude toward our emotions without the interfering overlay of shame, the less potential there is for falling into the trap of codependency, the less we look to have our emotions validated by others, and the less we prioritize the emotions of others over our own. The power struggle between the Empath and the Narcissist instead becomes a fluid exploration between two equally unhealthy poles with the potential for finding the healthy moderate flow. In doing this highly rewarding emotional work, the better we will be able to fully engage in the work of Cycle Three, claiming the self-acceptance and empowerment.

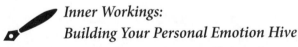

Inner Workings:
Building Your Personal Emotion Hive

With the preceding Emotion Hive Chart, take some uninterrupted time in a quiet place to breathe into your sacral chakra with the intention of opening yourself to gaining clarity on your relationship to your emotions. For each of the six outer emotions, take a moment to connect to the energetics of that emotion, paying particular attention to where and how you experience it in your body. It may be helpful to remember a time in your life when you recall that emotion being strongly alive in you. Or if it feels too hard to connect with the main emotion, focus instead on one of the nuanced reflections. If you do not remember a time you felt Peace, perhaps focus on Relaxed instead. If you are at a loss to recall a time you felt Anger, perhaps Irritated is more accessible. For each of the six, determine for yourself what the main message of that key emotion is for you. You can even ask the emotion to tell you how it will let you know, through your body, that it is trying to convey something to you. Befriend each of the key emotions, and by extension, all the nuanced reflections. Either in your mind or written out on a piece of paper, place yourself in the position of that emotion on the Emotion Hive Chart and anchor your acceptance of each emotion (i.e., "I embrace my anger and commit to listening to its message about appropriate boundaries") in each of the six spaces. Then imagine moving to the center space, to the position of Love, and feel how the six walls that form the safe center of Love are supported by Anger, Fear, and Sad, as well as by Joy, Empowered, and Peace. Feel also how Love emanates out to the six Key Emotions, allowing them to express freely in healthy ways. These emotions, and all those that continue to flow out from these, are your birthright. They are the expression of your Inner Child and are a precious gift in your life. The Love Hive honors that gift with a safe, protected sanctuary. You can use this technique with the opposite focus as well. If you find yourself in a situation and you can't identify how you are feeling about it, drop back into the Emotion Hive and allow your intuition to direct you toward the cell that feels the most accurate. Drop into that cell to explore the nuance until you are able to identify the particular shade of the emotion you are feeling with accuracy and then ask the emotion what it is trying to convey to you about the situation.

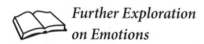 *Further Exploration*
on Emotions

Brackett, Mark. *Permission to Feel: The Power of Emotional Intelligence to Achieve Well-Being and Success.* Celadon Books, 2020.

Greenspan, Miriam. *Healing Through the Dark Emotions: The Wisdom of Grief, Fear, and Despair.* Shambhala, 2004 (reprint edition).

Smith, Tiffany Watt. *The Book of Human Emotions: An Encyclopedia of Feeling from Anger to Wanderlust.* London: Profile Books, 2015.

Eleven

. . . .

Journey to Meet Grandfather Sun and Grandmother Moon Meditation

One of the earliest challenges we meet in the journey toward wholeness is making the difficult choice to balance our needs with the needs of others. In the dualistic Empath/Narcissist paradigm, we prioritize self to the exclusion of other or prioritize other to the detriment of self. Neither of those approaches is respectful or honoring of the energy that flows between us. Both of them are reflective of codependent patterns, are informed by shame and fear, and keep us separate and isolated.

> Co-dependence is a disease of lost selfhood. It can mimic, be associated with, aggravate and even lead to many of the physical, mental, emotional or spiritual conditions that befall us in daily life.

> We become co-dependent when we turn our responsibility for our life and happiness over to our ego (our false self) and to other people.[15]

There is a degree of hope that can be found in the truism that I first heard from a wise Druid, Kristoffer Hughes of the Anglesey Druid Order: all water is one water. This awareness of loss of self in another, this challenge of honoring—or even identifying—emotions, this befuddlement over validating needs, this is not yours alone. It is part and parcel of the experience of being human.

---

15. Charles Whitfield, *Co-Dependence: Healing the Human Condition*, 3.

This meditation takes you deeper into the inner landscape that you have already experienced in order to explore the harmonizing potential of Cycle Two. As you journey in this landscape, have the courage to suspend judgment and be open to exploring what may perhaps be an unfamiliar perspective.

Meditation

Close your eyes. Focus on your breath. Allow your breath to drop you into a deep place within yourself. Each inhale connects you to those places within that may hold tension, discomfort, or unease. Each exhale invites you to release those tensions into the cosmos, bringing you to the balance place in the center of the Above and the Below that connects Spirit and human: the place between where magic happens.

You find yourself back at the place you were before: the mouth of the victorious cave, holding the seeds of your future glory. You allow yourself to feel the first tender shoots of inner confidence, hearing the soft trickle of a distant stream flowing. In the soft light of early dawn, you feel the delicate warmth of the sun's growing rays. It is one of those crisp, beautiful mornings in which the sun and moon share space and you can see them both in the clear, cloudless sky above. You gaze at those two celestial orbs, noting how different their energies feel to you and yet how perfectly balanced they are and, as you do, you feel a gentle nudge on your shoulder and a soft "chuff" in your ear. With a touch of trepidation, you slowly turn to look into the timeless eye of your vanquished dragon. That which was foe has returned to your side as ally, friend, and guide. Bowing its head, it offers its back and, with a grateful gesture, you settle yourself between neck and wings, easing yourself into a solid seat just as you feel the muscles ripple under your legs. The dragon launches itself off the edge of the precipice and propels itself—and you—upward toward the two heavenly bodies that had captured your attention.

Allow yourself to revel in the journey, the dips and the swoops of each wing beat, and surge upward. The flight awakens so many emotions in you: of excitement, and wonder, and perhaps just a touch of fear that makes you ensure your grip is secure. You rise higher and higher, getting closer and closer to the cosmic home of the moon and the sun. Just as you feel you are a short finger-stretch away from touching the face of the silvery moon, you close your eyes, immediately feeling another dragony swoop.

This swoop feels different. Not a brief dip before the next climb in altitude. This is more like the exhilarating freefall from the highest peak of a roller coaster. The emotions soar in you as you surrender to the experience and when the freefall slows and you feel your dragon land on what seems to be something solid, you open your eyes.

Slipping off your dragon's back, you see that you have been brought to a place where a silvery river winds through an arid land. In the distance, you see that two figures await you by the banks of the river and you start to move toward them. As you get closer, you see that they are two ancient beings: a silvery old woman and a coppery old man. Their eyes crinkle as you near them and you feel nothing but love and kindness from them: from Grandmother Moon and Grandfather Sun. They have much to teach you about the nature of flow.

Grandmother Moon reaches out and touches your cheek with her soft, wizened hand. Her touch is like liquid love, quenching a thirst within that you forgot you even had. You feel the flow of the river course through you and you know the moon. You know her deep mystery, the pull of her phases, her glowing guidance on the darkest night. You feel the gaze of her empathetic eye and know you are ever cradled in the loving arms of Grandmother Moon. As her touch releases, you find yourself brought out of your lunar reverie, back to her eyes, and you know to the depth of your being that you have been seen.

As you smile and thank Grandmother Moon for the gift of her empathetic love, you feel a hand rest upon your shoulder: the firm, steadying hand of Grandfather Sun. His anchoring touch holds you solidly in place as the banks hold the river, and in that focused guidance you know the sun. You know his direction and clarity. You know his constancy, even in the moments when his strength seems to wane. You know his dedication to a singularity of purpose, his commitment to supporting growth. And you also feel the edge of a narcissistic self-centeredness that makes you almost want to pull back, that brings up a tickle of unease until you hear, like a summer's hum in your ear, "But, of course, I am self-centered. Everything revolves around me. Tell me, what would it feel like for you to put yourself in the center of your own life for once?" You feel the truth of that land solidly in your very cells as his touch releases and you are brought out of your solar reverie. You turn and look into the eyes of Grandfather Sun as you thank him deeply for his gift of your self.

Shifting your gaze so you are able to hold both Grandmother Moon and Grand-father Sun in your vision, you are struck once more by how beautiful and perfect the symmetry of their energies. You see how seamlessly they balance each other and in the clarity of that awareness, you begin to feel how it is balanced within yourself: Sun and Moon, Narcissist and Empath, inward-focused and outward-focused, need-informed and feeling-informed, directive and intuitive, logical and emotional, self and other. You know there is room within to house all those energies and, in fact, those precious seeds that you still carry tucked away require all those energies in order to grow.

Allow yourself to take this in, to feel it in your blood and breath. Know that you have awakened and embraced the inner balance and harmony necessary to actualize the life of your choosing.

 Stones to Deepen
the Meditative Experience

Fire Opal intensifies emotional connection and awakens a zest for life.

Merlinite blends earthly and cosmic vibrations and helps us to remain open in spite of bad experiences.

Mystic Merlinite supports in releasing deeply held emotional patterns and old wounds, clearing the way for soul retrieval.

Septarian brings unconscious knowledge forward to assist with change.

Shattuckite, called the "Stone of Reconciliation," helps to calm the mind and create harmony.

Watermelon Tourmaline balances masculine and feminine energies.

Twelve

· · · · · · · · · · · · · · · · · · · ·

The Hermetic Principle of Gender Contemplation

Though considered to be the seventh and last principle (or Universal Law), the Hermetic Principle of Gender perfectly aligns with the energies of Imbolc and the movement between the two poles of thaw and freeze that invite us to start to anticipate the life that is gathering strength for its immanent burst forth.

Though several of the Hermetic Principles can be difficult to access or comprehend in the fullness of their implication, this principle tends to spark the most confusion, or even reaction. The automatic assumption associated with the word "gender" is to attribute "maleness" or "femaleness" to the equation. In an age that is increasingly challenging rigid gender definitions, stereotypes, and roles, this principle can be seen as problematic. Recalling the ancient genesis of alchemy and the Hermetic arts, one can turn to etymology to gain a deeper understanding of the underpinning of this principle. The word "gender" stems from the Latin "genus," meaning "family" or "nation." It is more on par with the French word "genre," which branches from the same root. Thus gender is not about the "state of being male or female in relation to the social and cultural roles that are considered appropriate for men and women"[16] but about identifying the two main camps of approach when it comes to how to move through the world.

----

16. *Collins English Dictionary, Glasgow*: Harper Collins, 1991.

Gender is in everything; everything has its Masculine and Feminine Principles; Gender manifests on all planes.[17]

The Hermetic Principle of Gender invites us to explore the dynamics inherent in duality in order to fully appreciate how necessary both are in the act of creation and manifestation. Looking at some of the oppositional energies implied in this principle, we find:

Active	Passive
Directive	Receptive
Deductive	Intuitive
Objective	Subjective

These qualities, in and of themselves, are fairly neutral. There is no implication of good or bad, right or wrong. They are more like directional signals, pointing to options in the approach of any situation. However, fairly quickly, given certain societal assumptions and expectations, we can see that the dynamic begins to take a bit of a different turn when we start to explore further opposite qualities.

Spirit	Matter
Light	Dark
Conscious	Unconscious
Mind	Body
Will	Desire
Thinking	Feeling
Masculine	Feminine

At a fairly distinct point in history with the triumph of the Roman Catholic Church in the West, the separation of Spirit and Matter was solidified with a most definite slant against Matter and, by association, all qualities that fall within the realm of that energetic. The Age of Reason (1715–1789) is defined by Rene Descartes'

----

17. The Three Initiates, "The Kybalion: Chapter II. The Seven Hermetic Principles," www.sacred-texts.com (Yogi Publication Society, 1912), https://www.sacred-texts.com/eso/kyb/kyb04.htm.

philosophical proposition "cogito, ergo sum," which translates as "I think, therefore I am." The import of this statement was meant to eliminate existential questions, with the emphasis being on providing a solid circumstance to prove existence. But what it also did was highlight that it is our thinking that validates our existence. This, coming on the heels of several centuries of absolute Church rule and the danger to life and limb that threatened if one opposed said rule, cemented the authority of Mind and everything aligned with that particular energetic. Taken to an extreme, we start to see where the overlay of shame touches any aspect of self that is not ruled by the mind. The Hermetic Principle of Gender removes the impetus to prioritize one aspect of the dynamic above the other, restoring both to their equal and necessary input, so we are able to honor:

Grandfather Sun   Grandmother Moon

Mankind cannot live by reason alone. To do so will create the barren wasteland found in such teaching tales as The Fisher King. And, as young Percivale learns in his quest, if we want to restore life to the land, we need to care enough to override what we have been taught is the proper approach, and meet the challenge with what our hearts tell us is right.

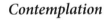 *Contemplation*
Contemplate how the Loving Hynni of Ebb and Flow reflects the Hermetic Principle of Gender: the waves that allow us to touch upon both ends of the spectrum and each moment between the poles.

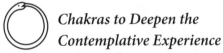 *Chakras to Deepen the*
Contemplative Experience
Connect with the **sacral chakra** to open yourself to fluid and cleansing water energies. Cradled and protected by the bones of the heart-shaped pelvis, this chakra supports the flow of the full spectrum of emotions through the experience of our life, from the quietest murmur to full-on flood. The energy that emanates to and from the front of this chakra informs us of the feelings that are current, related to what we are experiencing in the here and now. How open and healthy we are in receiving

their message will determine how future energies will unfold. The energy that sits in the back of this chakra is informed by past experiences: how supported we were in expressing our feelings and the degree to which we still carry the legacy of the emotional climate of our upbringing. Any issues with lower back, ovaries, testes, and appendix, all of which share nerve endings and tissue with the lower back, could be indicative of a blocked *back* sacral chakra

The higher-vibration chakra that sits in the cradle of our abdomen is the **Tenth Chakra of Harmonious Balance.**[18] As the higher reflection of the sacral chakra, experienced when we have released the constriction of shame, it helps us to take what we have learned of balancing the masculine and feminine within and infuse that inner dynamic with the depth of soul. The Tenth Chakra reflects the integration of the Hermetic Principle of Gender in its highest embodied expression.

....

18. Stone, *Soul Psychology*.

Thirteen

Cleansing and Purification Ritual

Early spring brings the first tender moments of thaw, inviting the waters of alchemical Dissolution to wash away the grit of negativity that may still be sticking to the psyche. As our energy becomes clear of the old heaviness of the past, our emotions can run as clear as fresh spring water, guiding us toward our pure intent. This ritual invites you to open yourself to the sense of sitting beside a sacred well as you "gather" reeds to weave protective love into a three-armed Brigid's Cross for your Inner Child. (See Appendix E for illustrated steps.)

Symbols to help connect to ritual focus	• Items that help connect to the Inner Child around ages 3 to 6, including photographs of self as a child • Containers or little bottles of water (from sacred sources, local waters, or pristine melted snow) • Candles • Statues or photos of those deities associated with sacred springs or rivers; Spring or maiden goddesses; goddesses of love and beauty • An image of the Loving Hynni of Ebb and Flow
Optional: Stones from *Journey to Meet Grandfather Sun and Grandmother Moon* Meditation	• Fire Opal • Merlinite • Mystic Merlinite • Septarian • Shattuckite • Watermelon Tourmaline
Items needed for ritual activity	• A fresh unused candle (orange, if you want to align with Hynni) • A lighter • A cauldron • Water • 12 reed strands (pipe cleaners can be used instead) • Optional: Candle snuffer • Optional: A cup of loose-leaf tea or *Tea Leaf Fortune Cards*

Creating the Altar

On the left side of your existing altar or on a surface that can act as one for this ritual, set up an homage to your Inner Child, including a photo of yourself as a pre-school age child or any items you may had since you were a child. On the right side of your altar, set a cauldron filled with water. In my travels, I have collected sacred, special, and meaningful-to-me water from all over the world and also been gifted water from places I have not been by friends who know of my collection. All these waters are precious to me and, when I create my "sacred well" at Imbolc, I include a few drops from each of them. In the center, place a fresh, unused candle and the reeds or pipe cleaners.

You may also choose to decorate your space and your altar with those elements that speak to the theme of purification and new beginnings, such as those associated with Imbolc or Candlemas. You may also want to include reflections, representations, or symbols of gods and goddesses associated with water, spring, love, and purification.

When you are done preparing your space, take a moment to feel how the energy you have created affects you. You will want to ensure that there are elements that speak to the general theme of the ritual or the festival itself. This reflects the "Above," the realm of the transpersonal or mythic. You will also want to ensure that there are elements that represent you on the altar. This reflects the "Below," the realm of the personal.

In the Hynni approach, the Intuitive Reflection for this Cycle is tasseomancy. If you would like to include tea leaf reading as part of your ritual, prepare a cup of tea, allowing the loose leaves to float in the boiled water. You can sip this tea during the ritual so that by the end you will just have the dregs and sodden leaves in the cup. If this feels complete, take some time to prepare yourself for ritual (see Appendix D).

The Ritual

If you have a picture of yourself as a child on the altar, begin to focus on that, taking some time to look into the eyes of that child and, when you feel ready, light the candle in the center of your altar, holding the intention to connect with that emotional part of yourself. You may even feel, as you do, your younger self join you in this liminal space by your "sacred well," sitting, so to speak, by your side.

It is love for the Child Within that is the impetus for crafting your Brigid's Cross. This is the part of you that tells you how you feel about what is happening in your life. It is the part that guides you to remember the truth of who you are. It is the part that informs you of your needs, reassures you of their validity, and urges you to always remember that you matter. And so, holding love for that part of yourself in your heart, you reach for the first of the strands you will be using to form this three-legged protective charm. Touch the strand to your heart, blessing it with love for your Inner Child, then dip it in the water in your cauldron, anointing it with a Divine blessing for your Inner Child, and bend the strand in half. Take the second strand, blessing it with both your own love and with that of the Divine and then, bending it in half, slip it over the first strand about 1/3 of the way down from where the first strand was bent, pointing toward the left. Take the third strand, bless with your heart energy and dip in the waters of the cauldron, then slip it <u>over</u> the second strand and <u>through</u> the loop of the first strand, pointing toward the right. You should now have three arms to your cross—one pointing straight down, one pointing to the left (toward "ten o'clock"), one pointing to the right (toward "two o'clock").

Before continuing to weave, take a moment to contemplate these three arms. They can represent the Above, the Below, and the Synthesis. They can represent your Inner Child, your Higher Self, and the Adult that acts on behalf of both. They can represent your feelings, your reason, and the Self that honors them both. However you represent these three arms, know that they always serve to protect that which is most precious—your Essence.

Continue to weave, first blessing the strands, then adding them to your cross, building upon the foundation created by the three arms until all the strands have been woven.

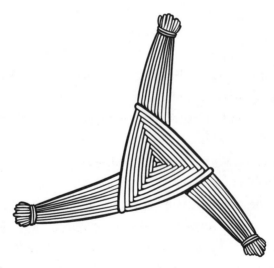

When it is done, shift your attention to your Inner Child, letting that child know that this beautiful weaving reflects your love and commitment to Self. Take all the time you need, resting in this moment, gazing at the candle before you, sitting in a pool of love with your Inner Child by your "sacred well." You can also use this time to consult the leaves, if you have been drinking tea during the ritual. With the barest of liquid left in the cup, flip the cup upside down onto the saucer, give it several firm turns counter-clockwise and flip it upright again. Use your intuition or your "Inner Child eyes" to discern any shapes or symbols you see in the cup and allow your "Inner Child imagination" to play with what their significance may be to you, particularly with respect to your Essence and deepest desires. If you choose to use the *Tea Leaf Fortune Cards* instead, pull three cards and approach reading them as if they were symbols found in a cup, letting your own interpretation overlay whatever words may be on the cards themselves.

Closure of Ritual

When you are ready to leave this space, bring your conscious awareness back to your breath. Taking one last moment to anchor the connection to your sense of your Essence, using either your breath or a candle snuffer, release the flame of the candle before you. What has been experienced in ritual lives forever in your cells. It need only be called forth from within when you choose.

Take some time to move through the directions once more, thanking the elements for helping to hold space and keep you safe through the ritual. Start again in the North with earth, then move through the East with air, the South with fire, the West with water, ending with the Below of the material plane and the Above of the cosmic plane. Thank and bid farewell to the deities who have been a part of this ritual with you and know that the wheel may turn around you, but you are—as they are—ever at the center.

Clearing Ritual Space

If you have been using an existing altar, you may decide to keep some items on your altar over the course of the cycle as a way to continue to hold the energy of what you have experienced and embodied in the ritual. Find a safe place to store items that you may want to keep for future rituals, such as the Essence candle, until next time. If you like, leave the water in the cauldron on your altar to evaporate, imbuing the room itself with the loving energy that was generated in the ritual.

 *Tasseomancy Recommendations*

Hepburn, Rae. *Tea Leaf Fortune Cards*. Stamford, CT: US Games, 2011.

Lyle, Jane. *Cup of Destiny*. New York: Shelter Harbor Press, 2013.

Fourteen

Love Is the Highest Law

The power of Cycle Two is the healing that comes when we know in every cell that we are loved and loveable, and when we realize that every emotion is a movement toward love if we allow it to flow as it needs with awareness, respect, and true empathy.

There is a wide, wide ocean of possible emotion that is waiting for us to explore and experience. In all the various depths, temperatures, colors, and qualities of those waters, we remember that all water is one water. We may find ourselves experiencing a seemingly endless array of situations, relationships, dynamics, and feelings, but when it comes right down to it, there is one emotion that is by far the greatest force in the Universe and that is love. Love is the energetic force that brings integration to opposites and helps us to see past the illusion of separation.

In the pain of codependency, we lose sight of the love that is the necessary supportive environment we need to foster healthy relationships within and without. We may negotiate away self-care, self-regard, and self-respect in order to appease or placate the other and in no way, shape, or form is this a reflection of love. It is said that we need to love ourselves before we can truly love another and that is the truth. If I change who I am in order to make you happy, I am not acting from a place of love toward either of us. I am acting from a place of agenda and control. When I love myself, I give myself the gift of being my true, authentic, flawed self and love you enough to know that you are entitled to have whatever feelings you have about that.

The Gift from the Inner Child at Imbolc is allowing the warmth of love to provide the thaw that will lead us to the great awakening of an empowered self.

Key Aspects of Cycle Two[19]

Archetypal Themes	Healing Themes	Indication of Crisis	Healing Practices
Gifts from the Inner Child Love; purification; new beginnings	Emotions and emotional fluency; Pre-school Child, honoring full range of emotions; neglecting needs	Overwhelmed by emotions; an inability to identify or experience emotions; excessive or extreme reactions to current situations; difficulty in relationships with others; discomfort or shame regarding sexuality	Exploration of Emotion Hive; contemplation of the Hermetic Principle of Gender; activation of Loving Hynni of Ebb and Flow
Elemental Reflection	**Intuitive Guidance and Tool**	**Alchemical Reflection**	**Affirmations**
Water	Aquatic guides; tasseomancy (tea leaf reading)	*Dissolution* The release of held pain that comes through the accessing and expressing of emotions.	I go with the flow; I release with ease; my emotions run clear; I am able to share my feelings with others; I am cleansed by blessings that surround me.

....

19. More information on Key Aspects can be found in *The Great Work: Self-Knowledge and Healing Through the Wheel of the Year* by the author (Llewellyn, 2015).

Part Three

Cycle Three
March 22–May 2

New Paths to Dispute Resolution

The Centering Hynni of Esteem

As Below	**As Above**
Conflictual	Cooperative
Alchemical	Sense of Self
Separation	Nurturing
Defensive	Empowerment
Defenses	Boundaries

Synthesis
Renewal
Resurrection
Preparation

Fifteen

Ostara and the Celebration of Life

The Vernal Equinox or Ostara is marked astronomically when the sun crosses over the equator, for a brief moment holding that absolute balance between night and day before moving us slowly but surely into increased daylight hours. This is the time we move solidly into the Light Half of the Year according to the ancient Celts, knowing that we have come through another difficult and potentially dangerous dark time. The sense of *Resurrection* and coming back to life is a main archetypal theme of this festival. The word comes from the Latin root "resurgere" meaning "to rise again." In all aspects of nature, and in many ways within ourselves as well, there is the sense that that which has been languishing or steeping underground is surging forth again to claim life with confidence and competence. The energy of this festival is different than that of Yule. This is not the celebration of the hope and optimism that comes with the birth of the Divine Child. This is the celebration of *Renewal* that comes when we know deep in our souls that we have the skills and tools necessary for seeing ourselves through the tough times, the courage to release that which will keep us stuck in the dark, and the wherewithal to set intention for the course that will bring us to our best future. There is a certain aspect of "claiming" that differentiates this festival from Yule and brings a nuance to the archetypal energies of the celebration: the recognition that it is our own strength that has seen us through the dark and helped us navigate the sometimes treacherous path back into the Light. This is different than the celebration of the miraculous arrival of embodied hope, which carries a passive resonance in comparison. Ostara implies that there has been effort and sacrifice and out of that effort, life has returned.

Harnessing competence is the culmination and resolution of the psychological developmental conflict of the School Age Child. In childhood development theory, we go through unconscious internal polarities to come to a place of inner mastery. For the School Age Child, that polarity is industry versus inferiority. At Ostara, with the archetypal theme of *Preparation* and readying the ground to receive the seed that is the potential of our future harvest, this sense of competence awakens the confidence that we have what it takes to be able to coax and guide those seeds into fruitful abundance.

When, instead of being fueled by competence, we are informed by inferiority and low self-esteem, we are still caught in the dark. The Shadow reflection of this Cycle is an inability to or difficulty with resolving conflict that has less to do with communication skills than it does with a lack of connection to one's own empowerment. If we have not successfully integrated the "powers" from Cycles One and Two (i.e., knowing our needs and honoring our emotions), encountering any type of conflict holds too great a potential for throwing us back into the dark (i.e., shame). Like Orpheus' attempt to lead Eurydice out of the Underworld, if we have not truly heard the message while we were in the dark, we are destined to continue to live there or, at the very least, continue to look back.

Conflict is experienced when there is static on the line of intersection between myself and another. The less I am in tune with my own inner life and the more I require validation from the other, the fuzzier the boundary between us and the higher the potential for conflict. The Vernal Equinox shows us that, in the interplay between the light and the dark, one is not more important than the other. They are both necessary for the ongoing seasonal dance and growth cycle. The more I am able to acknowledge and honor this, the less potential there is for conflict and the more potential there is for creation.

Though, of course, the Spring Equinox would have been experienced from the dawn of time, the festival and celebrations associated with it have changed from place to place and through the ages. The festival that we know of as Ostara is, in fact, a modern creation. As Kerri Connor notes in her book on Ostara, "It was Gerald Gardner, while creating Wicca, who pulled together customs from different traditions and came up with the seven sabbats and then added in the Vernal Equinox, bringing the total sabbats to eight and putting them approximately six weeks apart."[20]

But that does not mean that the ancients were not acutely aware of the spiritual and symbolic significance of this time. El Castillo, the massive temple at Chichen Itza, was built around 1000 CE in such a way that, at both the Vernal and the Autumnal Equinox, it appears as though a serpent is slithering down from the top of the pyramid to the bottom step, representing the return of the feathered serpent god, Quetzalcoatl or Kukulkán. Machu Picchu, the remarkable mountaintop city of the Incas, built in the fifteenth century CE, houses a giant pillar at the top called the Intihuatana, which loosely translates as "the place where the sun gets tied."[21] At midday on both equinoxes, the sun is positioned directly above this pillar so it casts no shadow, seeming to sit or "be tied" there. The Druids refer to this time as *Alban Eilir*, meaning "the light of the Earth." The ancient Romans celebrated the *Hilaria* on March 25, the last of several festival days dedicated to the goddess Cybele. This particular day celebrated the joyous resurrection of her lover, Attis. *Passover* (Jewish) does not necessarily fall on the Vernal Equinox, but it is considered a spring holiday that commemorates the emancipation of the Israelites from slavery in Egypt. *Easter* (Christian), the celebration of the resurrection of Christ, first began in the second century CE, and was observed with the timing of the Jewish holiday in mind. *Nowruz* (Persian) is perhaps the oldest of all these festivals that center around the Spring Equinox. Dating back some seven thousand years and translated as "new day," this festival marks the start of the Iranian New Year.

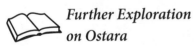 *Further Exploration on Ostara*

Connor, Kerri. *Ostara: Rituals, Recipes & Lore for the Spring Equinox*. Woodbury, MN: Llewellyn, 2015.

....
20. Kerri Connor, *Ostara*, 20.

21. Norman, "The Intihuatana Stone in Machu Picchu," Annees de pelerinage, May 14, 2017, https://www.annees-de-pelerinage.com/intihuatana-stone-in-machu-picchu/.

Sixteen

The Shadow of the Enemy at the Gate

Ostara brings us to a threshold, stepping across which opens us to light and the opportunity for growth. Many ancient myths present otherworldly beings or gods and goddesses as guarding these liminal places that move us from one distinct reality to another. Often, they are the keepers of the key needed to open the door that allows one to cross into new life. The boundary places are recognized to be power places. Places where magic happens. Places worth defending. In our inner psychological life, this power place is the threshold that invites true knowledge and acceptance of self. When we are able to step into the truth of our life from that place of empowerment and unquestioned self-worth, we do experience a life of magic. Enfolding the precious Divine Child into the core of our Being opens us to a life of wonder. Sadly, this is not the norm, rather the opposite. The knowledge of ourselves as precious remains locked in the shadowy depths of the Underworld and we climb into the light as partial Beings, the key hanging uselessly on a chain at our waist.

When we are carrying much of darkness within us, it is impossible to have a solid sense of self. It is impossible to connect with one's own identity and be our own advocate. It is impossible to know who we are outside of others' identification of us. When you do not have a sense of your own worth and value, you cannot feel that anything you do, say, or want is valid. Your wants, needs, and dreams become invalid. In invalidating yourself, you actually make yourself an invalid, weakening yourself and disconnecting self from the source of strength within.

It is a fascinating phenomenon that when we start to become aware of how we deal with our own boundary places—the meeting place of self and the other—that we very often go to extremes of reaction. This can be expressed in the Empath-Narcissist spectrum addressed in Cycle Two, but it can also take the form of the Victim-Bully dynamic. Having explored the Shadow in two separate cycles now, it is starting to become clear that whenever our inner experience is informed by shame, it is going to create issues. More often than not, we see ourselves as powerless and the other as all-powerful and we grasp any means at our disposal to keep ourselves safe. Defenses are employed when there is a perceived threat and we feel that we must activate some sort of protection. These can take many forms and be employed on any of the four aspects of Being: physical, emotional, mental, or spiritual. All defenses serve one common purpose: to make sure that the threat or the danger—perceived as the Other—is kept at a distance.

On a surface level, it might appear that having an understanding of defenses and when to use them is a beneficial thing. It may seem that this is a skill that one would want to explore and develop. It certainly has been the way of the world for thousands of years. Building up militaries and arsenals in order to <u>defend</u> that which is yours and <u>attack</u> those who pose a threat to it has gone on for so many millennia it seems woven into the fabric of how we know to be human. If this is the way we do things from a global perspective, then this is naturally how we do things in our smaller, personal world. The macrocosm is reflected in the microcosm. We are given the message through many means and in many forms that we must learn to defend ourselves. But as we have also learned through history, and what can also be seen reflected in the interpersonal, is that this defensive approach to maintaining safety only leads to casualties on all sides. The problem with defenses is that they are by their very nature *defensive*! They are unconscious and reactive. They distance and isolate. They tend toward annihilation rather than fortification. And, because, most especially in the personal and interpersonal realms, they are always focused on the external as being at the root of the issue, they never help get to the core of the problem, which is the internal relationship. Defenses will always keep us locked in some level of the wrangle of a control drama. We focus so much on fighting the wolves at the door that we ignore the poison arrow that has slipped through all the armor, piercing us in our most vital and vulnerable spot—our identity, our sense of self, our self-esteem. What we need to do is stop expending our energy on battling that which is external and focus instead on drawing out the poison that is coursing through our veins. When we find ourselves in a battle, focusing on that which is outside of us and drawing upon all our defenses to keep that at bay, we have already lost the war.

We have been trained to think that the threat coming from the outside is the one that has the potential to cause the most damage, and so we arm ourselves and ready ourselves to defend ourselves against what we anticipate will be the enemy at the gate. The truth is that it is often the internal messaging that does the most damage. Best represented by the pre-cellphone horror film, *When a Stranger Calls*, we have all internalized to some degree the experience that necessitates the chill-inducing warning: "The call is coming from inside the house."[22] That which has the greatest power to destroy us lies within, not without. As long as we are focused on battling the "enemy" that lies outside of us, the toxin that lies within has the opportunity to deepen its hold. There is a psychological term for that. It is called "projection." We reflect onto the other that which we are not able to face within ourselves, and we attack it on the outer playing field, rather than face the dark or the demon within. At this time, when we are encouraged to step from the dark into the light, we have to address that internal threat once and for all. If we do not, we are doomed to reactionary dynamics that will always see the other through the lens of danger. The ground in which we plant the seed for our future harvest will be tainted with toxins, resulting in a blighted harvest.

When it comes to addressing how we approach disputes with another, there is a range of how we may meet that challenging intersection, all informed by how solid, balanced, and healthy we are in our own sense of self or not. One way to understand this range is to see the varying degrees through alchemical and energetic reflections. If one is familiar with the alchemical stages of healing and the chakra energetic, it provides a familiar context to various options regarding new paths to dispute resolution. It is in our lower chakra that we process many of the challenges of our human experience. When blocked in these chakras, we are locked in codependence patterns, overlaid by shame, and are very far from an experience of empowerment. This is reflected in the ways in which we engage when it feels our boundaries are threatened.

....
22. *When a Stranger Calls*, Melvin Simon Productions (1979).

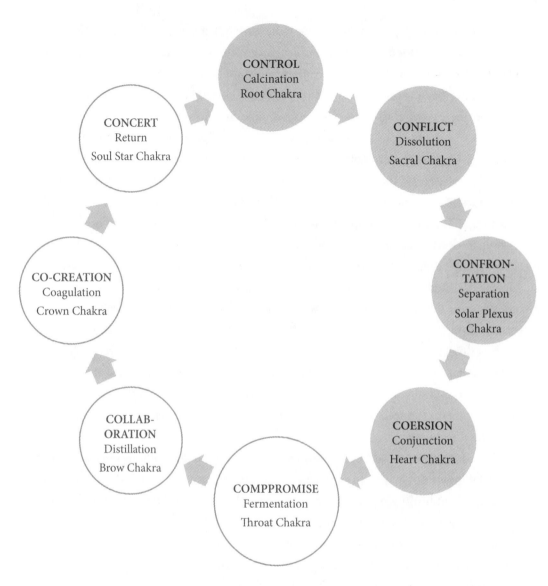

Control is our attempt to wrest power over the other. It is the Shadow aspect of the root chakra, indicating fears around security needs. There is no trust that the other will be open to negotiation and so we respond by attempting to remove that option. We maneuver and manipulate to ensure our needs are met. This generally results in a total disregard for the needs of others. The degree to which we control others indicates the degree to which we actually have no faith in ourselves.

Conflict brings the manipulation of control into open opposition. I often hear people talk about their fear of confrontation when in fact it is the fear of conflict that drives us to drop down into control or causes us to activate rigid, impenetrable defenses. Conflict is the Shadow aspect of the sacral chakra, which often feels dangerously informed by emotions that are infused with shame. The hurt that tells us we are unlovable. Or the anger that tells us we matter little to others. Or the sadness that tells us we are discardable. These are not healthy reflections of hurt, anger, or sadness, but the toxic messaging clouded by shame that keeps us separate from others. It is these sharp, painful emotions that will very often bring us into pitched conflict. This is what it feels like to be triggered and it is this we strive to avoid. Conflict brings no benefit to anyone involved. The best rule of thumb when you find yourself engaged in conflict is to muster every internal resource you have in order to choose to walk away. The dispute or disagreement needs a more empowered approach and that will never be found in the midst of battle.

Confrontation quite literally translates as the ability to be "up front with" our differences. It does not carry the same level of potential threat that open conflict does; however, there can still be an edge to confrontation especially if one is coming from the low self-esteem indicative of a blocked solar plexus chakra. It is in this level of "dispute resolution" that we particularly find the defenses, especially the mental defenses. We are not in the "Machiavellian" type dynamic of control, nor the "berserker" type dynamic of conflict. From a Shadow perspective, with confrontation, we are standing on the ramparts and shouting "Your mother was a hamster and your father smelled of elderberries."[23] It is a fairly easy shift to release the need for defense and start to move into a more empowered, communicative mode of dispute resolution.

Coercion is a sneaky, manipulative form of control that likes to present that there is care being afforded the other, but the truth is it is still just a covert way of controlling someone else to get your own way. It can involve barter with little or no intention

....
23. *Monty Python and the Holy Grail*, Python (Monty) Pictures (1975).

of follow through; "guilt trips" (which are actually "shame traps"); or the duplicity to show a certain friendly face until one has achieved the desired end. In many ways, coercion can be even more devastating than the previous Shadow paths of dispute resolution because it presents from heart chakra energy but there is no true caring involved. In the experience of the other, it can come across as gaslighting and can do incredible damage to both self-esteem and ability to trust for that person.

Once we have addressed the heaviness of shame and drained the poison of its toxic messages from our veins, there is no need for manipulation or control. In doing the healing work of Cycle Three, we truly leave the Shadow in the Dark Half of the Year, claiming our gifts, knowing our strength, and stepping into the Light Half of the Year from a place of empowerment. And, as Marianne Williamson says, "As we let our own light shine, we unconsciously give other people permission to do the same."[24]

The first step in claiming our own light is being able to recognize when our defenses have been activated, when our shame has re-engaged. If we are looking for a key from those guardians at the threshold, there is no better key to empowerment than this: know your defenses and recognize when they have been turned on!

Shadow of Cycle Three: Defenses

All defenses fall within the Shadow work of Cycle Three; however, a further delineation shows how different defenses can align with the energies found on the Wheel of the Year

------

24. Marianne Williamson, *A Return to Love.*

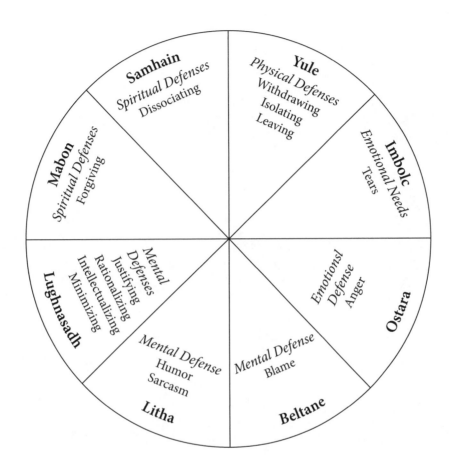

Samhain
Spiritual Defenses
Dissociating

Yule
Physical Defenses
Withdrawing
Isolating
Leaving

Mabon
Spiritual Defenses
Forgiving

Imbolc
Emotional Needs
Tears

Lughnasadh
Mental Defenses
Justifying
Rationalizing
Intellectualizing
Minimizing

Ostara
Emotionsl Defense
Anger

Litha
Mental Defense
Humor
Sarcasm

Beltane
Mental Defense
Blame

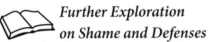

Further Exploration
on Shame and Defenses

Burgo, Joseph. *Why Do I Do That?: Psychological Defense Mechanisms and the Hidden Ways They Shape Our Lives*. New Rise Press, 2012.

Potter-Efron, Ronald. *Letting Go of Shame: Understanding How Shame Affects Your Life*. Center City, MN: Hazelden Publishing, 1989.

Underland-Rosow, Vicki. *Shame: Spiritual Suicide*. Waterford, 1995.

Seventeen

The Light of Boundaries

Early spring, aligned as it is to the energetic of water, introduces us to inner equilibrium, to the nourishing flow of healthy emotion. It attunes us to be able to recognize when a feeling is coming from a healthy source like a rain-fed aquifer, rather than an unhealthy source, like a stagnant old still water pond. Late spring, aligned as it is to the energetic of air, introduces us to outer equilibrium, to the differentiating clarity brought with the acute awareness of just what is within my domain and thus my responsibility and what is not. The Vernal Equinox is a beautiful metaphor that helps shed light on that distinction. Night is not day, nor is day night. What is relevant for the domain of the night is not necessarily relevant for the realm of day. It is perfectly clear in the balance of light and dark, less so in interpersonal relationships, and yet, in reality, it is really that simple. What is mine is mine and really none of your concern. What is yours is yours and really none of my concern. In interpersonal relationships what is key to remember is a clear delineation between what is mine and what is yours. The muddier this delineation is, the more the night bleeds into the day or the dark into the light, the more likely we will resort to conflict or control to try to grasp some semblance of equilibrium.

So, what is mine and what is yours? It is not as complicated as one might think. The following chart is adapted from the work of Charles Whitfield to use as a guide to bring the fresh breeze of clarity on the space between you and another.

MINE
My feelings
My experiences
My Choices
My consequences
My beliefs
My deams
My spirituality

YOURS
Your feelings
Your experiences
Your Choices
Your consequences
Your beliefs
Your deams
Your spirituality

Whitfield's Boundary Delineation[25]

To recognize and respect these elements as being wholly yours, outside of anyone else's reach to muck or meddle with, does not mean we operate in the world from a place of egocentric selfishness. It actually means that we stand centered in our own self. The admonition to discard self through the shame-based accusation of selfishness to replace it with the equally shame-based but more socially acceptable selflessness does a disastrous disservice to self and is, in fact, contemptuous of spirit. The greatest gift you can give your family, your employer, your friends, and, indeed, the world is that of your full, claimed, embraced, celebrated, empowered Self.

When we come from Self, we are centered in self. Our emotional center of gravity rests in a healthy, flowing solar plexus chakra that is informed by an internal sense of identity. We know who we are, what we like or dislike, what our beliefs are, what our hopes are, what our strengths are. We can accept what our limitations are, what our misguided choices have been, and mistakes we have made, all without going to a place of shame. It is not that we are unconcerned with the feelings or experiences of others. Not at all. It is just that we are acutely aware that it is not our business to overstep a line—just as we would most probably experience some uncomfortable or

....

25. Adapted from *Boundaries and Relationships: Knowing, Protecting, and Enjoying the Self* by Charles L. Whitfield.

angry feelings if someone overstepped a line with us. Knowing where you end and another begins is a key building block in creating a foundation of healthy self-esteem and empowerment. Having attained esteem, usually through innumerable experiences in which we have forgotten that differentiation and found ourselves back in the dark, we are able to identify, establish, and maintain healthy boundaries without defensiveness.

Defenses are externally focused. We are overly concerned with where the other person is coming from, what they might think of us, how they might hurt us. When I am defending, I have put my centered sense of self in the other and the only outcome is disequilibrium.

Boundaries are internally focused. I know who I am and where I am and draw that line in the sand, dedicated to not stepping over it myself and iterating, reiterating, and iterating again its firm yet loving existence. Boundaries are the three little pigs in a house of bricks. The wolf can blow all he wants. Nothing is going to budge.

We know we have mastered the ability to implement a healthy boundary when there is no fear-based charge around how we think the other person is going to respond. This is huge. So many times, I have heard someone expound on what they would love to say to another, sharing hurt feelings or expressing a need, but when I suggest having the conversation, the response is, "Oh no, I can't. They would get mad at me" or "They would think badly of me" or "They would hate me." Whenever we prioritize the other person's reaction over our need to communicate, we are back in the Shadow of defense. Boundaries put our own needs in sharp focus, at the center of our attention, but they are also respectful and appropriate. They do not disregard the other or try to control or manipulate. Boundaries, as in the diagram above, pay attention to what is within our own domain, have consideration for what is in the other's domain, and make room between the two for some air to breathe.

When we are solid, for the most part, in our own empowerment, attentive to the empowerment of others, and comfortable with communicating healthy boundaries, we are able to move out of the reflections of dispute resolution that are still concerned with power struggle, and into more expansive and far more exciting possibilities.

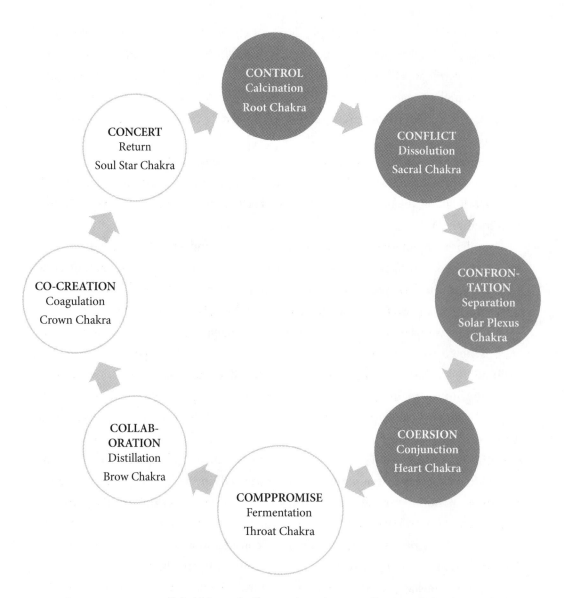

Compromise can still feel like a challenge, though it is reflective of the throat chakra and our ability to communicate and express. It is also connected to the alchemical stage of Fermentation, a stage that allows another layer of that which keeps us stuck and heavy to die. Compromise requires that we surrender some aspect of our perspective for the greater good. If there is any part of unhealthy ego still at play, this will be impossible.

Collaboration brings us to the level of dispute resolution that no longer feels like there is any aspect of the spark of discord. With collaboration, there is still the element of difference. We can still be coming from opposite ends of the spectrum or issue. But, informed by the brow chakra, we are able to see past the edges of our own boundary to appreciate the other's perspective. The alchemical stage of Distillation purifies substance through the repetitive action of warming and cooling, allowing a refinement with each round. Collaboration is very similar. Taking two differing perspectives and moving them through the distillation process allows for a resulting vision that pulls the best from both, acknowledging the competence and ability of both to contribute to the overall wisdom of the task.

Co-creation is the reflection of dispute resolution filtered through the crown chakra. In co-creation, we are able to see that what appear to be disagreement and conflict are actually the very things we need to inspire our growth or to bring out the very best in the issue at hand. It sees the static created when opposing forces come together as holding great potential for inspiration and brilliance. It does not shy away from differing viewpoints but rather invites them to offer the creative spark that can lead to unexpected brilliance. There is no shred of unhealthy ego in this approach to dispute resolution. Embodying the final alchemical stage of healing and the attainment of the Philosopher's Stone, coagulation, in co-creation we know ourselves to be whole regardless of whether we are seen and heard or not. We know this to be true of the other as well. We are able to put any consideration of needing to have our input recognized aside and instead are able to focus on the task at hand: what is the best course moving forward for the greater good of all concerned?

Concert is less a distinctive tributary on the new paths to dispute resolution than it is a way of being. Concert is defined as "being in harmony or accordance." As such, it invites us to coordinate our own energies (including our ideas, perspectives, and abilities) to the energies of others in order to come to the greatest level of cohesion and alignment. It requires a wise depth of perception to be able to discern the most harmonious engagement. This is not always about agreement. Sometimes it is about speaking up. Sometimes it is about pushing back. Sometimes it is about walking away or holding the peace or ceding to a differing view. It requires the resolve of the soul star chakra to truly know oneself to be in unity with community. When we know that our own song contributes to the melody of the Universe, the Music of the Spheres, and that we really can never take a misstep if we are true to Self and Spirit, then we really are in concert with the harmonious whole. This is the silent final stage of the alchemical healing process: the return to the knowledge that we are not separate.

Not Spirit from Matter. Not Earth from Heaven. Not you from me nor me from you. When you know that to battle another is only to fight yourself and choose to lay down the sword for good, this is the attainment of the highest wisdom.

This does not require us to sacrifice the needs that we have worked hard to recognize and claim. Nor does it require us to ignore the vital messages from our emotions. We hold fast to what we know is ours, honoring the human part of us that does experience differentiation. And we give ourselves the gift of healthy boundaries on all four aspects of Being: physical, emotional, mental, and spiritual.

Light of Cycle Three: Boundaries

All boundaries fall within the Essence work of Cycle Three; however, a further delineation shows how different boundaries can align with the energies found on the Wheel of the Year

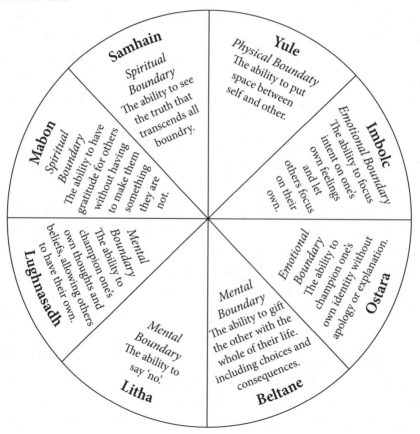

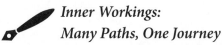 *Inner Workings:*
Many Paths, One Journey

To fully experience the different energies and outcomes of the new paths to dispute resolution, take some uninterrupted time in a quiet place to breathe into your solar plexus chakra with the intention of opening yourself to the benefits and drawbacks of each of the eight possible paths to take when faced with difference or opposition. Think of a time when you found yourself in opposition with an individual. Allow yourself to drop fully into what that experience was like for you, paying particular attention to how you feel in your solar plexus chakra as you do. As you think about this situation and how you responded to it at the time it occurred, allow yourself to become aware of which dispute resolution path you took at the time. How much of your shame was involved? How much unhealthy ego was at play? Did you come from Control, Conflict, or Confrontation? Were you up front with your needs and feelings or did you employ some aspects of Coercion? Do you feel you responded from a place of empowerment and empathy? Did you follow the path of Compromise, or Collaboration, or Co-Creation? Whichever path you feel you took at the time, allow yourself to review that same situation from each one of the paths, paying attention not only to how you feel as you walk that path in your mind, but how it feels after you have walked it and whether that path itself moves you into shame or into empowerment. When you have completed all paths, take a moment to make a promise to yourself of which path you will always strive toward. It may not always be the case, but the awareness that the choice is there can often make all the difference.

Eighteen

Journey to Encounter Your Personal Power Animals Meditation

Empowerment is the experience of knowing that the source of one's vitality, impetus, and momentum stems from an internal, not an external, place. So much of the personal journey from shame to reclaim is about recognizing self from beyond the cacophony of others' voices and to attune to the inner flow of thoughts and feelings. This can be a delicate process to attain and requires consistent attention to maintain.

The center of our torso provides an enormous amount of information to us. It is unceasingly eloquent. However, it requires the loyal "guardians at the gate" to ensure that the message remains untainted from external agenda. It is fine for us to receive input and guidance from others. It is a gift to have a life full of friends, family, supports, and cheerleaders, but we do want to ensure that we employ these inner guardians who "check the credentials" to make sure that what passes over the threshold is only that which will be beneficial to us. It is not that we are trying to shut out others and isolate ourselves from any interconnection, nor does this mean that we won't at times encounter that which challenges us. But it reflects the balanced, and in truth, empowered belief through which we know absolutely that when we come from this "centered-in-self" place, a bit of challenge allows us to stretch and grow. We are not afraid of disagreement. We are not thrown off-kilter by opposition. We do not cave when others attempt to wrong us. We are able to entertain the possibility that the other may have access to a greater truth or wisdom than we have, filtering it through the "torso-land" or the "torso-rejection" that informs us clearly what page we are on.

If it lands as truth, empowerment allows us to have the humility to admit as much. If it lands as "not our truth," empowerment allows us to have the integrity to admit as much. And the inner guardians stand beside us, ready to step in and implement a firm and respectful boundary, if need be.

This meditation explores the familiar inner landscape you experienced previously through the lens of three elemental energies, inviting you to meet the Power Animal or Guardian that shows up in each of these three realms in order to work with you. As you journey to encounter these guides, be open to accepting the companionship that will continue to walk with you long after this meditation has ended.

Meditation

Close your eyes. Focus on your breath. Allow your breath to drop you into a deep place within yourself. Each inhale connects you to those places within that may hold tension, discomfort, or unease. Each exhale invites you to release those tensions into the cosmos, bringing you to the balance place in the center of the Above and the Below that connects Spirit and human: the place between, where magic happens.

You find yourself back at the banks of the river that flows through what was an arid land. You observe now that the land is not as dry and empty as it first appeared. You see that there are places and patches, mainly along the edge of the river, where delicate shoots are starting to appear, reaching upward toward the mid-morning sun. You too feel yourself stretch for those rays, noticing that there is growing warmth in their touch. Looking up into the sky, you notice with a bit of a pang that the moon has disappeared in the strengthening light, but you do see the sun and, looking upon the face of Grandfather Sun, you too feel a stronger sense of self, a more centered sense of strength, and a greater appreciation for the value of being self-centered. You feel a glow within your torso that echoes the glow of the mid-morning sun and you know, absolutely, that this glow within is precious. <u>This</u> is your greatest asset. And in that realization, you know that this must be both cherished and protected.

You find yourself drawn to the banks of the river, lying down on the soft earth with your feet resting on the edge of the water, gazing up into the bright, morning sky. You feel grounded and safe, open and receptive, clear and focused. You are aware of the elements that support you—of earth, water, and air—and you are aware of how they move within you. Each has its benefit, its gift, its strength. Each has its own way of supporting you in your being and in your journey. As you connect with each of these elements, you become aware that there is movement within each of these realms. You feel the pulse or a beat on the earth. You hear a splash or feel a ripple in the water. You hear a whoosh or feel a shift in the winds. Creatures are approaching, one in each element and you feel the welcome anticipation as you would the approach of a soul friend.

Scooting over the bank and scuttering to your side comes a creature of the earth. Slipping up to the bank and emerging at your feet comes a creature of the water. Swooping down from on high and landing gracefully at your head comes a creature of the air. You greet each in turn with both joy in your heart and honor in your countenance.

Take some time to dialogue with each. Each one reflects a different source of Essence energy for you. Each one offers a different approach to self-regard and self-protection. Each one serves as a reminder to maintain your own personal healthy boundaries, but each does so in its own unique way. When you are confident that you have fully absorbed the message from each of your power animals—when you are filled with confidence—rise from the place where you lay, knowing it is time to continue your journey, knowing that your power animals are always with you, either walking beside you or walking in spirit.

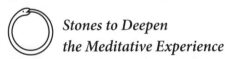 ### Stones to Deepen the Meditative Experience

Chrysanthemum Stone awakens one to one's true purpose and helps to forge through obstacles with joy.

Healerite is a powerful protector and healer, said to shield the auric field and protect cellular structure.

Rhodizite, usually used in sets of three, is a Master Healer and helps to increase potency.

Nineteen

The Hermetic Principle of Cause and Effect Contemplation

Continuing our esoteric journey backward through the Hermetic Principles, Cycle Three, the time in which we focus on nurturing empowerment and self-esteem, brings us to the sixth principle: the Hermetic Principle of Cause and Effect, or, as it is sometimes known, the Law of Causation. In this season of resurrection and the growing sense, particularly as experienced through the School Age Child Within, of our impact on the world around us, we begin to recognize that what we do matters.

It does seem at first glance that this principle is not all that far removed from Newton's Law of Motion as presented in physics. These three laws all speak to the nature of consequence when one object acts upon another object. The Hermetic Principle takes this application as seen in the physical world and applies it through a different lens. It reveals the impact of causation on more places than the physical realm and thus highlights the absolute importance, not just of our competence and ability in the world, but of our personal responsibility and accountability to that world. We have the opportunity to pay attention to the consequences of our actions. In *The Kybalion*, the Hermetic Principle of Cause and Effect is presented as:

Every Cause has its Effect; every Effect has its Cause; everything happens according to Law; Chance is but a name for Law not recognized; there are many planes of causation but nothing escapes the Law.[26]

The Kybalion goes on at length about Chance and how, from the perspective of Universal Law, there really is no such thing as chance. This is reflective of Jung's concept of synchronicity. We can appreciate that that which follows an identifiable cause falls within the realm of the physical laws, which deal in linear time and linear space. But that which appears to be linked acausally (i.e., synchronistically) falls under the purview of the Hermetic law. Or to put it far more simply, just because we can't see the connection between things or events does not mean one is not there. In fact, according to spiritual law, we know absolutely that the connection <u>is</u> always there whether we can see it or not and so we can actually use that to guide the manifestation of that which is in alignment with our Essence.

At its core, this principle teaches us about empowerment. It advises us to be aware of what our choices and actions are, to be aware of the application of Free Will, and to take good care not to be "carried along like the falling stone, obedient to environment, outside influences and internal moods, desires, etc."[27] We need to know who we are, what is important to us, what our values are, what our goals and visions are. Others may be able to give us an inkling or make a suggestion, but ultimately, it is up to us to determine what that inner realm is, what inhabits it, what informs it. And once we are well clear on that and have made a commitment to honor, champion, and protect that, we can be sure that what happens outside of us, our life experiences, and the people we attract into our lives will respond.

Care needs to be taken with this principle, for if one has not addressed the dark Shadow of shame, there is a danger that this interweaving of cause and effect will be misconstrued from a place of victimhood. "It's my fault." "This always happens to me." "What's wrong with me that I attract this into my life." If you find thoughts of this frequency inhabiting your mind, it is important to know that you are locked in an

....

26. The Three Initiates, "The Kybalion: Chapter II. The Seven Hermetic Principles," www.sacred-texts. com (Yogi Publication Society, 1912), https://www.sacred-texts.com/eso/kyb/kyb04.htm.
27. The Three Initiates, "The Kybalion: Chapter XII. Causation," www.sacred-texts.com (Yogi Publication Society, 1912), https://www.sacred-texts.com/eso/kyb/kyb14.htm.

erroneous causal perspective and missing the higher truth of synchronicity. There is always something to learn or an opportunity to grow. Sometimes that lesson is learning to say "no" or taking the opportunity to walk away. And the bottom line, always unquestionable, non-negotiable truth is that there is never something <u>wrong</u> with us, however much we may be living and choosing from fear-based beliefs. At our core, we are always a reflection of the Divine. The inner sun always reflects the strength of the outer sun. The more that we can connect to that shining light within, nourishing the potential that lies in the seed of our Soul, the more we will experience the magic and wonder of serendipitous causation.

Contemplation

Contemplate how the Centering Hynni of Esteem reflects the Hermetic Principle of Causation: that nothing happens by chance and so, that which is reflected within is going to impact on what we experience or how we choose to act.

Chakras to Deepen the Contemplative Experience

Connect with the **solar plexus chakra** to open yourself to clarity, focus, and centered direction. Emanating from the center of your torso, this chakra is reflective of the inner sun that brings bright discernment and focus to our experiences, tasks, and goals. In the context of the *Magnum Opus*, this chakra is aligned with the element of air, which brings fresh perspectives and insight—literally, the ability to see inside our own motivations. It connects us to the validity of our choices and actions if they are informed by respect and love and helps us to know when we may need to take a stand for what we know is best for us. The energy that sits at the back of this chakra has the potential to skew the clarity of our forward motion, if we are still being directed by the pain of the past. Unhealed past trauma cannot help but inform a sense of self and this chakra in particular can be negatively influenced by the wounds that are still acutely painful to the touch.

The higher-vibration chakra that sits in the center of the torso is the **Eleventh Chakra of Calm Wisdom.**[28] As the higher reflection of the solar plexus chakra, it

....

28. Stone, *Soul Psychology*.

helps us to remain centered in the midst of chaos, having worked hard to diminish the trauma from the past. It helps to keep us grounded in the here and now of our experiences, knowing that what we have experienced in the past brought us to where we are today and that is okay. In that, it inspires us to tell our story and share our journey with others, not from a place of trauma and woundedness, nor from a place of ego, but knowing that there is a universality to our story that may be helpful to others. In its integration of the past with the present, the appreciation for the impact of the present on the future, and the embodiment of the wisdom that comes with experiences, the Eleventh Chakra reflects the message inherent in the teaching of the Hermetic Principle of Causation.

Twenty

Planting the Seed of Intention Ritual

As this spring festival celebrates the solid return of life, it is necessary to awaken the energies within to harness and honor if we are to be successful in bringing our hopes and dreams to fruitful manifestation. This ritual is an invitation to plant the seed of your future intention, drawing upon the clarifying perspective brought by the alchemical stage of Separation that allows you to see who you are and what is important to you, different perhaps from who others are and what may be important to them. As you sow, so shall you reap. This is the time to be intentional about what you sow, planting a seed that represents the intention reflective and supportive of True Self.

Symbols to help connect to ritual focus	• Ostara symbols (bunnies, chicks, lambs, eggs) • Spring flowers • Statues or photos of those deities that reflect Nature; an image of the Centering Hynni of Esteem
Optional: Stones from *Journey to Encounter Your Personal Power Animals* Meditation	• Chrysanthemum Stone • Healerite • Rhodizite
Items needed for ritual activity	• A fresh, unused candle (yellow, if you want to align with Hynni) • A lighter • A cauldron • A small ceramic planter • A small amount of potting soil • A seed of your choice (although sunflowers are perfect) • A variety of paints and paintbrushes or paint pens • Optional: A glass of water (if using paintbrushes) • Optional: Candle snuffer • Optional: Oracle deck

Creating the Altar

On the left side of your existing altar or on a surface that can act as one for this ritual, place the paints, paintbrush, and glass of water, or the paint pens, whichever you will be using. On the right, have your cauldron that contains your one seed. In the center, place a fresh, unused candle, the small ceramic planter, and a small bowl of potting soil.

You may also choose to decorate your space and your altar with those elements that bring a sense of the very energy and vitality of life coming back from the dark. This may include symbols that are associated with the Vernal Equinox, Ostara, Easter, or other spring festivals and holidays through the ages. You may also choose to include an image of the Centering Hynni of Esteem, which reminds us that what we carry protected within ourselves is the very seed of our future potential.

You may also want to include reflections of the Divine on this sacred space you are creating. This may be statues or photos of the gods and goddesses that are particularly connected to this time.

When you are done preparing your space, take a moment to feel how the energy you have created affects you. You will want to ensure that there are elements that speak to the general theme of the ritual or the festival itself, as well as those items that are going to be used in the ritual. This ensures that both the "Above," the realm of the transpersonal or mythic, and the "Below," the realm of the personal, are represented. If it feels complete, take some time to prepare yourself for ritual (see Appendix D).

The Ritual

Allow yourself to connect with the rising energies of the season that are pulsing beneath you in the earth and surrounding you in the very air you are breathing. Find the resonant energies within yourself, that place that is yearning to burst forth. As Anaïs Nin said, "And the day came when the risk it took to remain tight in a bud was more painful than the risk to blossom." This is that day. Light the candle in front of you and take some time, gazing at that flame, allowing yourself to explore that sense of the you waiting to emerge. Pay attention to any words that come to mind that describe what you are feeling, or visions of what you want to manifest in your life, or symbols that have meaning for you. Take the planter in front of you and, in your own time, allow these words and symbols to take form. Decorate the planter, inside and out, if you choose, with everything that is reflective of your True Self, your hopes and dreams, and the strength you have within to make those dreams come true.

When your design feels complete, fill the planter half full of the potting soil. Shift your attention to the cauldron on your right. Within it lies the seed of your future manifestation, which has been incubating in the cauldron but is now ready to be planted in the waiting earth. Take that seed and hold it in your hand. Feel the energies that run through the earth. Feel those energies run through you like a current. Feel that current culminate in your palm and be transferred into the seed. Feel within yourself the joy of embracing the risk to blossom. Touch that place in you that knows how to persist. There may have been dark times in the past. There may be tough times in the future, but you have wings, and the Essence that lies within knows how to soar regardless.

Take all the time you want or need to gaze upon the light of the candle that is reflective of your Light, and know that what you have had the courage to plant, you have the strength to guide into being. Use this time to pull an oracle card, receiving a message from the Divine regarding your strengths and abilities, including guidance to help you feel confident in moving into your future.

Closure of Ritual

When you are ready to leave this liminal space, bring your conscious awareness back to your breath. Commit to nurturing this seed that you have planted. When it is strong enough, if you have the ability to do so, plant it outside and watch it continue to thrive. Taking one last moment to anchor the connection to your sense of your Essence, using either your breath or a candle snuffer, release the flame of the candle before you. What has been experienced in ritual lives forever in your cells. It need only be called forth from within when you choose.

Take some time to move through the directions once more, thanking the elements for helping to hold space and keep you safe through the ritual. Start again in the North with earth, then move through the East with air, the South with fire, the West with water, ending with the Below of the material plane and the Above of the cosmic plane. Thank and bid farewell to the deities who have been a part of this ritual with you and know that the wheel may turn around you, but you are—as they are—ever at the center.

Clearing Ritual Space

If you have been using an existing altar, you may decide to keep some items on your altar over the course of the cycle. If your altar receives ample sun, you may choose to keep your planter there until the weather is warm enough for transplanting.

 *Oracle Deck Recommendations*

Salerno, Toni. *Gaia Oracle*. Woodbury, MN: Llewellyn, 2013.

Marashinsky, Amy. *The Goddess Oracle*. Stamford, CT: US Games, 2006.

Walden, Kelly Sullivan. *Hero's Journey Dream Oracle*. Woodbury, MN: Llewellyn, 2018.

Baron-Reid, Colette. *Wisdom of the Oracle*. Lifestyles (Penguin Random House), 2015.

Twenty-one

You Are Whole Within

The power of Cycle Three is the healing that comes when we know in every cell that we are empowered, that our lives are our own to define, that the source of our power lies within, and that we are really only answerable to our Higher Self.

This is not to say that we won't experience pain. The world is imperfect, as are we. To be empowered is not to say that there won't be those who try to take that power from you. There are those who hate and harm. And this may not even be solely on a personal level. History is strewn with whole bodies of cultures that have had their pride and sense of worth stripped from them. The past several thousand years of history have been informed by attempts to hold power over others and the devastating degrees of control leveled on persons or peoples to try to maintain that control. In Canada, we are just now addressing the horrors of residential schools and the "Sixties Swoop," both methods through which indigenous children were taken from their families and placed into what was deemed "better" circumstances (i.e., Church-run schools and white families). A report by Justice Edwin Kimelman in 1985 called the practice "cultural genocide."[29] The Truth and Reconciliation Commission of Canada, created to investigate both the practices themselves and their terrible legacy, was active from 2008 to 2015, at which time it released a summary

---

29. "The Sixties Scoop Explained—CBC Docs POV," Www.cbc.ca (www.cbc.ca, 2019), https://www.cbc .ca/cbcdocspov/features/the-sixties-scoop-explained.

report of its findings which included ninety-four calls to action.[30] As of October 2017, only seven of those had been implemented. The first slaves were brought to America in 1619.[31] Four hundred years later, the experience of many, or in fact the majority of, Black Americans continues to be informed by prejudice, inequity, and control. Individuals who are members of cultures that have experienced ongoing culturally-targeted atrocities have an even harder journey to claim the gift of empowerment. The journey from the underground darkness of shame to the renewal of life in the light of Self is long, arduous, and potentially strewn with dangers. It is understandable that one who has navigated those treacherous paths would be loath to surrender what has been so hard won. The attention being paid to cultivating awareness around cultural appropriation is indicative of the need to establish solid and functional boundaries, especially in the face of blatant disregard for the depth and nuance of culture-specific teachings. When people treat you like you are worthless for decades or if your people are treated like they are worthless for centuries, it is an act of courage to claim your worth: a necessary act of courage.

Whether addressing the personal or the cultural, coming to an understanding that connecting to worth, sense of self, and empowerment is informed internally, not externally, is imperative. The life you have waiting for you, as Joseph Campbell would say, is dependent on releasing your grip on the life you were handed by others. Break free of the limiting ties that try to keep you small, and focus on the small diamond-shaped seed that you hold within the safety of your torso. There is great potential there—as great as the oak that lies within the acorn. Nurture that and know that you are whole within.

....

30. Joseph, Bob. "Truth and Reconciliation Commission Calls to Action." Truth and Reconciliation Commission Calls to Action, February 1, 2016. https://www.ictinc .ca/blog/truth-and-reconciliation-commission-calls-to-action.

31. History.com Editors. "Slavery in America." History.com. A&E Television Networks, November 12, 2009. https://www.history.com/topics/black-history/slavery.

Key Aspects of Cycle Three[32]

Archetypal Themes	Healing Themes	Indication of Crisis	Healing Practices
Nurturing Empowerment and Self-Esteem Resurrection; renewal; preparation	Empowerment; self-identification; School Age Child, competence, defenses; defensiveness; fear of Conflict/Confrontation	A shaky sense of self-esteem; inflated guilt over little incidences; challenges or uncertainty while in the company of others; feeling not in control of one's own life and choices; an inability to establish healthy boundaries	Exploration of healthy boundaries; contemplation of the Hermetic Principle of Cause and Effect; activation of Centering Hynni of Esteem
Elemental Reflection	**Intuitive Guidance and Tool**	**Alchemical Reflection**	**Affirmations**
Air	Bird guides; oracles	*Separation* The sorting through of what is self from that which is not-self (i.e., expectations of others)	I am open to a fresh perspective; I experience freedom in my life; I am comfortable saying "no"; I am responsible for my own feelings and experiences; I am important and valuable

....

32. More information on Key Aspects can be found in *The Great Work: Self-Knowledge and Healing Through the Wheel of the Year* by the author (Llewellyn, 2015).

Part Four

Cycle Four
May 3–June 13

Fanning Your Spark into Flame

The Bridging Hynni of Synthesis

As Below
Inhibitors of
Inner Spark
Alchemical
Conjunction
Imbalanced
relationship
Core issues

As Above
Enhancers of Inner
Spark
Empathy
Union and
Partnerships
Core meaning

Synthesis
Union
Passion
Synthesis

Twenty-two

Beltane and the Passion for Life

With the shift to the new seasonal energy and the arrival of early summer, a vital, new vibrancy starts to take hold. Beltane heralds the synthesizing of Spirit with matter, which is the necessary foundation for any manifestation, success, or harvest. Beltane celebrates the activation of enlivening Spirit into inert matter, fusing the two extreme poles into a single powerful, inextricable force. It is the implementation of the spark of life into the seeds in the earth, allowing for the interweaving of energies. It is *synthesis* and *union*, creating cohesion, resonance, and partnership between opposites.

The key energetic of this time of year is *passion*. You can feel the charge in the air. It is the gathering electricity that needs a fruitful place to land. If Cycle Two is about connecting to the love that opens us to a sense of belonging and the ability to embrace pleasure in life, then Cycle Four amplifies that love into the passion that urges us to union. In response to the electricity in the air, you can feel the current coursing through the land under your feet, calling forth the force of creation that is necessary for any realization.

The beautiful and, at times, forbidden tradition of the maypole dance acts as a lightning bolt, bringing the active and conceptual into direct relationship with the receptive and applicable. Again, if Cycle Two shows us how to flow from one pole to another, Cycle Four urges us to weave these two poles into one intertwined, unbreakable whole.

In any dance, it is helpful to be aware of the energies that inform the interactions and dynamic. There are many ways to enter the dance, as there are many dances that one can join. What we dance and how we dance tells a lot about the inner dance. If I lead the dance too much, dragging my partner around the floor, there is something in me that needs to be in control. In such a way, I may be limiting another's input, containing their expression, controlling their destiny. But if I always follow in the dance, if I allow the press of another's hand to dictate where I will move and how fast, I lose the sense of my own flow and rhythm. I lose the sense of the importance of my input. I lose the potential to celebrate the gifts I bring to any dance. If I dance alone, I don't have to worry about leading or following, but I lose the opportunity to weave with another in a way that can often challenge yet also affords great gifts and often unexpected benefit.

The metaphor of the dance beautifully reflects the Shadow that is potentially experienced in this cycle: giving and receiving love. As one of many key Core Issues, it is astounding how many individuals struggle with this dynamic and, interestingly, it is usually one side of the coin that poses more trouble than the other. Most of us do not have a hard time "giving" love. Shifting the focus to the other and making it about them, rather than ourselves, is a safe engagement, but it makes for very wobbly interactions. You cannot have a dance that only "to's" and never "fro's." You cannot weave the maypole if you only "duck under" and never "lift over." And yet, somehow we think that we can have healthy relationships when we give and give and give, and never account for the need to balance that with receiving. We don't account for the subtext that conveys to the other when we are so focused on what we can do to help the other and not how we can ease back and allow a gift to be received from the other.

There is a two-fold danger in this Beltane Shadow that results in a very chaotic pattern in the weave. The first danger is that of falling into the control drama of over-responsibility. In this codependent pattern, there is the unconscious but blatant assumption that the other is not capable of being responsible. If I take control of the dance, if I insist on giving without receiving, it is almost impossible not to hear the undercurrent of mistrust. It is only a matter of time before this becomes a burden, leading to energy depletion and burnout (work, relationship, or other types of burnout). Where there is a preponderance of responsibility, there is an eventual and inevitable depletion of joy.

The second danger is the way in which an inability to receive makes liars of us all. Because the truth is that the Child Within, even as wounded as they may be, desperately wants to receive love. When we focus so much of our attention on giving to others, we are denying the part of us that does want to receive but is afraid: afraid no one will love us, afraid the love will end, afraid we won't measure up, afraid the love will hurt. And so, it becomes safer to deflect. It becomes easier to always take the lead and never allow ourselves to relax into someone else's rhythm for a moment. We deny our desire to receive. We repress that spark of anticipation on days we might be celebrated, diminish the part of us that yearns to take hold of the gift, and dismiss any signs that there may be those who want to bring that love and joy into our lives.

To truly harness the powerful electric current that is present at this time, one must be aware of all those elements that either stop that force in its tracks or stir it to greater expansion. For there is nothing less than the bounty of the harvest at stake. The success of what is cultivated into fruition is dependent on how we lay the groundwork now.

Because the energy is unmistakably sexual at this time, with the weaving and the dancing and the tree implanted in the earth and the spark of passion that awakens the earthy body, this is one of a few festivals that fell out of favor for several hundred years. The lusty lasciviousness of the May Day celebrations were much frowned upon by the Puritans. There are few recognizable modern iterations of this festival.

Floralia (Roman) was dedicated to the goddess Flora (meaning "flower") and was celebrated from April 27 to May 3. The Romans also held a bawdier festival every three years called *Maiouma*, which lasted for a month. These were suppressed by the Emperor Constantine in the third century CE. Ancient Greeks celebrated the fertility goddess *Maios* on May 1, recognizing the triumph of summer over winter, which was also seen as the triumph of life over death. *Walpurgisnacht* or St. Walpurga's Night (German) is still celebrated on the eve of April 30 and the day of May 1. The celebration is named for an eighth-century English nun who was canonized for her success at ending pagan activities, but later morphed into a festival to protect oneself from witches, especially after the notorious period known as the "Burning Times" (the fifteenth to seventeenth centuries). *Las Mayas* (Spain) is part of an extended celebration from May 1 to 9, in which young girls sit for hours on public altars decorated with flowers before attending church. This festival also includes *Fiesta de las Cruces* during which crosses are decorated with flowers. Serbians still celebrate *Prvomajski uranak*, which translates as May Day Dawn. It is tradition to go out into nature on May 1 to camp and have barbecues. *Morris dancing* (UK) captures the energy and intent of the maypole dance but without the pole and ribbons. Morris Men, wearing bells on their shins, dance to awaken the earth by waving handkerchiefs and tapping sticks on the ground. *May Basket Day* (USA) was a widespread tradition in the nineteenth and early twentieth centuries. Flowers and goodies were gathered in April and placed in a basket that was hung on the door of a loved one on May 1.

This is a time to open our hearts, to celebrate the power of passion, and to step into full, courageous engagement with life. The dance that is brought with May is one of joy for all that can be manifested through connection, celebration, and a little hard work, as long as we are able to respect that the dance has a rhythm that honors the necessity of opposites. As we celebrate the dynamism of difference and raise up our own uniqueness, we are able to see with true eyes how diversity brings a richness to life that cannot be denied nor disparaged.

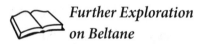 *Further Exploration on Beltane*

Marquis, Melanie. *Beltane: Rituals, Recipes & Lore for May Day.* Woodbury, MN: Llewellyn, 2015.

Readisch, Linda. *Night of the Witches: Folklore, Traditions and Recipes for Celebrating Walpurgis Night.* Woodbury, MN: Llewellyn, 2011.

Twenty-three

The Wounded Heart's Shadow

Deep at the heart of the existential question, there is one single irrefutable truth. It can quickly become convoluted, complicated, twisted, and bastardized, but when it comes right down to the bare bones of it, we all just desperately want to be loved. We want to be entwined in the joyful energies and the intersection with another who can see who we are at our core, can accept our flaws, and celebrate our uniqueness. Beltane and the exploration of union and partnership places this universal truth right at the center of the stage. This is not to say that we all yearn to be in a romantic relationship, but that having connection with someone who can appreciate us for who we are—in partnership and/or friendship and/or companionship—is an imperative to the soul.

This time of year is not about separation. It is about the fusion of Source with the energies of the Earth in a burst of exuberance for life. Across the wheel, sitting in the Dark Half of the Year, is the festival which reflects the separation aspect of Spirit and matter. As challenging and sometimes isolating as it may feel, when we embrace the release from the tangible and material in its natural time, we find that we are connected to that which is far greater than ourselves. But at this time of year, when the air is warming with the strengthening sun and the trees are awakening to their innate beauty, this is not the time for separation. Here we focus on union, grounding that Spirit into the earthy matter or the Earthly mater. In doing so, we have the opportunity to connect more fully with others. We have the opportunity to see ourselves as part of something which is greater than ourselves, but in the human, relational realm.

The Shadow of this time comes from losing sight of the joy that connection, union, and synthesis can bring. It comes from seeing ourselves as separate: from Spirit, from others, from Self. When we are imbued with shame, it overrides the truth that we carry deep in our hearts, covering it with the Inhibitors that act like interference or static on the line along the pathway between Spirit and matter. The pure, activating, enlivening spark that burns within and carries the potential for a conflagration that would light up the sky itself becomes diffuse, muddy, or nullified by the mucky overlay of the three Shadow attitudes that are not at all about the enhancement of life but rather the denial of life

The first Inhibitor is *entitlement*, the Shadow attitude toward experience. Increasingly, one hears complaints of the rise in entitlement, the idea that some individuals seem to carry that they are owed something. For the most part this charge is laid at the feet of the Millennials and Generation Z. The irritation that many feel when faced with entitlement is that it appears, on the surface at any rate, to be coming from a place of arrogance. There is an energy around this attitude that what is coming (or should be coming) to the entitled person is their due, their birthright, and that there is nothing that they need to do, no effort that needs to be made, in order to account for this due. There is a perception that the entitled person considers themselves to be above everyone else and endlessly deserving. This could not be further from the truth. Entitlement is the shield for the quaking, insecure heart. Entitlement, much like grandiosity, puffs itself up like a kitten trying to make itself look bigger than it actually is, but underneath all that standing-on-end fur is a very tentative soul that does not feel adequate or capable of providing for self. In some cases, it is past pain or hardship that creates a sense of entitlement: an unconscious karmic tally that tries to see the interweaving dance of life as a tit-for-tat exchange. But there is also the "participation medal phenomenon," which, more often than not, creates the unhealthy groundwork for entitlement in adulthood. With all the best intentions for creating a level playing field, instilling a sense of value in experience, and an eye to alleviating, if not eliminating, the potential for shame, especially with regard to ability and achievement, the actual result appears to be the internalization of a message: "You don't believe I am capable." Rather than reduce shame, it solidifies it into the mantra of a results-driven covert perfectionist. A very painful place to be! Helicopter parents and snowplow parents, in hoping to instill a sense of unconditional love and worth, run the risk of creating deep-rooted shame that is even harder to put a finger on because it is shrouded in the cushion of bubble-wrapped experience. A glaring example of this is in the recent university admissions scandal in the US, in which several Hollywood celebrity parents were found guilty of fraud, having paid to rig SAT scores to ensure university acceptance. Most telling is that the response of one celebrity's child who, upon learning of the deception, asked, "Why didn't you believe in me? Why didn't you think I could do it on my own?"[33] It is this inability to allow for the empowerment lessons that come through consequences (both of success and challenge) that creates the bedrock of entitlement. It shuts down the capacity to take responsibility for oneself: for one's opportunities, choices, and consequences. Instead, it hands that responsibility over to others in that puffed-up way as a buffer against the shame and sense of inadequacy that is the true bedrock of entitlement.

On the heels of entitlement comes the second Inhibitor, the Shadow attitude toward challenges or the way in which we rise to meet whatever life has to offer us. If we are already informed by the shame that underpins entitlement, the response to any true challenge that presents itself is *resignation*. It speaks to the inner belief that one does not have the capacity to achieve success, and it is devastating. Resignation tells us that nothing will ever change and that what we do does not matter. It is another massive shovelful of suffocating dirt on the spark of enthusiasm, healthy risk, and potential to live fully and courageously. The fear of being ineffective, incapable, or wrong stops us from even trying to step into the arena. It shuts down the capacity to care, which ultimately walls up our heart behind a slab of stone. The answer to the question "Who cares?" must always be "I do. I care. I always care. Regardless of how hard it may be or how scary it may be, I care. For to care is to be fully alive. To care is to risk attaining bliss. To care is to have the courage to claim your right to your own authentic life. And it is always worth it because you are always worth it."

When we do not resonate to that message and instead it falls into the deep dark void of our sense of worthlessness, we encounter the third Inhibitor of our spark, the

33. Hautman, Nicholas. "Felicity Huffman's Daughter Amid Scandal: 'Why Didn't You Believe in Me?'" Us Weekly, September 6, 2019. https://www.usmagazine.com/celebrity-news/news/felicity-huffman-details-daughters-reaction-to-college-scandal/.

Shadow attitude toward others: *isolation*. It is this which ultimately keeps us from weaving the dance of intimacy with others. In direct opposition to the "pufferfish" response in which we try to make ourselves look bigger than the tiny inadequate being we feel ourselves to be, isolation is the way in which we make ourselves invisible and try not to be seen by others. We remove ourselves from engaging with the world and with others in order to keep ourselves safe and ensure that no one has the opportunity to see how flawed we think and believe ourselves to be. Isolation is very different than solitude. There are times when we need to be alone. There are times when choosing to enter into a time of quietude opens us to hearing the inner voice more clearly. It opens us to a stronger connection to Higher Self and Spirit. But that is very different from isolation. Solitude is stepping into relationship with that larger than one's Self. Isolation is withdrawing from relationship because one is terrified of being truly seen.

These three Shadow attitudes are informed by the Wounded Child and serve to anchor shame (lack of worth, lack of esteem, and lack of self-acceptance). They act like heavy earth thrown over our inner spark, diminishing its light and threatening to extinguish its glowing guidance. The result is lack of engagement with life, lethargy, and depression.

In order to start to shift this heaviness that sits in our heart and overshadows our ability to engage fully with life, we need to address the faulty inner programming that is jamming our circuits. We need to look to core issues. Charles Whitfield, an American doctor and author with decades of work in trauma recovery, clarifies the difference between an issue and a core issue as:

> An issue is any conflict, concern, or potential problem, whether conscious or unconscious, that is incomplete for us or needs action or change. A core issue is one that comes up repeatedly.[34]

Every one of us will have at least one of these issues that actually hold the potential to move us toward our Essence and our truth, if we are able to recognize what our own core issue is—or what the multiple core issues are. From a spiritual perspective, our task in this lifetime is to grapple with the meat of our core issue or issues in order to incapacitate the hold they have had over us. The active engagement with

....
34. Whitfield, *Wisdom to Know the Difference*, 4.

this issue becomes the impetus of my life purpose and when I have come to a level of understanding and mastery around that, it becomes my higher purpose to bring that wisdom to others who may be grappling with the same thing. If I struggle with abandonment, my life purpose lessons will provide me with ample opportunities to feel abandoned until I am able to resolve that issue to an appreciation that, as long as I remain true to myself, I can never actually be abandoned. The attainment of this wisdom is the completion of the lesson. In seeking to resolve the pain of the core issue, we need to address the masks and defenses, the addictions and negative beliefs that constellate around its life-nullifying message.

As a general rule of thumb, psychotherapy recognizes fifteen core issues that show up in the dance of relationships, specifically in unhealthy, codependent dynamics. The more wounded the heart, and the more active the Inhibitors, the more virulent the core issues will be, causing devastating issues around disengagement with life, anxiety, panic attacks, and countless other ways in which we hold love (including self-love) at arm's length away from us.

Much in the same way that addictions and compulsions work, although you may recognize that there are several core issues you can recognize as active within yourself, there is likely just one that is the hardest to address: your one true <u>core</u> core issue. You may learn to respect your needs, find a balanced approach to perspective, and place boundaries when people around you act outrageously, and yet continue to feel insecure in friendships and relationships. The resolution of neglecting needs, all-or-nothing thinking, and difficulty resolving conflict are all indications of solid, courageous growth. The clearing of that debris reveals the deep roots of the true core issue: the fear of abandonment. It is imperative to gain that clarity in order that we may start to rebuild a broken heart with a soft healing.

Shadow of Cycle Four: Core Issues

All core issues fall within the Shadow work of Cycle Four; however, a further delineation shows how different core issues can align with the energies found on the Wheel of the Year

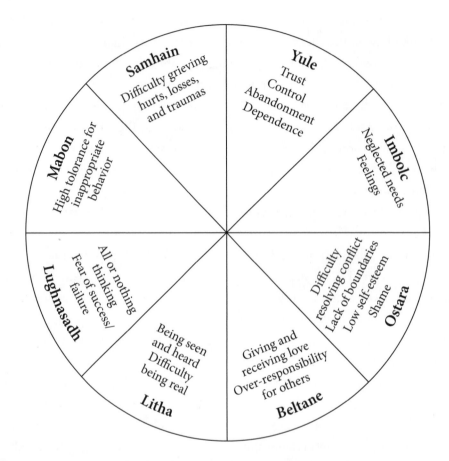

Assessing where we stand with regard to our core issues is not about wronging ourselves. That will result in nothing but a further entrenchment of the Inhibitors. We assess where we stand in order to gain a greater sense of how to place the first step of the dance that will reanimate the heaviness of our life with enlightened Spirit. We meet the challenge of the core issues head on in order to afford ourselves the possibility of our greatest heart's desire: to be loved for who we truly are.

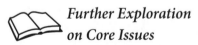

Further Exploration on Core Issues

Whitfield, Charles. *Wisdom to Know the Difference: Core Issues in Relationships, Recovery, and Living.* Muse House Press, 2012.

Twenty-four

The Light Heart's Gift

There is a corollary truth to that of our desire to be loved and that is this: if we are here on the "earth plane" having a human experience and life, we <u>will</u> experience pain. There is absolutely no getting around that. The challenge is to come to a place where we understand implicitly that we are not defined by our pain nor it is a commentary on our value and worth.

To aid us in the soul task of dropping into all that life has to offer without being overwhelmed by hardship or despair are the Enhancers. These three Light attitudes keep our focus on the Spirit that is interwoven into all our experiences, and help keep us from dropping too deeply into the Shadow depths of the cauldron of transformation.

The first Enhancer is *gratitude*. Gratitude is not something that we feel in response <u>to</u> something. It is an attitude that we carry within that reflects upon every moment of our lives. Gratitude is not permission to spiritually bypass in response to terrible, painful circumstances. We still need to feel what we feel and use those feelings to inform us on what feels like our inner truth as the best approach to address the situation. It is not that we are grateful for the pain itself, but that, in the face of the pain, we are grateful in the inner knowing that we are never separate from Spirit and so we have access to the tools we need to support ourselves in any situation. We note the painful experience and set our gaze on how to move through that experience with our Essence intact. When we are able to connect to that which uplifts, even in the face of hardship, we are well on the way to attaining the Philosopher's Stone.

Closely connecting to gratitude is the second Enhancer: *acceptance*. Acceptance is the attitude toward challenge that moves us into a place of being able to activate change.

Awareness + Acceptance + Action = Change

Acceptance is not a passive energy. Rather, with unfiltered acknowledgment of the state of how things are, it calls us to action. Where there is no acceptance, there is denial, which only serves to keep us in the dark. With acceptance, we can harness the courage to change that what no longer serves.

Connection is the third Enhancer; it recognizes the importance of others in our lives and ourselves in the lives of others. When we recognize the implicit value of connection, we see our place in the world and others in our life as a gift, in all the various imperfect reflections it may show up. We know that relationship is the playground through which we learn how to resolve the core issue that gives shape to our particular Shadow, using it as a catalyst to draw our eyes upward to a meaning and purpose that is reflective of a higher self-truth. Connection reminds us that it is only through relationship that we grow.

It is interesting that we can often see the benefit of stretching ourselves physically to support physical health, but we are more tentative when it comes to emotional and mental health. I may not enjoy the pain of the individual workout, but I can see the benefit in the context of strengthening my body for running the marathon that is my heart's desire to experience. I may balk at cutting gluten out of my diet, but I absolutely see the value of not having a painful, bloated, gassy stomach and so I make that disappointing choice in order to feel better in my body. We can see the benefit of challenging the status quo and making the tough choice in the physical realm, but we think that it is very different in the emotional or mental realms. When we are informed by our Essence, rather than our Shadow, and when we attune our ears to hear the voice of our Higher Self rather than have it be drowned out by the pain of our Wounded Child, we have shifted from the Inhibitors to the Enhancers. It does not mean the choices will be any easier. It does mean that we will know that we are supported and that we have the inner strength to implement healthy choices. It means that we have attuned our eyes to see the core issue and we have attuned our hearts to reflect the core meaning. Rather than see our pain and challenge as punishment or somehow conveying the message that we do not deserve love, connection, or intimacy, we are able to see that there is a bigger meaning to the story of our life than getting caught up in the particularities of our pain.

Light of Cycle Four: Core Meaning

All core meanings fall within the Light work of Cycle Four; however, a further delineation shows how different core meanings can align with the energies found on the Wheel of the Year

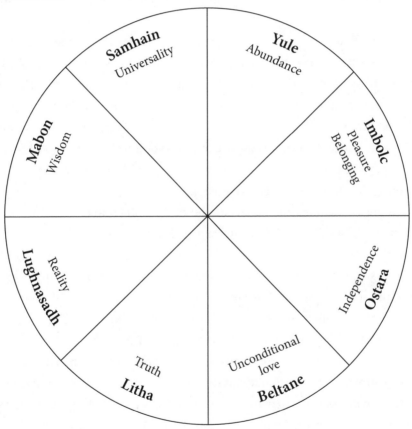

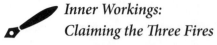

Inner Workings:
Claiming the Three Fires

Fire is the great transformer. It has the power to shift earth into ash, water into steam, air into "the unbearable lightness of being." In the alchemical stages of healing, one can see three distinct types of fire, used in different ways to achieve a transformative end.

There is the intense, dramatic fire of Calcination right at the beginning of the process. In this first alchemical stage of healing, fire scorches everything to the ground, resulting in the "dark night of the soul." Devastating as this experience may be, it is necessary to rid ourselves of the inauthentic dross in order that we may start to move into alignment with our truth.

There is the slow, steady burn of Fermentation's fire. Much like the process of simmering, this fire applies a consistent heat that allows for a longer, more controlled transformation. Though Calcination <u>feels</u> more profound due to its intensity, Fermentation is where matter becomes infused with Spirit and the true profound shift takes place.

The final fire is the Eternal Flame of Coagulation. It is the "fire in the mind," the sacred fire, the burning bush. It is the fire that is so bright the sun seems dim in comparison, and yet it does not burn. It ignites our souls with the remembrance of truth and meaning. It is this fire that is contained in all fires. It provides the forceful impetus behind the calcinating fire. It provides the careful direction of the fermenting fire. It is ever present, whether we acknowledge its presence or not.

These three types of fire can be seen as the three Nurturers of our Inner Spark. They help to support the three Enhancers and to challenge the three Inhibitors.

Reflecting the energy and intensity of the fire of Calcination is Passion. Passion has the potential to move mountains but also to level things to the ground. It is the motivator of caring, propelling us to keep going, even if we do not feel equal to the task. Passion inspires us to approach all our experiences with an open heart.

Courage provides the constancy and stamina needed to maintain an open-hearted approach to challenges in order to see them as opportunities to grow rather than a commentary on our value. Stemming from the Latin *cor* meaning "heart,"[35] courage supports us in risking to actively face our challenges, reflecting the power of the

....

35. "Courage | Origin and Meaning of Courage by Online Etymology Dictionary," Etymonline
   .com, 2019, https://www.etymonline.com/word/courage.

fermenting fire to imbue the wisdom of Spirit into even the rottenest of situations. Courage compels us to embrace the action of caring.

Love is the energy of caring that reflects the Eternal Fire and fully brings the presence of the Divine into our lives, our situations, and our relationships. It invites us to always maintain an open-hearted approach to others, knowing that they too are reflections of Spirit in matter, even if their Inner Spark is compromised and diminished under the sludge of the Inhibitors.

Take some time to sit with a situation or a relationship that has caused pain or posed a challenge. Something that you suspect may have caused your heart to harden. If you are able, try to identify which core issue from the chart in chapter 28 may be at the root of what is going on for you. As you hold the sense of that constellation of self, situation, and core issue, imagine them as three branches of a single tree that have been stacked together and explore what might transpire as you apply, one by one, the three different fires.

The Beltaine fires were believed to have magickal properties. Their flames, their glowing embers, their ashes, and their smoke were all believed capable of granting health and protection.[36]

You may find as you explore with your inner intuitive vision that the situation or relationship responds better to one of the Three Nurturers than the others. Allow yourself to gain clarity on what that would look like in practical application, what it would look like in action. Take that action through to the possible, anticipated outcome. Listen to the message of the flame, ember, ash, and smoke, and allow the sense of the core meaning to be revealed.

Three things are continually increasing:
fire or light,
intelligence or truth,
and spirit or life—
and these things will end by predominating
over all others.[37]

....

36. Marquis, *Beltane*, 22.

37. Bonewits, I. (n.d.). The Ancient Druid Order 1.3 by the British Circle of the Universal Bond. http://www.neopagan.net/AODbooklet.html

Twenty-five

Journey to Honor the World Tree Meditation

At this point in the journey, in the cycle through the year or the movement through our lives, we have arrived at an interesting place. Energetically and, in truth, psychologically, we are at a crossroads. The heart chakra is the meeting place of our spiritual selves and our human selves. That which is above flows down into us through the crown and settles in the heart with all the knowledge of lessons and patterns. That which is below flows up into us from the root and settles into the heart with all the experience that has brought us to this place. That may be times of wonder, beauty, and grace and that may be times of confusion, pain, and despair. At this time, when we have moved out of fledgling energies and are starting to gain some solid steps, how these energies come together and how they begin to impact on each other will create the circumstances that determine our future. We are as trees with our roots reaching down deep into the earth, drawing from the past to inform our current circumstances and our branches reaching up toward the cosmos, stretching out and growing in all directions. If the past flowing into the present carries more impetus than the awareness of lessons and potential for growth, especially if that past has been devastating or traumatic, there may be a challenge in expanding into a life of courage and passion. The water that flows up from the roots must meet the energy drawn from the light in order to create a healthy environment within for continued life.

Experience + Knowledge = Wisdom

This is the time when we have the opportunity to step into a whole new way of being an adult. As has been said in many different ways in earlier cycles, the experiences we had in childhood certainly have the power to shape us, but at a certain point we have the freedom to wrest that power back. This is the point. This is the crossroads. This is the opportunity to step onto the road of your own life, for the road that others chose for you is no longer an option.

This meditation takes you further along the journey into your inner landscape to the place where your World Tree[38] stands. Reminiscent of Yggdrasil and yet imbued with your own unique personal shape, the communion with your World Tree opens you to a deeper appreciation for all that has brought you to where you are in your journey, and it invites a broader anticipation for all that you may experience in the days, months, years, and decades to come.

Meditation

Close your eyes. Focus on your breath. Allow your breath to drop you into a deep place within yourself. Each inhale connects you to those places within that may hold tension, discomfort, or unease. Each exhale invites you to release those tensions into the cosmos, bringing you to the balance place in the center of the Above and the Below that connects Spirit and human: the place between, where magic happens.

You rise from the banks of the river feeling a solid sense of self within. In your journey thus far, you have faced the inner dragon and made it your friend; you have been touched by the light of the sun and the mystery of the moon; you have met allies who champion your progress. You feel all these guides and supports coming together within you, feeling strong and sure.

As you turn to scan the landscape, you notice that the daylight is growing stronger as well. It is late morning and there is far more warmth in the rays of the sun that alight on your face and skin. You notice also that in the time you spent by the banks of the river, the land has burst forth with life. Delicate shoots of grass carpet the ground that sprouts forth a sea of tiny colorful flowers. It is truly a sight for the eyes, beautiful to behold, and you feel the energy rise within you to meet such beauty. And in the center of the scene a towering, majestic tree rises before you, so massive

....

38. There are many depictions of the World Tree around the world. It is perhaps most commonly known as Yggdrasil of Norse mythology. In Mesoamerica it was seen as the ceiba tree. The Greeks and Romans saw the olive as the sacred World Tree. In Hindu mythology, it was a sacred fig.

it is astounding that it did not capture your attention before. Attached to the highest branches are almost impossibly long ribbons that dance around the trunk of the tree as they are caught by tendrils of wind.

As you draw nearer to the tree, you notice that not only is the air around it almost electric, but that there is a definite difference that you can feel in the energies coming from different parts of the tree. You find a welcoming space amongst the tree roots and nestle in, stilling your body so you can more fully experience these differing energies.

Starting with the area around where you sit, you can sense three distinct energetic emanations. It brings to your mind faint echoes of the realms from the Norse Eddas,[39] particularly Helheim (the Home of the Dead), Niflheim (the World of Fog and Mist), and Muspelheim (the Land of Fire). The roots of the tree do not feel perhaps quite so dark and challenging as these realms, but there is a definite sense of Shadow lurking here, drawing up remembrance from deep, deep in the Earth of times so long ago that held the potential to numb your hopes. Take some time to explore these energies, getting a sense of how they can potentially inhibit the movement of growth and how that might be shifted until you feel your awareness drawn upward, soaring to dizzying heights until you feel yourself perched within the swaying branches.

Here too you feel the three distinct energetic emanations that seem to mirror those you just felt. Again, echoes of the Eddic realms bring to mind Alfheim (the Home of the Elves), Vanaheim (the Home of the Vanir), and Asgard (the Home of the Aesir). These elevated energies inspire, expand, and enhance you. As the branches reach out and up to the cosmos, so you can feel the gathering current of potential and vision coursing down the branches toward the trunk. You realize that this current was the electric charge you felt in the air around the tree as you approached. With that realization, you find yourself dropped solidly into the trunk of the tree.

You explore this space between root and branch. This is the middle ground, and it brings to mind thoughts of "Middle Earth," of Midgard (the Home of the Humans), Jotunheim (the Home of the Giants), and Svartalfheim (the Home of the Dwarves). This in-between place—the trunk of the World Tree—feels so stable, solid, and centered. The

....

39. For source information about the Nine Worlds found in Norse mythology, read the Poetic Edda, *Völuspá*.

energies here feel so nurturing. From this place informed by both the Above and the Below, you know in your heart that all things are possible.

With a breath, you find yourself once more nestled in the roots, feeling the whole of the tree reflected in the whole of you. One of the multicolored ribbons dances past on the wind and, as you reach out to touch it, it comes instantly loose from its moorings on a high branch of the tree and flutters to your feet. You pick it up and tuck it into the same place that protects your precious golden seed, knowing that it will always connect you to this transformative place of power and magic.

 *Stones to Deepen
the Meditative Experience*

K2, known as the Stone of Empathy, helps us resolve inner conflict and let go of the desire to fight with others.

Morganite brings a lightness to the Spirit, attracting an abundance of love into one's life.

Nirvana Quartz gently removes stuck energies to help move one toward enlightenment.

Prairie Tanzanite opens one to the knowing of "I am" and acceptance of being a Spiritual being having a human experience.

Star Ruby reverses a tendency to self-neglect and replaces pessimism with optimism.

Twenty-six

The Hermetic Principle of Rhythm Contemplation

In the passionate energy of the budding early summer, we find ourselves exploring the fifth Hermetic Principle, that of Rhythm. As we have welcomed the coming season with the dance, so we find there are many ways in which the movement of that dance is expressed in our lives, presented in *The Kybalion* as:

> Everything flows out and in; everything has its tides; all things rise and fall; the pendulum-swing manifests in everything; the measure of the swing to the right, is the measure of the swing to the left; rhythm compensates.[40]

The concept of timing is a key aspect of manifestation. There is a need to respect the natural rhythm that allows for the ideal circumstances of actualization. Life itself takes on an appreciation for rhythm. The annual cycle is but a rise of budding and fruition into the fall of harvest and decay. There is a time to plant and a time to harvest. There is a time to attend and a time to step back. The more we pay attention to the facets of this cycle, the more we can impact upon the factors that contribute to the fullness of success. Almanacs serve as helpful guides to empower us to read the tides to know how best to elicit a favorable outcome. In the world of nature, the growth cycle, the tidal cycle, the astrological cycle, we are comfortable with the Hermetic Principle of Rhythm.

....

40. The Three Initiates, "The Kybalion: Chapter II. The Seven Hermetic Principles," www.sacred-texts.com (Yogi Publication Society, 1912), https://www.sacred-texts.com/eso/kyb/kyb04.htm.

Need for awareness around the nature of rhythm is also imperative in relationships and this is where we can find it more of a challenge to see the wisdom and the truth in the principle. It speaks to the ability to nurture interdependence in all relationships, which is the mark of a healthy dynamic. When we can honor the interweaving of codependence and independence, the result is healthy interdependence.

Codependence is the loss of self in another. It is present when we have disconnected from our own internal source of power and turn to the other for definition, substance, and solidity. This is not healthy to maintain in a relationship, but, as we are human, we will find ourselves touching it on occasion.

Independence is the reliance on self to the exclusion of other. It is present when we are so focused on our ability to make do without help from anyone that we become remote and distant to others. We need to know that we are capable, but unrelenting independence often indicates an inability to relax enough to trust that others will be there.

In any relationship, there are going to be times when we need to melt into the support of the other, to seek affirmation or validation. And there are going to be those times when the other needs the same from us, to reach to us for support because they are not able to take another step without assistance. This is the healthy rhythm of the relationship dance. It is interdependence. It is this dynamic that acknowledges that today may be my day. That is okay. It is okay for me to be wobbly today. It is okay for me to follow while you lead. Because I know that tomorrow the rhythm of the dance will change. I know that there will be those moments when I take the lead because you are having a wobbly moment. I know that tomorrow may be your day. Interdependence is not a static stance, holding each other side by side, equally rigid. It is the intuitive movement to and fro that honors the shift in need and meeting of need moment by moment. It requires attentiveness and nuanced response.

The Hermetic Principle of Rhythm calls us to pay attention to the inner wisdom that tells us when the time is right. Like the process of birth itself, it reminds us that to try to force something to happen too soon can result in damage. When we ignore the natural pace and instead try to impose control, things can tear. However, to leave things too long can result in a different kind of trauma. When we refuse to be attentive to the danger of torpor, we run the risk of falling into lethargy and exhaustion that can leave us actually feeling drained, depleted, and depressed. When we see this Principle as represented by the hourglass, we can find the rhythm—the movement of the grains of sand from one side to the other—that hits the perfect balance between control and indifference. We can attune ourselves to our own perfect rhythm, trusting that we will know when to shift from one side to the other when it feels right to do so.

 Contemplation

Contemplate how the Bridging Hynni of Synthesis reflects the Hermetic Principle of Rhythm: the balance needed on both sides to create symmetry in the movement and harmony in the dance.

 Chakras to Deepen
the Contemplative Experience

Connect with the **heart chakra** to open yourself to the meeting point of the Above and the Below, of Spirit and human. The energy that flows through this center draws on the edges of either end of the spectrum and finds the spark in the place where they intersect. It is a place of gentle love, forceful courage, and the passion that brings meaning and movement to life. When the rhythm of the flow between Above and Below is steady and consistent, knowing each to be informed by and made stronger by the other, only then are we able to truly enter into the dance between Self and other in a way that enhances both. It is the healthy inner relationship between Inner Child and Higher Self coming together in the meeting place of the Adult Within that enables us to explore the best a relationship has to offer, adult to adult. The energy that sits at the back of this chakra can act like a tether holding us back or an open wound that leaks life force from us, inhibiting our ability to step fully into engaging with others. When the back of the heart chakra is blocked, we are overly directed by old hurts or traumas, often overcome with bitterness or regret. The healthy flow of energy from Above and Below through the heart chakra needs to touch both front and back, releasing the pain from past relationships in order that we can truly meet the current one.

The higher-vibration chakra that sits in the center of the upper chest is the **Twelfth Chakra of Samadhi.**[41] Translated from the Sanskrit, it is derived from the word meaning "to bring together." The implication of the term is that of directed concentration, a sense that one must bring together all the forces of one's mind toward an object or concept. It is the culmination of a yogic practice, indicating the achievement of union between the embodied soul with infinite spirit. When we are adept at experiencing the union of Self and Spirit within, and we are practiced at bringing that inner wholeness into relationship with others, we open ourselves to the possibility of attaining the Twelfth Chakra of Samadhi, connecting us to all life forms and experiencing the intricate, delicate dance that is life on all levels.

41. Stone, *Soul Psychology*.

Twenty-seven

Weaving Passion Ritual

Beltane is traditionally celebrated with a maypole dance, which not only represents the Earth's reception of the Divine spark necessary for conception if the planted seed is going to flourish, but also illustrates that we are not isolated but interdependent. As hard as it can feel sometimes to risk the trust required of intimacy, our human nature calls us to relationship and our Spirit nature yearns to dance with others. The alchemical stage of Conjunction is the first solid, though yet imperfect, coming together. This stage reflects the balanced relationship of two equal parts as they work to find harmony, similar to the way in which a maypole dance may start somewhat wobbly until the participants find the flow of the weaving rhythm. It is challenging, though not impossible, to weave a maypole alone. This ritual invites a solo dance through the technique of branch weaving to ignite passion, vitality, and courage into your life (see Appendix F for illustrated steps).

Symbols to help connect to ritual focus	• Trees and tree branches • Summer flowers (including posies and crowns) • Statues or photos of those deities that reflect sacred lovers (like Isis and Osiris) • An image of the Bridging Hynni of Synthesis
Optional: Stones from *Journey to Honor the World Tree* Meditation	• K2 • Morganite • Nirvana Quartz • Prairie Tanzanite • Star Ruby
Items needed for ritual activity	• A fresh unused candle (green, if you want to align with Hynni) • A lighter • A cauldron • A forked branch about two feet in length, ethically procured • Four different colors of yarn or ribbon (about five feet of each) *Possible color associations:* Red: Courage White: Innocence Orange: Playfulness Black: Mystery Yellow: Confidence Brown: Stability Green: Health Pink: Love Blue: Expression Grey: Reliability Indigo: Intuition Silver: Grace Purple: Faith Gold: Wisdom • Three wooden or glass beads • A fork • Scissors • Optional: Candle snuffer • Optional: Ogham oracle

Creating the Altar

With the change of the seasons toward summer and more constant and hospitable weather conditions, you can do this ritual outside if you choose. And if you are able to sit under a tree for this ritual, that would be ideal. If so, everything will be identical to the indoor version of the ritual, with the exception of the candle, which can be left out of the outdoor version.

Before you start the ritual, set out your materials. On your left, place the fork and four lengths of different colored yarn or ribbon. One of these will serve as the anchor color. The other three are the colors to be woven. Choose your colors with care. Intention has great impact, especially when it comes to weaving magic. On the right, have your cauldron, which contains three beads. In the center, place a fresh, unused candle and your branch.

You may also choose to decorate your space and your altar with those elements that amplify your connection to the vibrancy of life, and statues or photos of the gods and goddesses that are particularly connected to this time. You may also choose to include an image of the Bridging Hynni of Synthesis, which reminds us that in the dance with "Other," regardless of whether that "Other" is a person, a community, or a situation, the energies of each must be balanced.

When you are done preparing your space, take a moment to feel how the energy you have created affects you. You will want to ensure that there are elements that speak to the general theme of the ritual or the festival itself as well as those items that are going to be used in the ritual. This ensures that both the "Above," the realm of the transpersonal or mythic, and the "Below," the realm of the personal, are represented. If it feels complete, take some time to prepare yourself for ritual (see Appendix D).

The Ritual

As you sit in this place of the meeting place of the Above and Below, allow yourself to feel ever so deeply the power of the intersection point of those two very different energies. Take hold of your branch, paying particular attention to the meeting point of the two branches: the crux that creates a potent crucible for manifestation. In this moment, at this time of your life, what would you choose to dance into being? If there is a relationship to forge or a dream to realize, what would you choose to instill with the amplifying potential of passion? When you are ready to begin, light the candle before you and connect with the energy of your heart, the meeting place of your human and Spirit selves, and of self with other.

Take the yarn with the color you have chosen as your anchor color and tie the end just below the fork of the branch. Holding your branch horizontally so that one arm of the fork is above the other, wrap the yarn around the top arm twice, then bring the yarn down to the lower arm and wrap it once. Continue to wrap the arms, twice on the top and once on the bottom, moving horizontally along the branches. As you do, consider what provides foundation to your endeavors? What is the framework upon which you build? Who are the supports in your life? When you reach the top, tie the yarn securely to the top arm and cut off any excess.

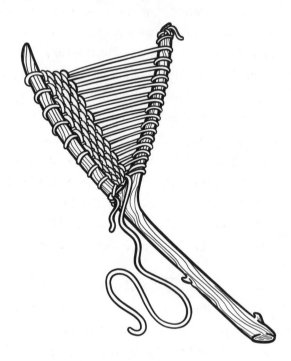

Take some time choosing the first color with which to work. What does it represent to you of what you are weaving into your life, what you are dancing into being, what passion you are amplifying? When that feels clear to you, tie one end of the yarn or ribbon to the top arm at the end closest to the wide opening. Begin to weave in an under-over pattern until you come to the end of the line, then shift direction and weave in an under-over pattern until you reach the wide opening again. Then weave again, back and forth until it feels that the time in the "dance" is right to reach into the cauldron and choose one of the beads. If this bead represented one quality in you that would help you dance your dream into being, what would it be? When the answer is clear to you, string the bead on your yarn or ribbon and keep weaving until either you come to the end of the length or it feels complete. Feel the rhythm of the weave. Feel the build of the "dance." On the last frame strand, knot your yarn to keep secure while you work with the other colors. Use the fork to push the strands into a strong and tight weave and then turn your attention to the remaining yarn or ribbon. Take some time choosing what color you want to work with next and what that represents to you. Repeat the entire process, starting with tying the yarn or ribbon to the anchor color strand closest to the wide opening of the branch and ending with securing the yarn to that strand when the color weave feels complete and then using the fork to push strands into a tight weave. When that is done, repeat the whole process with the last color. Pay attention to how your own energy shifts with the weave and how you feel as the pattern takes shape.

When you have come to the end of all three lengths of yarn or ribbon and your branch weaving is complete, take some time to charge it with the power of your intention. Hold the branch to your heart and, gazing into the light of the candle, feel the strong current of love, dedication, devotion, and passion that flows from that place into your weaving. When the candle contemplation feels complete, if you have an Ogham on hand, pull the tree that provides the best guidance for you at this moment.

Closure of Ritual

When you are ready to leave this liminal space, bring your conscious awareness back to your breath. Taking one last moment to anchor the connection to your heart and your passion, using either your breath or a candle snuffer, release the flame of the candle before you. What has been experienced in ritual lives forever in your cells. It need only be called forth from within when you choose.

Take some time to move through the directions once more, thanking the elements for helping to hold space and keep you safe through the ritual. Start again in the North with earth, then move through the East with air, the South with fire, the West with water, ending with the Below of the material plane and the Above of the cosmic plane. Thank and bid farewell to the deities who have been a part of this ritual with you and know that the wheel may turn around you, but you are—as they are—ever at the center.

Clearing Ritual Space

If you have been using an existing altar, you may decide to keep some items on your altar over the course of the cycle. Your beautiful branch weaving can hold the energy of your passion on your altar or, if you are able, place it in your garden to serve as an inspiring focal point.

 *Ogham Deck Recommendations*

Hidalgo, Sharlyn. *Celtic Tree Oracle*. Woodbury, MN: Llewellyn, 2017.

Matthews, John and Will Worthington. *The Spirit of Nature Oracle* London: Eddison Books, 2018.

Mueller, Mickie. *Voice of the Trees*. Woodbury, MN: Llewellyn, 2011.

Twenty-eight

Honor Diversity

The power of Cycle Four is the healing that comes when we know in every cell that as we are empowered, so it is imperative that all beings be empowered, and that difference, diversity, and variety makes for a stronger and more vital system.

In nature, we know that biodiversity is necessary to maintain a healthy balance of life within an ecosystem. The more diverse a system is, the stronger it is and, perhaps more importantly, the better able it is to survive and thrive in the face of adverse conditions or external stresses. Each element brings its own strength to the table that creates a powerful gestalt: the whole is greater than the sum of each of its individual parts. One plus one plus one equals wow!

The same holds true for any system, including human systems such as families, workplaces, and friendship circles. When we are solid in our own sense of Self, the presence of the other offers the opportunity for us to see ourselves in sharper relief and to hone some of our own rougher edges. Carl Jung, with all his expertise on dream analysis, explained that he went to someone else to interpret his own dreams because he could not see his own back. We are often too close to our own story. Diversity offers us that other view that can help us come to greater self-understanding.

Seeking the other perspective does nothing to threaten our own. If we know who we are, having an alternative affords an opportunity to assess. It is not a challenge to the status quo. Surrounding oneself with the psychological equivalent to "Yes Men" does nothing for soul growth and is actually indicative of a tenuous hold on self-esteem. Beware the evidence of the need for acquiescence. It suggests the groundwork for an unhealthy, unbalanced non-diverse ecosystem.

There is a saying that variety is the spice of life. There is richness of texture and flavor that is brought to the dish. The same is true of relationships. When we bring a variety of perspective, culture, age, and experience into our lives, we are made all the richer from that.

Key Aspects of Cycle Four[42]

Archetypal Themes	Healing Themes	Indication of Crisis	Healing Practices
Union and Partnership Union; passion; synthesis	Relationships; adolescent; identity in dynamic; developing interdependence; identifying core issues	A lack of passion for activities and ventures; resentment toward others; unhealthy relationship dynamics; lack of compassion or empathy for others; burnout (particularly as relates to healthcare workers and healers)	Exploration of Core Meaning; contemplation of the Hermetic Principle of Rhythm; activation of Bridging Hynni of Synthesis ⧖
Elemental Reflection	**Intuitive Guidance and Tool**	**Alchemical Reflection**	**Affirmations**
Fire	Wee guides (insects); Ogham	*Conjunction* Bringing disparate parts together in balanced relationship though maintaining distinction from each other	I embrace my human nature and my Spirit; I treat myself with care and respect; I am open to love; I am inspired and inspiring; I bring passion to my ventures and endeavors.

....

42. More information on Key Aspects can be found in *The Great Work: Self-Knowledge and Healing Through the Wheel of the Year* by the author (Llewellyn, 2015).

Part Five

Cycle Five
June 21–August 1

From Mask to Mandala

The Clear Hynni of Expression

As Below	**As Above**
Mask	Mandala
Alchemical	Peacock's tail
Fermentation	Truth and creativity
Being real	Archetypes
Subpersonalities	

Synthesis
Accomplishment
Acknowledgment
Gathering strength

Twenty-nine

Litha and the Inner Adult

As the sun moves into its full strength at the Summer Solstice or Midsummer, we are afforded a moment's respite. Much of the work involved in laying the groundwork for a solid, hopefully abundant harvest has been done. All of the work in gathering said solid, abundant harvest has yet to be done There is nothing for it at this time of year than to appreciate the long, languid days soaking up the strength of the sun, having turned the next part of the work and the growing cycle over to the natural forces. Some maintenance may be required, but for the most part, it is up to the sun and the rain to bring the work to its fulfillment.

In taking the time to appreciate the momentary pause, it can be important to recognize the work that has been done so far. At this midpoint in the Great Cycle of the Magnum Opus, we turn our faces to the glowing sun that we welcomed with its tentative, delicate rays at the Winter Solstice and we bask in the awareness of our *Accomplishment*. It has been no small feat to bring us to where we stand in this moment, and to take even the smallest moment to allow the full weight of that to land is so important.

There is a tendency in our society to accentuate the negative and mask the positive as far as our accomplishments go. This tendency makes it even more difficult to challenge the hold shame has over our lives and invite a healthy sense of Self back into the driver's seat. The full summer sun invites *Acknowledgement*. It invites the revelation of all we have done, all we have attempted, all we have prepared, all we have dreamed. This moment of fulfillment before the slide back down into wane. It is the pause to take stock of all that was, is, and will be before setting off along the next part of the undertaking.

Late spring reminded us that there is an inherent strength we have within, and it was that strength that brought us through the dark into the light. This late summer festival reminds us that this is the time for *Gathering strength* in preparation for the work that is yet to come. If we expend our energy at this time that is meant for acknowledging the journey we have taken thus far and resting up for the next part of the journey, then we will have potentially wasted valuable resources and jeopardized the possibility of our future success.

There is a secondary benefit to taking this moment of pause. When we are moving and building and working and shaping, it can be challenging to stop long enough for others to catch sight of who we really are. There can be a lot of splash and distraction in the need to be ever-doing. When we stop long enough to allow the sun's light to illuminate us, we also invite our own Light to shine forth. We risk actually being seen.

The Core Issue in Cycle Five is that of being seen and heard or rather all the ways in which we feel that does not happen. Instead of experiencing the glory of the manifest sun, we feel invisible. This creates the Shadow reflection: That it doesn't matter what we say or do, others will not see us, recognize us, appreciate us, validate us.

The shift from early to late summer is reflected in the movement from adolescent to adult. In adolescence, we explore different identities and passions, homing in on the experience of self that feels true. In adulthood, we begin to take that true experience of self out into the world. We engage in work that feels reflective of our interests. We settle into friendships and relationships that feel aligned with our values. We express who we are through how we are in our lives, if we have graduated into adulthood with a healthy foundation. If instead we are informed by shame, we will not carry that confidence of self into our self-expression. Instead of feeling comfortable being seen and heard, we are horrified at the prospect of being exposed. Instead of putting our ample energy and resources in creating a fulfilled life, we unconsciously pour those resources into crafting numerous and intricate masks to hide our strength, ability, and accomplishments. If we cannot see it within ourselves, there is no way we are going to risk others seeing our perceived flawed truth. Adulthood becomes a complicated task of trying to make one's way in the world while at the same time trying to hide one's truth from the world.

To further complicate this foray into adulthood, often we have already internalized the message that what we say or do does not matter unless it is witnessed and validated by others. So, very often in adulthood, we are operating by three contradictory faulty beliefs.

1. Whatever we do only matters if it is seen and heard by others (validation)
2. Nothing we say or do is going to result in being seen and heard by others (abandonment)
3. Even if we were, it is dangerous to be seen and heard by others (vulnerability)

When distorted by Shadow, the power of this festival can turn against us. What we most yearn for, we fear the most. We want to be seen and heard and yet, we dread the possibility that that may actually occur. In looking to the archetypal energies, we find a key to the path that lies ahead and to our future success.

Summer, by its very nature, begs us to escape the mundane and commune with the great outdoors. As such, there are not as many traditional celebrations for this time of year. The celebrations tend to be the experience of nature itself. That said, there are a few examples of Midsummer festivals from the past and even fewer in the present. The ancient Romans celebrated *Vestalia* from June 7 to 15, honoring the sacred hearth fire of the goddess Vesta. The ancient Greeks celebrated *Kronia*, during which regular social mores were overturned. This is reminiscent of the Roman celebration of Saturnalia, which was celebrated at the Winter Solstice. The ancient Celts named the day *Alban Heruin*, meaning the Light of the Shore. Many indigenous tribes in North America, including the Sioux and Blackfoot, still celebrate ceremonial *Sun Dances* around the time of the Summer Solstice, which often involved emotionally charged acts of bravery to overcome great pain. *Midsommar* (Sweden) is a highly popular holiday considered to be the second most important holiday after Christmas. Interestingly this is the festival that sports the maypole in Sweden, called the midsommarstång. The *Revetlla of Sant Joan* (Spain) is celebrated with fireworks and wild revelry. A bit later than the Summer Solstice but falling into the time frame of the season are the national celebrations of several countries, which also tend to include fireworks and revelry. Canada celebrates *Canada Day* on July 1. It shares this day's celebrations with Rwanda, Somalia, Hong Kong, and Burundi. The United States celebrates *Independence Day* on July 4. More contemporarily, Russia began the beautiful and highly creative tradition of *White Nights*, to celebrate the time during which the phenomenon of the "midnight sun" is experienced. This natural occurrence of extended daylight in countries close to either pole, North or South, lasts from around May to July with the height occurring around the time of the Summer Solstice.[43] Another modern festival that reflects the celebration of creativity and expression at this time is the modern pan-European Fête de la Musique. Begun in France in 1982, this Summer Solstice festival is a celebration of music, especially music played outdoors, that is now held in over one hundred countries.

The Summer Solstice invites expression. It nudges us into the Light whether we are comfortable in that place or not and encourages us to celebrate our stepping into the independence of self and the autonomy to choose our own way.

 Further Exploration
on Litha

Blake, Deborah. *Midsummer: Rituals, Recipes & Lore for Litha.* Woodbury, MN: Llewellyn, 2015.

43. It is an interesting juxtaposition that the cycle that contains the White Night celebration of the Midnight Sun is the same cycle that reflects the Hermetic Principle of Polarity.

Thirty

· ·

The Shadow Mask of Subpersonalities

When we turn our face to the full force of the summer sun, what is the face we present? Is it a shining reflection of our Essence, the true core of Self and identity? Or is it the dim, dented, ill-fitting mask that has been foisted upon us by others?

If we carry a deeply rooted belief that we are inherently flawed, the innate survival impulse is to hide what we believe to be our true face from the world and to try to adopt a face that we feel—or that we have come to experience—is acceptable to others. This false face goes by many names. Carl Jung referred to this as the "Persona." Further to Sigmund Freud's delineation, it has been called the "Unhealthy Ego." Jay Noricks refers to it as a "part." Hal and Sidra Stone use the term "subpersonality." Whatever the name, the function serves the same purpose: these masks we wear are the personal protective gear in which we shroud our True Self so that others may find us palatable and acceptable.

There can be some confusion over the difference between a mask and an archetype, and increasingly the terms are often used interchangeably. Though it may seem like semantics, there is actually a considerable and significant difference between the two.

The term "archetype" comes from the Greek word *archon*, meaning "ruler." Plato, who coined the term, saw archetypes as being the conceptualized "ideal form" of something that then has a diluted multiplicity of tangible forms represented in the actual physical world. For every breed of dog from mastiff to teacup Chihuahua, there is concept of "dog" that permeates the sense of each one. It can be hard to put one's finger on exactly what that is, but we have a sense of knowing that a dog is a dog and not a cat or a platypus. Jung applied this premise psychologically in his concept of the collective unconscious. In our inner reality, we carry the sum total of all our personal experiences in our personal unconscious. Anything that has ever happened to us, in all its sensory input, is stored in our memory, but there is so much information we carry when taking into consideration all experiences from in utero to present, it would be beyond overwhelming to have it all in our readily accessible memory banks. So most of the information regarding our experiences lands in our personal unconscious. It's there but we don't necessarily need to have easy access to it. But Jung postulated that there is a deeper unconscious layer that connects all of humanity, in which we share the sum total of all our collective or shared experiences. This is the realm of the collective unconscious and it is here that the archetypes reside. Universal and innate, it is not that we may or may not carry these archetypes within us. We <u>all</u> carry <u>all</u> the archetypes within, regardless of whether we experience them in our lives or not. Archetypes are informed by Spirit (Plato's Ideal Form) and are "a priori," meaning that they exist within us before we have even begun to experience our human life. Archetypes negate the concept of being born "tabula rasa" or as a blank slate. It is more like being born with a booklet of coloring pages, each with its own big, bold simple outlined design for you to color however you like. Whatever life presents you with, your unconscious will automatically flip to that page and start coloring, even scribbling outside the lines if you so choose.

This is very different than the idea of a subpersonality or mask. Subpersonalities are shame-based, adapted personalities that are unconsciously created as a result of painful or traumatic experience. They are not innate within us. Technically, this is called "a posteriori," meaning that we are not born with these energies latent within us, just waiting to come forth given the requisite life experience. They develop after we are born as a direct result of lived experience. From a psychotherapeutic perspective, they specifically develop as an unhealthy coping mechanism to try to mitigate unease in what is consciously or unconsciously perceived to be a hostile environment. But, as with so many coping mechanisms that are born out of fear, that which was created to protect always ends up carrying a cost that is often too steep to bear.

If I enlist the People-Pleaser to ensure that my acquiescence helps me fly under the radar, at some point I will feel the weight of never pleasing myself.

If I engage the Martyr in order to feel a sense of purpose through my sacrifice, it is a matter of time before bitterness fills my heart.

If I accept the never completed "to do list" from the Perfectionist to reflect a sense of worth through my doing-ness, I may as well add "succumb to burnout" to the list right away, for it is just a matter of time before it all becomes too much.

Every subpersonality comes with a cost. When I live from a place of inauthenticity and prioritize your perception of me over my own experience of self, that is going to take something from me that at some point may prove to be too much. My sense of self-worth, my valuable time, my kindness and compassion, my physical health, my resources, my peace of mind. All these and many, many more become the toll that is exacted when what we express in the world is out of alignment with our truth.

Every subpersonality has an agenda. As they are not concerned with authentic self-expression in the world, subpersonalities are shapeshifters, morphing into that which will be the least threatening role or the most acceptable to others. As such, the subpersonality's agenda is always controlling the relationship dynamic: "I will be what you need me to be in order to keep my fragile sense of self hidden from your judgmental gaze and thus keep myself safe."

In working with subpersonalities or masks, it is not a question of <u>whether</u> you have put on an inauthentic way of being but <u>which</u> one or ones do you use. Because shame (including lack of self-esteem and fear of vulnerability) is so widespread, truly in epidemic proportions, we all employ masks. For some, this veiled way of engaging with others might be the only way they ever know. This mask becomes so familiar it becomes confused with the true face that lies hidden—and safe—underneath.

It is true that when we go out into the world, we need to take on some shape or other. It is exactly the same as wearing clothing. What is important to discern is what informs what I wear? If I put this outfit on because I love how I look and feel in it, then I am reflecting my inner Spirit in my external expression. If I choose this outfit because I know it is acceptable in a particular environment for a woman my age, then I am allowing the externals and need for acceptance to determine my expression— especially if I find I don't actually even really like that particular outfit and I can't wait to take it off when I am safely in my own home again.

As we have already seen, there is a strong connection between the energies of late spring and those of late summer. If we have addressed the dark at the Spring Equinox and claimed our Light and strength, then we will have the confidence and esteem to express through the voice of our True Self. But if it still feels that there is a pit in the stomach and a rock in the heart, that self-acceptance and self-love has not taken hold. Applying the mask is the only option for expression that feels like it has any semblance of safety, but the highest cost it exacts on us is the belief that no one will love or accept us for who we truly are.

Tragically, the question I hear most often in some form or another is "What's wrong with me?" Subpersonalities are the psyche's way of trying to alleviate the pain of that question. But they don't get to the true heart of the issue, which is that nothing is deeply, inherently wrong with you in the first place! When that is truly understood, it is a game-changer and your life will never be expressed the same way again.

Shadow of Cycle Five: Subpersonalities

All subpersonalities fall within the Shadow work of Cycle Five; however, a further delineation shows how different subpersonalities can align with the energies found on the Wheel of the Year.

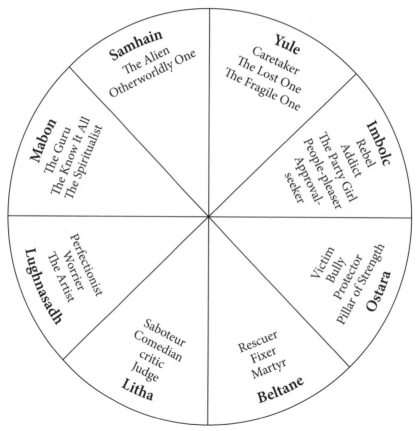

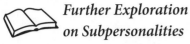 *Further Exploration on Subpersonalities*

Antony, Martin M., and Richard P. Swinson. *When Perfect Isn't Good Enough: Strategies for Coping with Perfectionism.* Oakland: New Harbinger, 2009.

Carson, Rick. *Taming Your Gremlin: A Surprisingly Simple Method for Getting Out of Your Own Way.* New York: William Morrow, 2003.

Rowan, John. *Subpersonalities: The People Inside Us.* Abington, UK: Routledge, 1990.

Temple, Della. *Tame Your Inner Critic: Find Peace and Contentment to Live Your Life on Purpose.* Button Rock Press, 2019.

Thirty-one

The Light of Archetypes

Something very interesting happens in the slow steady heat of the summer sun. This cycle affords the opportunity to change into a whole new form. At what point does the seedling become the tree, the water-logged leaves become the healing tea, the adolescent become the adult? What is the turning point? Alchemy says this is the point. The fifth stage is where the magic happens and that which we have been working on for so long undergoes an irreversible transformation. In fermentation, as a result of the slow, steady application of heat, the goop that originally appeared to be just a pile of rotting stuff changes in its very essence. Alchemically, this is evidenced by the appearance of the "peacock's tail," a wash of color that plays over the substance, that signifies the moment the rot becomes infused with Spirit. Numerologically five indicates opportunity, usually through crisis. The fives in the tarot suits are all indicative of the greatest challenge in the suit, and yet, all hold the potential for the resolution of that crisis if one is able to stay the course and be open to the lesson. In the major arcana, it is the Hierophant who is numbered five, highlighting this invitation not only to learn the lesson, but specifically to see the presence of Spirit in that lesson.

Under the slow, steady heart of the summer sun, we are illuminated and the whole of who we are has the opportunity to shine forth. As the previous chapter described, if we are informed by Shadow and shame, this may well be a very uncomfortable experience. Throwing our darkness into high relief can be very painful. But with a gentle approach and a commitment to continue to shine light on the issue, this pain can resolve into a higher appreciation for the gift of our lives and ourselves. If we breathe through the discomfort until that peacock's tail, we can experience the revelation of the higher truth that, in spite of all our imperfections, we are the embodiment of Spirit. We may be flawed, but we are also whole. And holy. As the esteemed psychiatrist and founder of the integrative psychological approach known as psychosynthesis, Roberto Assagioli said:

> It is certainly true—that there is a multiplicity within the self but the will is essentially the activity of the self which stands above the multiplicity. It directs, regulates, and balances the other functions of the personality in a creative way.[44]

There is a beauty in the recognition that we are both in the flow of the river of our lives and observing the river at the same time. There is always going to be the potential for turbulence—little eddies that might rock the boat—but the flow of the river itself is timeless and awe-inspiring. We experience the flow of the river in our human selves, but this cycle, especially alchemically, infuses us with the wisdom that there is something far greater than our own minute experience. The archetypes bring us in touch with the powerful, timeless, unifying energy of Spirit.

Archetypes are "conceptual energy containers" that exist in every single person. They rest within the psyche as potential waiting to be filled with content until such as a time as our "river flows in that direction." Each and every one of us has the archetype of the Divine Child within us. Our life experience may disconnect us from that remembrance very early on, but that energy is within us, which means we can always find our way back to it. Each and every one of us has the archetype of the Mother. We will most definitely fill that container with very different experiences, both positive and negative. We can never know an archetype. They are beyond our capacity to access. Archetypes are the essence of Spirit travelling forth into existence via the vessel of our souls. What we <u>can</u> know is the personal content with which that archetype has been filled through our life's experience. Thus, when we think we are mov-

---

44. Keen, Sam. "The Golden Mean of Roberto Assagioli." Sam Keen-Thinking Out Loud, December 17, 2009. https://thesamkeen.wordpress.com/interviews-by-sam/interviews -by-sam/the-golden-mean-of-roberto-assagioli/.

ing toward the archetype, what we are actually doing is opening the possibility for a deeper understanding of self. And in doing so, especially as we allow the constant warmth of the summer sun to illuminate, illuminate, illuminate, we have the opportunity to transform the pain that has kept us separate from our truth, our will, and our choice. We have the opportunity to allow the peacock's tail to awaken us to our own self-realization process. And we have the opportunity to step into a transformed relationship with the individuated Self. For Jung, the symbol that represented that Self is the mandala.

> The mandala is an archetypal image whose occurrence is attested throughout the ages. It signifies the wholeness of the Self. This circular image represents the wholeness of the psychic ground or, to put it in mythic terms, the divinity incarnate in man.[45]

At this time and in this cycle, when we begin to pay attention to the Adult Within and how we might choose to express who we are in our lives, having an appreciation for what informs that expression is some of the most important work we can do. When we are able to address and challenge the shame within and reclaim our Light, we release the masks we have worn in order to attain the approval of others, and in doing so reclaim the mandala of the Self. We reclaim our birthright as healed, whole, and holy. We may be flawed, but we are not broken. We may make mistakes, but we are also informed by a fundamentally healthy psyche that has its own inherent wisdom, providing us with the very tools, situations, relationships, and dynamics that will move us exactly where we need to be, should we choose to act from a place of Light.

....

45. Jung, *Memories, Dream, Reflections*, 334–335.

Light of Cycle Five: Archetypes

All archetypes fall within the Light work of Cycle Five; however, a further delineation shows how different archetypes can align with the energies found on the Wheel of the Year.

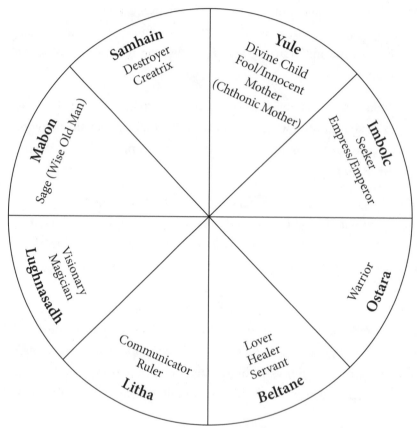

Inner Workings:
Crafting the Mandala of Self

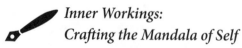

In his psychology of personality types (or typology), Carl Jung presented that there are four main functions that everyone has: sensing, feeling, thinking, and intuiting.[46] For each individual, one of these is going to be the dominant approach, the natural

....

46. Jung, *Collected Works of C.G. Jung, Volume 6: Psychological Types.*

"go to" response. One of these will likely be repressed or relegated to the deep corners of the Shadow. This can be seen through an elemental lens as well. Airy people tend to think first. Earthy people tend to approach with their senses. If you are a feeler first, thinking may be the last place you go to assess the best approach to a situation.

At the same time as Jung was developing his psychology of type, an American educator, Katharine Cook Briggs, was exploring the elements behind personality by researching biographies. She came up with four temperaments (meditative, spontaneous, executive, and social) before reading Jung's work on typology. Hugely influenced by Jung's approach, Briggs and her daughter, Isabel Briggs Myers constructed the Myers-Briggs Type Indicator, which is one of the most widely used personality assessment tools in the world.[47] As with Jung's work, understanding that we all contain aspects and elements of all attributes, the MBTI guides one to identify which of two opposite traits feels most applicable in four different categories. With one letter from each pair, the result is a combination of four letters that corresponds to one of sixteen possible core personality types.

Take some time to consider which end of the spectrum you feel most applies to you with each of these four categories and then determine from that which type you are according to Myers-Briggs (see chart at the end of the chapter).

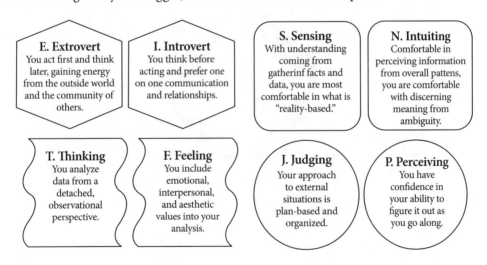

---

47. Her book on the subject, published five years after Jung's, was called *Meet Yourself: How to Use the Personality Paintbox* (1926).

If the personality type that is determined through this process feels like it highlights something of an Essence reflection within you, then this is a helpful template to serve as a foundation to craft your own mandala of Self. This can be done either physically or meditatively, though it is more powerful to have an actual drawing that is representative of Self at the end. Starting with a circle to represent the wholeness of Self, divide that circle into four quarters. Those four parts can represent each of the four categories above; or your physical, emotional, mental, and energetic selves; or earth, water, air, and fire. However you feel called to do so, fill in each of the four quarters with colors, symbols, or any other design elements which represent your connection—from an Essence perspective—to that quarter. When you are done, sit back and observe how you feel as you take in the image you have created of your wholeness, your Self.

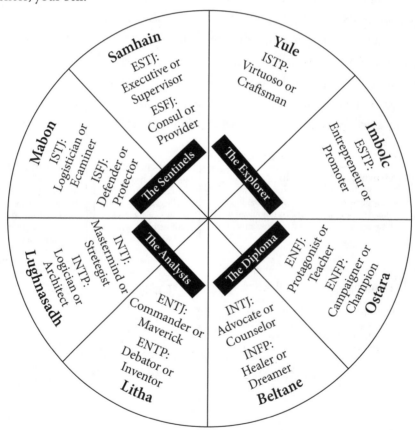

Thirty-two

Creating a Mandala Prayer Bundle Meditation

There can be a challenge when we come to the fifth cycle. It is when the sun shines most intensely. Where there is the brightest light, there is also the most pronounced shadow. But we come to this place with much experience and considerable skills that allow us to shift perspective from crisis to opportunity. It is not our pain that defines us and this is the place where we can see very clearly what <u>does</u> define us. This is the place where we can choose who we will be, how we respond, and how we share the truth of our journey. It is in the full force of the sun that rides high in the sky that our transformation comes and what we know of ourselves on the inside can be brought out into the light of the outside.

Every tradition has its method of communicating with the Divine, some more tangible and material than others. Hindu tradition involved *pujas* which translates as "worship" or "consecrate" and may be derived from the word meaning "flowers." South American shamans, specifically Peruvian shamans, perform an ancient ceremony called the *despacho*, which translates as "sending a message," along the lines of "sending a dispatch." Though there are many types of despachos, they all carry the sense of communicating with the Divine, specifically from a place of gratitude for the understanding of our place in the very fabric of life. The Ayni Despacho specifically has reciprocity or balance as its focus, recognizing that when we are out of balance, the world around us will be out of balance. This acknowledgment of interconnection and intention of being in right relationship with the world is expressed through the creation of a mandala crafted of natural elements, a prayer of gratitude offered to the Divine. Tibetan Buddhism has a similar practice of connecting with the Divine through the creation of a sand mandala. Approaching the mandala as a cosmic map that positions the human in relation to the Divine, these sand mandalas are recognized as temporary constructs, reflecting the impermanence of life, to be destroyed upon completion.

Whether despacho, puja, sand mandala, or prayer bundle, the way in which we communicate with the Divine speaks volumes to our relationship with Self.

Meditation

Close your eyes. Focus on your breath. Allow your breath to drop you into a deep place within yourself. Each inhale connects you to those places within that may hold tension, discomfort, or unease. Each exhale invites you to release those tensions into the cosmos, bringing you to the balance place in the center of the Above and the Below that connects Spirit and human: the place between, where magic happens.

You find yourself still seated in between the roots of the awe-inspiring tree. There is a definite weight of heat in the air, and you look up to see that the sun has now moved directly overhead. As you have been safely tucked within the fold of the tree, the day has progressed and you know that, much as it would be lovely to stay beneath its canopy, especially in this heat, it is time for you to move on once more. You feel the pull of some unnamable but unmistakable draw. You touch the pouch that holds your golden seed and the Spirit ribbon, knowing that there is a soul task that calls to you, awakening something within you.

As you rise from your place, you notice that you hold yourself differently. You feel different in your body. It is hard to pin down, but the best that you can account for is that you feel more anchored in your body than you have in a long time, and yet at the same time you feel more uplifted and expansive than you have in a long time as well. You feel as though you have both roots and wings, and this awakens a different inner dynamic—clearer, surer, more focused.

You begin to walk, choosing a direction that pulls invitingly on your heart. As you walk, you notice in great detail the lush richness around you. You move through a landscape in full blooming. There is a luxury of plants, flowers, herbs, shrubs, and trees. There is a symphony of sounds, calls, cries, hoots, and whistles. All of nature has come alive and you feel that richness of nature reflected within. Everywhere your eye lands, there is growth and color, and you find that there are certain items that seem to specifically call to you. An herb here. A feather there. A berry here. A branch there. With gratitude in your heart, you accept the gift of these particular items, gathering them up and tucking them into the pouch at your waist. You have a sense that there is a special meaning to each of these items for you. That each one is somehow reflective of and resonant with how you feel within. The quality or properties of the herb, flower, or tree that reflects a skill or gift that you recognize in yourself. The feather of a bird or tuft of fur from an animal whose medicine resonates with one of your core values. Whatever the item, explore how it represents some aspect of Self. Not only in its qualities, but also pay attention to the colors and textures to which you are drawn as you walk. You have a sense that what you feel within—the strength of the Self that flows there—is being reflected in the richness of the land around you. And just as you feel yourself fully immersed in the wonder that is this landscape, it begins to change. The land begins to climb ever so gradually, and you become aware of how close you are to a magnificent mountain range with a certain alluring peak that you know in your soul is what has been calling to you since you began this journey. You know that this peak is the culmination of your journey and that you will achieve that destination in time, but for now, you feel the urge to honor the journey thus far, to gratefully acknowledge what has been and humbly accept what is to be.

You set yourself at the base of the mountain and empty the pouch that holds all your gathered treasures. With great care, you tear at the seams of the pouch, turning it with your deconstructing expertise back into the simple square fabric it was before being worked upon and crafted. You lay the fabric down flat on the ground and begin to shape your own intricate and evocative mandala. Over each item you have gathered, and even more that come to you appearing magically in your hands as you work, you gently blow a prayer of gratitude before placing it on the cloth. Using color, texture, intention and inner knowing, create a beautiful mandala that serves as your voice of Self to the Divine. It is both a claiming and an offering, emanating gratitude for all that was, is, and will be. This design you are creating honors your relationship with the Divine, reflecting the reciprocity that you hold with the Divine, the profound balance in the dynamic between the Above and the Below.

Take some time to regard the beauty you have crafted, the beauty that you are, the beauty of Spirit at work in your life. And the last item that you place, in the very center of your bundle, is your golden seed, that precious kernel that you battled the dragon to attain. Offer that Seed of Self as the very center of your prayer bundle and then, when you are ready, bring the edges of the fabric together so that all the items in your mandala are safely contained within. The very last item is the Spirit ribbon that was gifted to you by the World Tree. Wrapping the ribbon around the bundle and tying it securely, your offering is complete. This is your gift to Spirit and you place your bundle in front of you, under the intense noonday sun. Astoundingly, the moment you remove your hands, the bundle bursts into flame. Your gift has been accepted and you know that who you are—in the fullness of who you are—is accepted and acceptable and can be expressed and shared with the world. From here on in, the path is all up.[48]

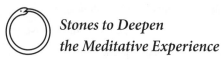 *Stones to Deepen*
the Meditative Experience

Purpurite helps one to break out of old patterns, repairing emotional damage and helping one to express the truth.

Stone of Solidarity (also known as the Stone of Sanctuary) is known as the "bridge-builder," encouraging respect, honesty, and trust that operates from a place of knowledge.

Tiffany Stone (or Bertrandite) integrates sweet, positive energy that assists with implementing positive change and bringing success to endeavors.

....

48. This meditation is easily translated into a beautiful ceremony. Crafting a physical prayer bundle is a powerful process. If you choose to do this in actuality rather than meditatively, there are three ways to offer the bundle to spirit. Burying in the earth invites a slow process of transformation. Releasing to water often allows for emotional release. Burning in fire, particularly at significant times such as the Summer Solstice, invites rapid transformation.

Thirty-three

The Hermetic Principle of Polarity Contemplation

The Principle of Polarity presents a view of existence in which opposing qualities are seen to be simply different expressions of the same theme. Not that they are completely different concepts having no relation to each other, but that they are connected and inform each other. If one finds oneself at either end of the poles, that reflects the expression of an imbalance in the theme, quality, or element that will lead to dis-ease. An expression that is too high along the scale is sharp. It issues forth in the world with a preponderance or excess of the quality. An expression that is too low along the scale is flat. It has little or no momentum to lift the quality into a place of healthy functioning. The gift is in recognizing that the importance of knowing what lies at either end of the pole is what is necessary to be able to calibrate the perfect pitch. *The Kybalion* describes the Principle of Polarity in that:

> Everything is Dual; everything has poles; everything has its pair of opposites; like and unlike are the same; opposites are identical in nature, but different in degree; extremes meet; all truths are but half-truths; all paradoxes may be reconciled.[49]

The idea of the Golden Mean in which happiness in life is found through achieving the balance point between two extremes is a very Aristotelian idea. The Greek

49. The Three Initiates, "The Kybalion: Chapter II. The Seven Hermetic Principles," www.sacred-texts.com (Yogi Publication Society, 1912), https://www.sacred-texts.com/eso/kyb/kyb04.htm.

philosopher Aristotle presented the example of bravado and cowardice representing the two polar opposites along a spectrum of courage.[50] At the one extreme end, there is bravado or rash action that races into a dangerous situation with no acknowledgment of danger's existence. At the other extreme end of the spectrum lies cowardice, which is so completely overcome with the awareness of the danger that it is incapacitated by inaction. Both respond to the situation, but from completely opposite directions. In Aristotelian philosophy, the Golden Mean is expressed through the balance that lies between the poles. For Aristotle, between bravado and cowardice lies courage, which reflects the choice to move into action but undertaken with the full acknowledgment of the inherent danger. Courage is the perfect pitch found on the balance point between the two extremes. It is through this middle path, the path of moderation, that we find happiness (or *eudaimonia*).

Any quality we experience or any emotion that we bring to experience can be found somewhere along this scale. When we truly comprehend the power of the Hermetic Principle of Polarity, it is possible to see how dis-ease, unease, being out of that centered inner place, comes when we start to tip too far along toward one pole or the other. This is not to say that we can never experience the exquisite joy of bliss. It is merely to say that in allowing for an experience of bliss, we may also be open to an experience of despair, and in the wisdom held between those two, we may find contentment and peace.

Hynni	Excess	The Golden Mean	Deficiency
	Controlling	Cherished	Naive
	Turbulent	Connected	Frozen
	Arrogant	Empowered	Helpless

50. Aristotle, Bartlett, and Collins, *Aristotle's Nicomachean Ethics*.

Hynni	Excess	The Golden Mean	Deficiency
⊗	Manipulative	Courageous	Evasive
◁	Demanding	Authentic	Dissembling
✦	Hypervigilant	Intuitive	Confused
☆	Blissed out	Integrated	Resigned
◈	Enmeshed	Unified	Isolated

Looking at the key qualities of each of the eight Hynnis (energy vibrations), one can see the Light embodiment of each reflected in the Golden Mean, with the Shadow attributes falling on either pole in either excess or deficiency. As we move from unconsciousness to consciousness, from Shadow to Light, and from naiveté to wisdom, we come to recognize that we cannot control that which lies outside of us. When we try to do that, we get knocked off-kilter and off-center. We are driven from the middle path (or middle pillar). And any movement away from the Golden Mean is a bid to control. There is great, great wisdom in these words well known in recovery circles: God (or the name you ascribe to that which is greater than yourself), grant me the serenity to accept the things I cannot change, the courage to change the things I can, and the wisdom to know the difference. The middle path is the wisdom to know the difference.

The Hermetic Principle of Polarity reminds us that the path to happiness lies in striking the balance that is reflective of our psychospiritual truth, and invites us to share that truth with the world from a place of integrity. It acknowledges that there is a weaving of our human and Spirit selves that is always going to create a level of complexity and sometimes contradiction in how and what we express, but that we can accept that truth and share it in countless creative ways with others. It is not about acting a certain way in order to be seen and heard in a particular way. It is not about trying to control how others view us. But neither is it about not being engaged and involved. As long as we are human, there will be a part of us that cares how others see us and respond to us, but <u>we</u> need to have a care that that does not stifle our expression. Pay attention to the ways in which you may strike strident or you may murmur mutely, and find the Golden Mean to pitch-perfect expression of Self.

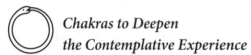

Contemplation

Contemplate how the Clear Hynni of Expression reflects the Hermetic Principle of Polarity: the vibrational emanation that takes our truth, whether in excess, deficiency, or balance, and amplifies it for the world to hear.

Chakras to Deepen
the Contemplative Experience

Connect with the **throat chakra** to open yourself to clear and authentic expression. We express ourselves in so many other ways in our lives than words. The choices we make, the causes we support, the stances we take, the people with whom we align ourselves. All these are filtered through the throat chakra as either authentically reflective of our deep inner truth or in disavowing the integrity of our Essence. We communicate who we are informed by fear or inspired by Spirit. Our values, our needs, and our emotions, as well as our dreams, our aspirations, and our inspirations, are all filtered through this gateway out into the world. The energy that sits at the back of this chakra is our will. It is the force of experience and commitment to self that flows into the energetics of that which flows out of us into the world.[51] When the back of the throat chakra is blocked, there is no will to give impetus, direction, and force to our choice. We may take action, but the chances are high that the arrow will fall to the ground well short of its target.

The higher-vibration chakra that sits in the center of the throat is the **Thirteenth Chakra of Mediumship.**[52] It expands the movement of true expression to the realms

....

51. Interestingly, Psychosynthesis, a branch of Transpersonal Psychology founded by Roberto Assagioli that introduced the concept that grew into subpersonalities, holds that will is the direct expression of the Self.

52. Stone, *Soul Psychology*.

of the non-physical, allowing the wisdom of those who have passed beyond the veil to intersect with our own wisdom in order to be shared with the world. When we are able to know ourselves as always connected to Spirit, expressing that truth as our authentic Self in word and action, we are able to raise our voice to be that vessel through which Spirit communicates in whatever way it shows up. This is not always through giving messages from the Other Side. There needs to be discernment, respect for boundaries, and allowance for personal choice in all matters of sharing messages. When you know yourself to be one with Spirit and when you know that physical existence and non-physical beingness are just vibrational degrees of the same thing, your voice and the voice of Spirit are one and the same thing. Messages from beyond the veil resonate with a truth that lies within you and you are a conduit for that message—not just in word but in all that you do and all that you are. It is through this high-vibration chakra that we activate the psychic ability of clairparlance. Rooted in the French *clair* meaning "clear" and parlance from *parler* meaning "to speak," clairparlance is the ability to listen with our hearts, attune to Spirit, and speak from that deep place of timelessness that has the ability to convey truth that transcends the fleeting now. And its topic is always how to manifest Spirit on Earth, how to heal the fragmented in order to come to a place of wholeness. Clairparlance is always about bringing Light to the pain that has been carried for too long, in all the myriad ways that can show up.

Thirty-four

Honoring Self Ritual

Sitting directly across the wheel from the Winter Solstice, this Midsummer festival invites the celebration of Light's attainment. The child has become the adult and, though there are many more miles on the road to travel, there has certainly been much work and effort that warrant acknowledgment.

Alchemically, this stage also has resonance with the Winter Solstice. Whereas alchemical Calcination of Midwinter brings abrupt change that comes with a shocking inferno, the steady heat of the summer sun is more reflective of alchemical Fermentation. All that has been experienced, all that has been constructed to this point—however imperfectly—has the potential to be transformed into something remarkable, if we allow the simmer to occur. This is the stage where true transformation occurs. There is a point in the simmer in which a subtle but monumental shift occurs, when things that were disparate start to gel. Alchemically this is known as the appearance of the peacock's tail, signifying that, through the patience of a slow, steady application of heat, Spirit has been irrevocably activated.

This ritual is an invitation to let the sun shine down on your accomplishments and craft a symbol that can reflect your own peacock's tail and serve as your guide to hold steady to your path.

Symbols to help connect to ritual focus	• A favorite photograph of yourself as an adult. • Any items that reflect your accomplishment (awards, certificates, completed projects) • Statues or photos of those deities that reflect the Sun's glory • An image of the Clear Hynni of Expression
Optional: Stones from *Creating a Mandala Prayer Bundle* Meditation	• Purpurite • Stone of Solidarity • Tiffany Stone
Items needed for ritual activity	• A fresh unused candle (light blue, if you want to align with Hynni) • A lighter • Outdoor version of ritual: air-dry clay • Indoor version of ritual: polymer clay • A cauldron • Small objects of meaning to you (crystals and stones, charms, flowers, herbs) • Optional: Candle snuffer • Optional: Tarot

Creating the Altar

As this ritual can be done indoors or outdoors, where you choose to do it will determine how you approach creating your altar. If you are able to sit high atop a hill surveying the landscape below for this ritual, that would be ideal. If so, everything will be identical to the indoor version of the ritual, with the exception of the candle, which can be left out of the outdoor version.

Whether on your existing altar or on a surface that can act as an altar for this ritual, take some time to set up an homage to some significant moments in your adult life. If you have a favorite photo of yourself as an adult, place it on your altar. Decorate the altar with items that reflect accomplishments you have achieved or those small private moments that fill you with happiness.

You may also choose to decorate your space and your altar with sun disks and decorations, or reflections of the Divine with statues or photos of the gods and goddesses that are particularly connected to this time. Images and statues of those animals that bring strength, power, persistence, and perseverance to mind, such as eagle, stag, boar, gorilla, lion, and ram are also beautiful additions to the altar at this time. If you choose, include an image of the Clear Hynni of Expression, which reminds the psyche that what begins as small energy within us has the power to become amplified out in the world.

Before you start the ritual, set out your materials. On your left, place a good portion of the air-dry clay or the polymer clay. On the right, have your cauldron, which contains all the small meaningful items you will be using in ritual. In the center, place a fresh, unused candle.

When you are done preparing your space, take a moment to feel how the energy you have created affects you. You will want to ensure that there are elements that speak to the general theme of the ritual or the festival itself. This reflects the "Above," the realm of the transpersonal or mythic. You will also want to ensure that there are elements that represent you on the altar. This reflects the "Below," the realm of the personal. If it feels complete, take some time to prepare yourself for ritual (see Appendix D).

The Ritual

Begin to focus on the items that reflect the accomplishments you are choosing to celebrate at this time, just some of all the accomplishments you have achieved thus far in your life. If you have a favorite picture of yourself on the altar, bring your attention to that person, allowing a sense of what energy resides within that person in the photo that has the capacity to do these wonderful things to come to your awareness and, when you feel even the lightest touch of what that is, light the candle before you and take the clay into your hands, beginning to work it gently and steadily until it becomes malleable.

As you work and shape the clay, take the time to think about each of the accomplishments you are celebrating at this time and the sense of the Self that is at the center of each of these events. Focus on the qualities about yourself that you cherish and allow the sense of those qualities to find expression in the clay. You may find yourself forming a representation of a beloved deity, or a power animal, or a symbol such as a star or a lightning bolt. Whatever it is, let the shape of it come from your Soul, not your mind. As you are nudged, reach into your cauldron and incorporate those items, and tokens that amplify this sense of Self, knowing that as you honor the Divine, so the Divine thrills in you. Let this honoring fill your every cell with the power of the sun. You may want to place a particularly special token in the very center of your statue or symbol, something that you know is there, but is not evident to the external eye. Something just between you and Spirit. Allow all the time you need to become clear on that sense of who you are, how your life has shaped you, how your Essence has informed your life, and how you might choose to shine your Light moving forward. If you have a tarot deck, invite Spirit to reflect the gift that is embedded in the journey of your life, as challenging as it may seem at times.

Closure of Ritual

When you are ready to leave this liminal space, bring your conscious awareness back to your breath. Taking one last moment to anchor the connection to your sense of your Essence, using either your breath or a candle snuffer, release the flame of the candle before you. What has been experienced in ritual lives forever in your cells. It need only be called forth from within when you choose.

Take some time to move through the directions once more, thanking the elements for helping to hold space and keep you safe through the ritual. Start again in the North with earth, then move through the East with air, the South with fire (put out the tealight in the cauldron at this point), the West with water, ending with the Below of the material plane and the Above of the cosmic plane. Thank and bid farewell to the deities who have been a part of this ritual with you and know that the wheel may turn around you, but you are—as they are—ever at the center.

Clearing Ritual Space

If you have been using an existing altar, you may decide to keep some items on your altar over the course of the cycle, including your air dried or oven baked representation of Self.

Post-Ritual

As is necessary with Fermentation, time is needed for that which was begun in ritual to cure. If you were working with air dry clay, it will need a solid 24 to 72 hours to completely dry, depending on how thick your statue is. If you are able to put it outside safely to soak in the heat of the sun that would be ideal. If you were working with a clay polymer such as Fimo, bake your statue or symbol in the oven at 110° C (230° F) for 30 minutes.

 Tarot Recommendations

Brooks, Toney (author) and Holly Sierra (artist). *Chrysalis Tarot.* Stamford, CT: US Games, 2015.

de Angelis, Davide. *Starman Tarot Kit.* Woodbury, MN: Llewellyn, 2018.

Hughes, Kristoffer (author) and Chris Downs (illustrator). *Celtic Tarot.* Woodbury, MN: Llewellyn, 2017.

Phelan, Ravynne. *Dreams of Gaia Tarot: A Tarot for a New Era.* Woodbury, MN: Llewellyn, 2016.

Ryan, Mark (author), John Matthews (author), and Will Worthington (illustrator). *Wildwood Tarot: Wherein Wisdom Resides.* New York: Sterling, 2011.

Smith, Pamela Colman. *Smith-Waite Centennial Tarot Deck.* Stamford, CT: US Games, 2013.

Thirty-five

Walk Your Talk

The power of Cycle Five is the healing that comes when we know in every cell that we are so much more than the individual, fleeting faces we show to the world and are able to draw upon the truth that transcends the ephemeral.

As has been previously noted, there is a strong connection between Cycle Three and Cycle Five, between late spring and late summer, between the solar plexus chakra and the throat chakra. When you know that you are whole within, even though there may be aspects of fragmentation, division, complexity, and confusion, you are better able to identify, own, celebrate, and express your particular talk. This is imperative especially when you find that you are flying in the face of differing thoughts, opinions, beliefs, and values. It can be very challenging to walk your talk when you are facing into gale force winds that threaten to bowl you over or whisk you away. But truth is not something that always needs to be spoken. It exists whether it is stated aloud or known in the heart. You walk your talk when you act in alignment with your soul. And that may be done without ever uttering a single word.

Having the confidence to walk your talk can be even more challenging in a society that has an attachment to labels. How we complete the statement "I am…" is of utmost importance. It is another place of intersection between solar plexus chakra and throat chakra. What we claim as the "I am" can give shape to the way in which we express ourselves in the world. And if we clutch others' labels of us to heart and begin to see ourselves through that lens, our voice can become very distorted indeed. It can be as damaging to a healthy self-perception to be hailed a genius as it is to be diagnosed as borderline, although there is far more prevalence of pathology in the current climate than those deemed extraordinary. I have encountered many people, usually young people, who have been labeled as having Borderline Personality. They exhibit the traits. They fit the profile. They accept the label. They believe the "I am" and take it on as an identity that then proceeds to inform how they see themselves moving through the world. Rarely is there a deeper inquiry into the suppression and silencing of the authentic voice that is trying to express the pain, shame, abandonment, and neglect that had been previously experienced.

It is powerful, and indeed necessary for healing—to come to a whole and unified experience of Self—to explore the shape of pain that may have been carried for so long and come to a truer expression in one's life. In particular, the Clear Hynni of Expression gives voice to the pain that informs perceived pathology. There is nothing inherently wrong with a label itself. What can be exceedingly damaging is allowing a label that is intended to present a general context to become the final word on identity. When we honor the truth of our psychospiritual nature, it is our Higher Self that is the final authority on how we complete the statement "I am ..."

Key Aspects of Cycle Five[53]

Archetypal Themes	Healing Themes	Indication of Crisis	Healing Practices
Shining our Truth and Creativity Accomplishment; acknowledgment; gathering strength	Voice; clear expression; truth; bartering integrity; choice; Adult's job description	Difficulty sharing thoughts and beliefs; repressed creativity; a sense that what they say doesn't matter; an excessive need to communicate; a depleted sense of will or belief in the efficacy of one's choices	Exploration of authentic presentation; contemplation of the Hermetic Principle of Polarity; activation of Clear Hynni of Expression
Elemental Reflection	**Intuitive Guidance and Tool**	**Alchemical Reflection**	**Affirmations**
Aether	Elemental guides (faeries, sylphs, merfolk, undines, gnomes, salamanders); tarot	*Fermentation* The "lesser Dark Night" that challenges us to look at where we still need to grow	My choices are informed by my Essence; my core self is pure and unchanging; I am balanced in all areas of my life; I communicate clearly and effectively; what I say matters; I express openly and safely

....

53. More information on Key Aspects can be found in *The Great Work: Self-Knowledge and Healing Through the Wheel of the Year* by the author (Llewellyn, 2015).

Part Six

Cycle Six
August 2–September 12

The Cultivation of Resilience

The Illumined Hynni of Vision

As Below
Rigidity
Alchemical
Distillation
All-or-nothing
thinking
Negative core beliefs

As Above
Resilience
Refinement
Visioning Self
Positive core beliefs

Synthesis
Pride
Ability
Strength

Thirty-six

Lughnasadh and Life's Harvest

Lughnasadh feels a bit like the "lost festival." Though we don't actively celebrate Litha or Midsummer to a large degree, it does feel like we acknowledge the energetics of it with myriad fun, outdoorsy activities. The beginning of August seems to come and go without much notice, enfolding into the generalized summer time frame. From the agricultural perspective, this festival is more closely aligned with fall than summer. This is the start of what will be many months of harvest, starting with the cutting of the grains at this time.

The festival itself translates as the Games of Lugh (the Celtic solar deity). It was a time for shows of strength and talents in honor of Lugh's foster mother Tailtiu who worked herself to death in order to provide for the needs of her people. The intention behind celebrating at this time is not to uphold the ultimate sacrifice, but certainly to acknowledge and own what we have worked hard to craft, create, and build for ourselves. One of the beautiful things about this festival is that, in a society that elevates humility, often to the extent of self-denigration, using shame to promote subservience, Lughnasadh unabashedly celebrates *Pride*, inviting the sharing of *Strength* and *Ability* in the arena of healthy, uplifting competition.

The Core Issue in Cycle Six is all-or-nothing thinking, otherwise known as "stinkin' thinkin.'" This is an issue of distorted perception in which we have lost the ability to see reality for what it truly is. There can be many motivations for this, but every one of them can be traced back to shame. It may be too scary to accept reality as it is because then I would have to take action and I do not feel equal to the task (and thus I end up back at shame). Or it may be too scary to accept reality because then I would have to accept responsibility and, if the result was not what I had anticipated, I end up back at shame. Or it may be too scary to accept reality because then I would have to engage in confrontation or conflict, and I do not feel strong enough (and thus end up back at shame). All-or-nothing thinking is the unhealthy defense mechanism that stops us from being able to accommodate nuance, variation, degrees, complexity, and living in the grays. You can easily identify when this defense shows up when you hear the language "always" and "never." Human beings do not exist in absolutes, so when the language of absolutes shows up, it is a tell that a shame has been triggered. Very often, especially when the all-or-nothing thinking is a by-product of perfectionism, it takes on the guise of comparison, usually with us being on the lacking side of the scale. When our shame tells us that we are not good enough—that we will never be good enough—perfectionism is the mask we wear to try to prove our worth to others, but to do so, it must always hold us up to some external standard that we will never be able to measure up to. All-or-nothing thinking tells us that if we are not perfect, then we are worthless, and it keeps us bouncing from one end of a self-destructive scale to another.

We need to be able to see ourselves—and have pride in ourselves—from the perspective of doing our best with the tools we have. Acknowledging our strength and our ability provides the solid ground we need to be able to see others and our situations with balanced discernment.

When approached through the lens of developmental theory, Cycle Five aligns with late adulthood. By the time we reach our fifties and sixties, we have gained a lot of experience, weathered a lot of challenges, and started to harvest the fruits of all that labor. If we have addressed the shackles of shame, certainly in releasing the tendency of all-or-nothing thinking, we are able to practice discernment, bringing a beautiful focus to the vision of our lives. We are able to home in on choosing all that serves us well and walk on past all that no longer aligns with our truth.

In looking at similar festivals to Lughnasadh, especially in ancient times, it is evident that pride in skill and mastery is a common theme. The *Olympic Games* (Greek) were held in honor of Zeus between August 6 and September 19; they were so named because they were held near Mount Olympus, the mountain upon which Zeus and the other Olympian gods and goddesses were said to live. Though there was a 1,500-

year hiatus between the ancient and modern Olympics, the traditional start date still stands, and the modern summer games are always held starting at the beginning of August. Mongolia also has its version of ancient, traditional games that are still held today. *Naadam Festival*, which means simply "games," is usually held earlier in July and includes competition in Mongolian wrestling, horse racing, and archery. It was through these games that ancient military leaders would choose warriors based on the skills they exhibited in competition. In Japan, the *Nebuta Matsuri* festival is held from August 2 to 7 in the city of Aamori, using lights and floats to commemorate an ancient brave warrior. In Oaxaca, Mexico, the *Guelaquetza Festival* celebrates the wide diversity of indigenous traditions and cultures in that State. Derived from the word meaning "offering," this festival has its roots in pre-Hispanic celebrations for the corn goddess, Centeotl.

In the wake of the attainment of the sun at Litha, Lughnasadh encourages us to bring forth our best game, see ourselves in our best light, and be positively fearless in the vision we bring to our lives. We have the gift of experience. We have been applying effort to the different scenarios, situations, and relationships in our lives long enough now to know what will bear fruit and what will languish on the vine. With the perspective of this experience and the discernment it offers, we can align our lives, for whatever time we have remaining, to hold the shape that is filled with the truth of our Essence.

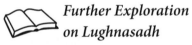 *Further Exploration on Lughnasadh*

Marquis, Melanie. *Lughnasadh: Rituals, Recipes & Lore for Lammas*. Woodbury, MN: Llewellyn, 2015.

Thirty-seven

The Shadow of Soul Debris

As challenging as it can be when we are overcome with emotions, or are battling to regain self-esteem, or are wading through the debris of grief, there is almost nothing as debilitating as the loss of vision and purpose. When we lose sight of who we are, it is like trying to drive down a country road at night with no headlights. It is terrifying.

The question of which came first, our thoughts or our feelings, may be much like the debate of which came first, the chicken or the egg. Developmentally, we engage with the world from an emotion-focused perspective well before we develop the ability to cognitively assess how healthy that response is. However, certain approaches to mental health such as CBT (Cognitive Behavioral Therapy) highlight the need to address unhealthy, unsupportive, or unsubstantiated thoughts as contributing to negative emotions and self-destructive behaviors. Interestingly, CBT's early roots lie in the REBT approach of psychologist Albert Ellis in the 1950s. Rational Emotive Behavioral Therapy drew upon the tenets of ancient philosophy, particularly Stoicism, that address our relationship to emotional pain and suffering, presenting that logic can be aimed at targeting the unhealthy or false beliefs that lead to painful or destructive emotions. In the 1990s, CBT as we recognize it today came into its own. CBT presents that our past experiences, particularly past trauma, pain, and experiences in which our needs were not met, create internal schemas in the mind that then become the lens through which we approach all current experiences. In the CBT approach, there are eighteen schemas in five general categories. These are easily translatable to many of the core issues outlined in Cycle Four, as all schemas are informed by the pain we carry in our hearts. They interfere with our ability to engage in healthy, supportive, and meaningful relationships, and they become the warped and misdirected vision we project onto others.

Cognitive Behavioral Therapy (CBT) Schemas	Noble Art Alignment
Disconnection & Rejection: Abandonment	*Core Issue (Cycle 4):* Abandonment
Disconnection & Rejection: Mistrust/Abuse	*Core Issue (Cycle 4):* Trust
Disconnection & Rejection: Emotional Deprivation	*Core Issue (Cycle 4):* Feelings
Disconnection & Rejection: Defectiveness/Shame	*Core Issue (Cycle 4):* Shame
Disconnection & Rejection: Social Isolation	*Spark Inhibitor (Cycle 4):* Isolation
Impaired Autonomy: Dependence/Incompetence	*Core Issue (Cycle 4):* Dependence
Impaired Autonomy: Vulnerability to Harm	*Subpersonality (Cycle 5):* Victim/Bully
Impaired Autonomy: Enmeshment/Undeveloped Self	*Core Issue (Cycle 4):* Lack of boundaries
Impaired Autonomy: Failure	*Core Issue (Cycle 4):* Fear of Success/Failure
Impaired Limits: Entitlement/Grandiosity	*Spark Inhibitor (Cycle 4):* Entitlement
Impaired Limits: Insufficient Self-Control/Self-Discipline	*Core Issue (Cycle 4):* Control
Other-Directedness: Subjugation	*Core Issue (Cycle 4):* Neglecting needs
Other-Directedness: Self-Sacrifice	*Subpersonality (Cycle 5):* Martyr
Other-Directedness: Approval-Seeking/Recognition-Seeking	*Subpersonality (Cycle 5):* Approval-seeker
Overvigilance & Inhibition: Negativity/Pessimism	*Spark Inhibitor (Cycle 4):* Resignation
Overvigilance & Inhibition: Emotional Inhibition	*Core Issue (Cycle 4):* Giving and receiving love
Overvigilance & Inhibition: Unrelenting Standards/ Hypercriticalness	*Subpersonality (Cycle 5):* Perfectionist
Overvigilance & Inhibition: Punitiveness	*Subpersonality (Cycle 5):* Critic

CBT has proven to be an effective tool for dealing with cognitive dissonance, particularly in cases of panic disorders, anxiety disorders, and phobias. When the pain of our past has created a present that is determined by fear, we are like that car traveling at night with no headlights. There is no light, no self-image, no sense of purpose or direction that one can see. Operating without light is to operate without power, without a sense of efficacy and worth. No wonder panic and anxiety are at an all-time high. Statistics from 2018 show that anxiety disorders affected more than forty million people in the US.[54] That is, one out of every five people in the US struggles in a debilitating way that can't help but affect their sense of self, sense of life, and sense of purpose. CBT offers many tools and templates for challenging the schemas that contribute to a contractive experience of life, including gaining clarity on the core negative beliefs that we have developed as a result of our past pain.

These core negative beliefs act as a befuddling and confounding GPS system. Instead of leading us where we need to go, or even want to go, they will always direct us to the place of our assumption. If you have programmed the location for "I do not matter" into your internal GPS because of all the times growing up that you felt rejected and abandoned; for all the times you felt invisible; for all the times you felt your voice was drowned out or silenced, then it is an absolute given that you will find yourself in that place. That is not even to say that you will attract people into your life who treat you as though you do not matter. Even if the people around you love and support you, treating you with respect, regard, and tenderness, you will not be able to see that. This is absolutely key! Your internal GPS will insist that you have arrived at the destination of "I do not matter," regardless of what might be the reality of the situation. This is what is meant by the term "projection." Projection means that you take your internal "operating system" or the vision of your belief system and you project that onto the movie screen of your own life. And, very sadly, especially when it comes to the tragically high numbers of people dealing with anxiety and panic, it is a horror movie that we are projecting onto our screens. There are a lot of people who have experienced a lot of terrible, terrible things in their lives. The true tragedy is that their lives continue to be informed by the illness or the ill will of others. They are trapped in the feedback loop caused by

....

54. Newman, Tim. "Is Anxiety Increasing in the United States?" Medical News Today. MediLexicon International, September 5, 2018. https://www.medicalnewstoday.com/articles/322877.

PTSD, the ongoing trauma experienced in the now that is directly and intimately tied to the unresolved and unhealed trauma of the past. Core negative beliefs are developed by a psyche trying to keep us safe, but unfortunately, they do so by ultimately holding us responsible for the pain we have experienced, instead of placing responsibility where it needs to be placed: on those who have done harm, whether through intent or neglect. Core negative beliefs, rooted in shame as they are, ultimately reinforce the perspective that we must be the cause of our pain, rather than challenging that flawed vision. They keep us locked in the darkness of our own shame and pain, negating a healthy sense of self and undermining a strong sense of purpose. Core negative beliefs are held in place by the debris of the past.

We are structured to be able to operate effectively in the dark as well as the light. Our eyes are designed specifically to be able to work in both daylight and at night. The human eye has two types of photoreceptors. Rods, which are found around the boundary of the retina, are responsible for vision at low light levels. Cones are located in the center of the retina and are responsible for vision in bright light. There are twenty times more rods than cones in the human eye. The very organ which is responsible for the vision through which we see the world and that is aligned with the brow chakra has twenty times the mechanisms for processing dark as it does light.

Additionally, the pineal gland is responsible for the production of serotonin, believed to be important in the regulation of mood and social behavior, amongst other things. It is considered a natural mood stabilizer. Seratonin synthesizes into melatonin when exposure to light is dramatically decreased. Called, the Hormone of Darkness, melatonin is linked to sleep cycles, guiding one when it is time to rest in the dark and when it is time to engage in the light. The pineal gland is also associated with the brow chakra.

In the heart chakra center of Cycle Four, we have come to embrace that we are learning to balance a human-Spirit life. In the brow chakra center of Cycle Six, we are invited to learn that life will always be an interplay of dark and light. That, in and of itself, does not have the power to define us, but it does have the power to shape our experience. Look to your thoughts. What are the beliefs you project upon the world? Are they working for you? If they are not, what keeps them in place?

I have often found it so fascinating, in the field of psychotherapy we can explore for weeks and months to come to the place where we are staring a core negative belief straight in the eye. My job is to help navigate the dark and unfamiliar woods to bring us to this place, which I am able to do in no small part because I have traversed those dark paths many, many times myself. But once we arrive there, my job is to step back because, truth be told, there is nothing more I can do. There is no trick to changing a core negative belief and no one can do it for you. It is as simple as realizing that the old GPS is faulty and choosing to switch it out. To do that, we need the insight to recognize that we have the power to implement the positive upgrade, the foresight to realize the difference it will make in our lives, and the oversight to see that it is carried out.

Shadow of Cycle Six: Negative Core Beliefs

All negative core beliefs fall within the Shadow work of Cycle Six and are intimately connected to the core issues found in Cycle Four; however, a further delineation shows how different negative core beliefs can align with the energies found on the Wheel of the Year.

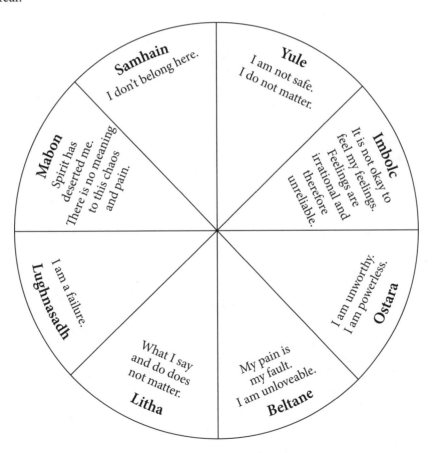

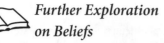 *Further Exploration*
on Beliefs

Achor, Shawn. The Happiness Advantage: *How a Positive Brain Fuels Success in Life and Work.* New York: Currency, 2018 (reprint edition).

Lipton, Bruce H. *The Biology of Belief* (10th Anniversary Edition). Carlsbad, CA: Hay House, 2016.

Thirty-eight

The Lightness of Soul Decluttering

The festival of Lughnasadh and the archetypal energies of Cycle Six are about connecting to the pride of Self, which opens us to be able to have the vision to see our best potential, to know that we have the ability to craft that vision into a viable future, and to know that we have the strength and fortitude to manifest it into reality. This is impossible to do when we are still trapped by the shame and pain from the past.

As long as we still carry the negative emotional charge of past traumas, we will continually be boomeranged back to the negative core belief that bloomed in us at the time of the trauma. This is called PTSD or post-traumatic stress disorder. It is like there is a part of our energy that is still living in that past, that is still stuck in that horror, and has lost its way to catch up with where the rest of our energy is in the present. This painful Shadow interferes with our inner soulful directional signal. We are disconnected from Essence, disconnected from our sense of self, disconnected from what brings joy and meaning to our lives. We have no sense of self. No image or reflection of our True Self.

Core negative beliefs are where we hold <u>all</u> the -isms: racism, sexism, ageism, sizeism, ableism, classism, heteroism. All these -isms will quickly lead to a gaping chasm because each one holds the vision of separation, hierarchy, and privilege, often masquerading as pride. This is not the soul-infused pride of Lughnasadh. This is a shame-based veneer that, when scratched away, reveals the rot beneath. Who are you? How do you see yourself? How does that inform how you see others? How does that impact on how you forge a vision for your life? One of the biggest challenges we have in our lives is to be able to see ourselves clearly. That requires challenging our core negative beliefs.

Derived from the Latin root meaning "to bounce back," resilience is about releasing the grip the past has on our inner relationship. Interestingly, Lughnasadh sits across the wheel from Imbolc, the time of year for clearing the fields of stones and debris in order to prepare for receiving the seeds. This is also a time from "clearing the stones from a field," but it is the fertile ground of our Mind that needs the attention in order to plant the seeds of vision, intuition, imagination, and insight. When we clear the heavy rocks of past pain—uprooting those core negative beliefs—from the forefront of our minds, the innate resilient nature of our souls bounces us back into the present. This is what Life Purpose is all about: healing the Shadow vision of the horrors of the past, retrieving our souls so that we are fully present in our lives today with an intact sense of self, planting positive core beliefs in the now-cleared ground, and inviting our Light-infused imagination to set our future's gaze. It requires resilience to integrate all of life's experiences, the painful and the sweet, but to do so offers us the gift of self-esteem. We know that our story will always be our story. It's not that the pain and trauma of the past never happened, but we realize that it no longer has the power to define who we are; it never had the power to define our worth; and it certainly doesn't have the power to shape our future.

Part of the wisdom that comes from seeing our journey clearly is recognizing that it is a process, not a goal. Just as in spring every year, the fields need to be cleared, we will continually be surprised by the errant thoughts or deep hidden beliefs that unexpectedly spring to the surface of our minds. The more centered in a solid sense of Self we are, the better equipped we will be to root them out, examine them and discard them if necessary, replacing them with a far more lush belief. When we are informed by soul (and not shame) with Positive Core Beliefs as our GPS (Guidance Per Spirit), we can never be lost again, no matter in what dark night we may find ourselves.

Light of Cycle Six: Positive Core Beliefs

All positive core beliefs fall within the Light work of Cycle Six and are intimately connected to the core meaning found in Cycle Four; however, a further delineation shows how different positive core beliefs can align with the energies found on the Wheel of the Year.

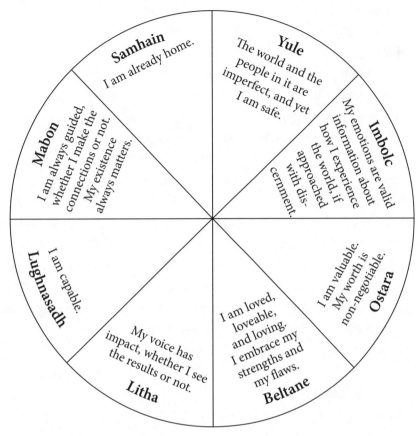

Samhain
I am already home.

Yule
The world and the people in it are imperfect, and yet I am safe.

Imbolc
My emotions are valid information about how I experience the world, if approached with discernment.

Mabon
I am always guided, whether I make the connections or not. My existence always matters.

Ostara
I am valuable. My worth is non-negotiable.

Lughnasadh
I am capable.

Beltane
I am loved, loveable, and loving. I embrace my strengths and my flaws.

Litha
My voice has impact, whether I see the results or not.

Inner Workings:
The Sacred Self Vision Statement

In creating a foundation for success, companies and organizations often utilize various methods for creating and maintaining integrity of purpose. All major corporations have mission statements to communicate focus of intent and clarity of direction. These short statements are helpful both to company employees, as a rudder to maintain course, and to customers, as an informative beacon, guiding them to companies they can believe in and trust. Mission statements generally consist of three parts: what the product is; who the product is for; and how this product is unique from all others. Another method that is sometimes used by corporations is that of the vision statement. Vision statements have a very different purpose: to capture the core essence of a company's ultimate aim or goal. A vision statement offers an image of what the world would look like or how life will be changed forever once the company fulfills what it set out to do right from the start. Mission statements focus on conveying information about what is being offered in the here and now. An example would be: We are committed to providing the best gadget with the most uses for the best cost to our customers. Vision statements show us the future. An example would be: We see a future focused on strengthening the bonds of community with all the leisure time our high-functioning gadgets create.

In any given moment in time, we sit at the crossroads of what was, what is, and what will be. We can sit at those crossroads as disempowered victims of our past, or we can seize the vision of a different future for ourselves. As was written by the thirteenth century Japanese Buddhist Nichiren Daishonen in his treatise, *Opening the Eyes*: "If you want to understand the causes that existed in the past, look at the results as they are manifested in the present. And if you want to understand what results will be manifested in the future, look at the causes that exist in the present."[55] This is the spiritual act of resilience. We learn from the past and utilize the wisdom gleaned from that to catapult ourselves into the future of our own making. To do that fully and effectively, it is helpful to have a vision statement.

Take some time to meditate upon what you have learned about yourself so far in this noble journey. Looking back at the time of deep winter (Cycle One), allow yourself to remember and reconnect with what you determined your Core Values to be. *An example might be: Diversity, Beauty, and Self-realization.*

Propelling yourself forward in your journey to the time of early summer and the celebration of the interweaving dance of your human nature with your Spiritual self (Cycle Four), allow yourself to remember and reconnect with that which you feel in your heart gives your life meaning. *An example might be: Belonging*

Feeling your feet directly beneath you in the current cycle that begins the movement into the harvest of all life's wisdom and meditating upon the Positive Core Beliefs from the chart above, allow yourself to feel which particular belief resonates with you at this moment in time. *An example might be: I am already home.*

....

55. "The Opening of the Eyes | WND I | Nichiren Buddhism Library," Nichirenlibrary.org, 2020, https://www.nichirenlibrary.org/en/wnd-1/Content/30. (pg. 279)

You may find that these three elements (Values, Meaning, and Belief) are all reflections of the same cycle, or you may find, as in the above example, that what jumps out is from a different cycle for each element. However, it shows up for you is perfect. The most important step is the next one. From those three elements which speak to your soul in this moment in your life, massage them into a vision statement that speaks to your Sacred Purpose.

An example might be:

Knowing that I am already home *and pulsing with the beat of* Belonging *to this great community called Earth, I gift my life's work to the championing of* Diversity, *the creation of* Beauty, *and the facilitation of* Self-realization *in all its forms. To this path I pledge my heart and soul.*

To craft such a statement for yourself becomes the security of headlights that can shine through the inkiest darkness so that you know, without a doubt, that you will never lose your way.

Thirty-nine

Wyrdwalking Meditation

What is Wyrd? Wyrd is the Anglo-Saxon term to describe the essential pattern that underlies the fabric of reality and existence as we know it. To the Chinese, it is the Tao: the path or the way. It is the Hermetic concept of the All, the One Mind that gives rise to the One Thing that is inherent in all things. It is this that the alchemical text, The Emerald Tablet, is describing, even going so far as to say that it is illuminating the pattern or the way. It is the flow of the Universe, the movement of becoming, of being, deconstructing, and becoming once more. In the spiritual novel *The Way of Wyrd*, the concept is described to the protagonist by an Anglo-Saxon sorcerer and mystic as:

> Wyrd existed before the gods and will exist after them. Yet wyrd lasts only for an instant, because it is the constant creation of the forces. Wyrd is itself constant change, like the seasons, yet because it is created at every instant, it is unchanging, like the still center of a whirlpool. All we can see are the ripples dancing on top of the water.[56]

It is not our role in this existence to try to understand the Wyrd. It is beyond our scope to be able to grasp. Nor is it our role to try to contain or control it because that is, quite simply, impossible. For one, we are not separate from it. I can no more control the Tao than I can stop the flow of my joy when I see a puppy. I can choose how I respond to it, of course. I do not need to bring every single puppy into my home in

....
56. Brian Bates, *The Way of Wyrd*, 73.

response to my joy. But I can recognize how it moves me and how it moves through me and start to shift myself to working <u>with</u> the pattern rather than against it. I can vibrate that joy out into my life and the lives of others in a thousand different ways. I can respond to the ripples on the water.

Jung was referencing Wyrd, though using completely different language, when he introduced the idea of synchronicity. Defined as "meaningful chance," synchronicity describes the underlying, hidden interconnection between two or more unrelated things. My mother passed away in January 2008. My father passed away in February 2011. My brother passed away in September 2017. Different years, different times of years. Each one of them crossed over on a Dark Moon night. To further intrigue, my mother's favorite play to direct as an amateur director was *Dark of the Moon*.[57] There was a beautiful stained glass from the set design from the last time she directed it that hung in my parent's home. And to add yet another layer, my dad had been in the last production of the play she ever directed. My brother had been in the one before that. All linked by the moon's dark face in so many different ways. Coincidence says that is just weird. Synchronicity says it is Wyrd. There is a message in that pattern that is eloquent in its message, whether it is heard or not.

The more we are able to brush the film of shame (and all the mental defenses it tends to kick up) from our eyes, the more we are able to see the patterns that have always existed. Raising our vibration does not cause synchronicity to occur. The Tao is. Raising our vibration allows us to begin to perceive the profound patterns as they have always been, even before we had the eyes to see.

This meditation invites you to see the patterns of your own life through the expansive lens of the Wyrd and, in doing so, brings a greater understanding to your life's experiences and a greater clarity to your life's purpose.

Meditation

The heat of the noonday sun has given way to the gentle warmth of late afternoon. Its amber light casts a soft glow over the landscape. Everything is touched with a golden tinge.

....

57. *Dark of the Moon*, written by Howard Richardson and William Berney, is a dramatic stage play first produced on Broadway in 1945.

In your journey, you have traveled long. You have traveled far. You have encountered wonders. You have endured trials. And now a path lies before you, leading you up to further untold wonders, a path that leads you as close to the stars as you can get while still having feet on this Earth. You look at the path ahead and know you now have a lightness in your Being that will bring ease to your climb. The release of challenges and fear at the World Tree and the gift of your prayer bundle blessing to the Divine have created a beautiful clarity of sight. You are fully in this moment. You are fully present in the Wyrd. And, as you begin the trek up the mountain path, reaching for the stars in every step, you have truly become a Wyrdwalker in every sense.

As you climb the path, pay attention to the landscape around you. How the flora changes the higher you go. The patterns that are discernible both in the stones beneath your feet and the clouds above your head.

You become acutely aware that the entirety of your experience is talking to you, so long as you attune your ears to hear. You become acutely aware that the fullness of your life experiences have always been talking to you, though you may not have always heeded the message.

As you come closer and closer to the summit of this particular mountain peak, you become even more attuned to discerning the underlying patterns present all around you. In the rarified high-altitude air, you can see so clearly. All of nature gives up a vision of fractals as if there is tangible structure under the patterns you see, and patterns emanating from the structure. You can go deeper within or pull further out and yet the patterns persist. With your inner eye you see that same fractal vibration in your own life. You know your path, your purpose, your gift, and you know you have always been vibrating to the resonance of that energy. You see with absolute clarity all the times you walked your path with sure steps. You know well the times you strayed, knowing now there was valuable information that came to you, even in those times.

There have been good times and challenging times. There have been times of despair and times of joy. There have been times of comfort and times of trial. The vibration has maintained, even if the amplitude may have changed greatly at times. But everything has always unfolded exactly as it needed to. You can see that now. The Wyrd is woven into every moment and underpins everything.

With this realization, you know what it is to be anchored in your own vision of Self, just as you crest the peak and step onto the elevated plateau that opens the world to your eyes and opens your eyes to that golden Seed of Self that you thought had burned with your prayer bundle. But here it is—at your feet, glowing softly in the light that is getting lower still in the sky. You pick it up and cradle it tenderly in your cupped hand. A part of you is so happy to hold it once more. A part of you knows it never left you. Another part of you knows that, whether you hold the seed or not, it is always with you. And that that is also Wyrd.

You are Wyrd.

Smiling softly, you look out over the expanse that lies before you and below you, taking in the scene. There below you, you see the World Tree. There far below you, you see the Timeless River. And there, across from you, but so far away, you see the cave—the place this all began.

You appreciate how far you have come, how much you have learned, and how much wisdom you have attained. You know this has changed—forever and always—how you see your life.

 Stones to Deepen the Meditative Experience

Ametrine, formed in the exact perfect conditions to bring amethyst and citrine into relationship, allows for the assimilation of higher perspective and guidance into our vision.

Atlantisite affords the opportunity to forgive ourselves for falling short of our best vision of self and awakening to the wisdom of ancient (mythic) civilizations, particularly Atlantis.

Auralite, comprised of twenty-three earth minerals and referred to as the Master Stone, is a powerful "code clearer" that helps in releasing negative beliefs and reprogramming with positive ones.

Quantum Quattro, brings together four powerful stones (Shattuckite, Chrysocolla, Dioptase, and Malachite) to open gateways to direct energy healing, bringing mental clarity, insight, and non-judgment.

♪ Forty

The Hermetic Principle of Vibration Contemplation

The Hermetic Principle of Vibration is the one universal law that managed the transition to the modern world, like the breakout star of all the principles. It had a sexy makeover into the Law of Attraction and went on to make millions.

This Principle, in its pure form, reflects that everything in the Universe is made up of energy and that energy is not inert. Energy moves. Energy vibrates. We see matter because it is energy that is vibrating so slowly that we can see it with the physical eye. That in no way means that that is all that exists. It is just what we can see.

As an example, we are accustomed to seeing light from red to violet, but we know that the rainbow spectrum of light is just a tiny sliver of the known range of energy vibration. Light is measured by its wavelengths. Imagine that you see a mountain range with peak after peak after peak. The distance from one peak to the next is equivalent to a wavelength. In essence, it is the frequency of vibration. You can imagine that peaks that are close together would be faster to reach and, of course, peaks that are a great distance apart would be far slower to reach. It is not so different with the wavelength of light. The sliver that is known as the visible spectrum has wavelengths that range from 700 to 400 nanometers (with 700 being on the slow red end of the spectrum and 400 being on the fast violet end of the spectrum.) Vibrating at wavelengths even slower than visible red, you find ultrared, then radar waves, then short wave radio waves, then TV waves, then alternating current waves. Vibrating at frequencies faster than visible violet, you find ultraviolet, then x-rays, then gamma rays, then cosmic radiation waves. If one were to account for the entire vibratory spectrum the numbers are beyond our ability to comprehend.

| Cosmic Radiation (10^{-14}) | → | Gamma Rays (10^{-12}) | → | X-rays (10^{-10}) | → | Ultra-violet (10^{-8}) | → | Visible (4^{-7}-7^{-7}) | → | Infrared (10^{-4}) | → | Radar (10^{-2}) | → | Short Wave Radio (10^{2}) | → | TV Waves (10^{4}) | → | AC Waves (10^{6}) |

To put this in some sort of context, the wavelength for cosmic radiation is 1/100,000,000,000,000 meters. The wavelength of alternating current is 1,000,000 meters. And what we can see with the visible eye is a minute sliver that falls somewhere between those two. It is enough to boggle the mind. What is known to us is a fraction of what exists in the known Universe and beyond, there is movement that far outreaches our ability to comprehend. As *The Kybalion* states:

Nothing rests; everything moves; everything vibrates.[58]

The Hermetic Principle of Vibration reflects this universal truth. Nothing is static. Existence is vibrant. In order to start to move into a place of wisdom and accept the ability to see reality for what it is, rather than what we may want to overlay upon it, we need to start with our own vibration. Do you vibrate quickly or slowly? Is the journey between your mountain peaks a quick jaunt or a long, leisurely meander, so to speak? There is no judgment in whichever it ends up being. We would not wrong red for its slower wavelength or, in other words, for its redness, so why would we wrong ourselves for a slower approach to process or a more considered engagement in a situation? If we are vibrating in alignment with our soul's truth, we are one with the One.

The Law of Attraction presents that "like attracts like." Elements that vibrate at the same rate are drawn to each other. If you want to attract a particular something into your life (wealth, health, fame, love) then you have to vibrate at the frequency of that something and it will show up. The term was first coined by Theosophy founder, Helena Petrovna Blavatsky[59] and was quickly hailed by the New Thought Movement of the early nineteenth century. It experienced a solid reputation through the work

....

58. The Three Initiates, "The Kybalion: Chapter II. The Seven Hermetic Principles," www.sacred-texts .com (Yogi Publication Society, 1912), https://www.sacred-texts.com/eso/kyb/kyb04.htm.

59. H. P. Blavatsky, H. P. *The Complete Works of H.P. Blavatsky.*

of Esther and Jerry Hicks and shot into stardom's stratosphere with the release of the film, *The Secret*.[60] The problem with this presentation of the Hermetic Principle of Vibration is that it does not always account for the reality of Wyrd. Just because I <u>think</u> I want wealth and fame does not mean that deep in the very essence of my being I truly want it. What I may be seeking is validation, acceptance, worth, or security and there are many, many ways to attain those. Nor does it necessarily reflect that wealth and fame are in alignment with my Higher Purpose. If I am truly being guided by Spirit and honoring the vibration of my own Essence, I know that wealth and fame do not unequivocally equate to happiness. Happiness unequivocally equates to happiness and that is a vibration within me, not anything that is bestowed upon me from externals.

The Hermetic Principle of Vibration is not about trying to achieve a particular thing in the world. It is the invitation to see your own wavelength upon an endless spectrum and start to live with the beauty of that vision as your compass.

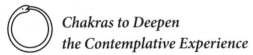 ## Contemplation

Contemplate how the Illumined Hynni of Vision reflects the Hermetic Principle of Vibration: the visual representation of four points of the compass (Above, Below, Within, Without) and the way in which the inner eye has the ability to expand toward multiple perspectives with the Divine as a guide.

Chakras to Deepen the Contemplative Experience

Connect with the **brow chakra** to open yourself to clarity, discernment, and vision. When it is healthy and flowing, the brow chakra gives us the sight required to pierce through illusion and respond to the reality of our experience and the world in which we live. It does not suffer denial, rationalizations, excuses, minimizing, or any mental justifications that allow us to get away with anything less than being fully in alignment with the core principles of trust, truth, respect, and love. When we align our vibration to that of higher truth and wisdom, clear sight gifts us with insight, oversight, hindsight, and foresight. We can see clearly in all directions, knowing what

....

60. *The Secret,* Prime Time Productions (2006).

it was that brought us to this point, what may transpire if we maintain this energy and vibration, how that brings purpose and meaning to our own lives, and how that allows us to be of service to that which is greater than ourselves. The back of the brow chakra informs with all the messages, beliefs, and programming that flow through the ancestral generations. If you have a crest or motto that has been part of your family heritage, this is the key that sits in the back of the brow chakra. This can be positive, supportive, and inspiring. If this generational programming is out of sync with a person's core value, this can cause a block in the back of the brow chakra which would need to be released before being able to solidly embrace one's own values and beliefs.

The higher-vibration chakra that sits in the center of the forehead is the **Fourteenth Chakra of Oneness.**[61] It is this chakra that is truly able to tap into the Tao and the Wyrd. It is this chakra that can see with absolute clarity that we are interconnected, that we are all notes in a single symphony and interconnected filaments illuminating a single complex tapestry. It brings awareness to the Divine Plan, not in the sense that there is a right and a wrong to the implementation of the Plan, but that there is a symmetry to the flow of life and that when we vibrate to this chakra the synchronicities that have always existed right before our eyes suddenly become revealed. We can see the beautiful order that underpins all of experience and we see how we ourselves are an integral part of that order. The Divine is limitless and you are part of and contained by that limitlessness. The Fourteenth Chakra invites us to touch that part of us that is as expansive, vast, and unlimited. We do not need to uphold that energy at all times. It is not for us to operate in our lives always from that perspective. That would be impossible and dangerous. But to briefly touch the face of the Divine and see it reflected in us gives us the clarity and inspiration to step fully and fearlessly into our lives.

....

61. Stone, *Soul Psychology.*

Forty-one

Illumined Vision Ritual

This first early fall festival is traditionally a time of pride and competition, celebrated in the games that allow one to show off one's great achievement or best ability. It is a time, on the threshold of harvest, in which the best vision of self can be projected out into the world. What we present of ourselves for others to see requires the continued refinement in the ways in which we see ourselves that is offered in the alchemical stage of Distillation. This ritual invites you to use the rewards of harvest to weave a "god's eye" through which to see the distilled Essence of your True Self with inspired clarity (see Appendix G for illustrated steps).

Symbols to help connect to ritual focus	• Wheat, corn, and other grains • Sunflowers • Statues or photos of those deities that reflect wealth and prosperity • An image of the Illumined Hynni of Vision
Optional: Stones from *Wyrdwalking* Meditation	• Ametrine • Atlantisite • Auralite • Quantum Quattro
Items needed for ritual activity	• A fresh unused candle (dark blue, if you want to align with Hynni) • A lighter • A cauldron • Six to ten stalks of wheat (pre-soaked for ease of working) with heads removed • Two stalks of wheat (headless) cut to about six inches long) • Two pieces of thick wire (about six inches long) • Two pieces of string • Scissors • Optional: Black paint pen • Optional: Candle snuffer • Optional: I Ching (three coins or a deck and an I Ching book)

Creating the Altar

Whether on your existing altar or on a surface that can act as altar for this ritual, place elements that bring the sense of work's culmination and fruition to mind, including those reflections of the Divine connected to wealth and prosperity. You may want to also include an image of the Illumined Hynni of Vision, which reminds the psyche that wherever you stand in your life, there are always multiple perspectives you can access to provide insight.

The last things to have on hand are those items that will be used in the ritual working itself. Place the soaked wheat stalks and the two wires on your left. Place the two lengths of string in the cauldron to your right. Place the unlit candle in the center in front of you.

When you are done preparing your space, take a moment to feel how the energy you have created affects you. You will want to ensure that there are elements that speak to the general theme of the ritual or the festival itself. This reflects the "Above," the realm of the transpersonal or mythic. You will also want to ensure that there are elements that represent you on the altar. This reflects the "Below," the realm of the personal. If it feels complete, take some time to prepare yourself for ritual (see Appendix D).

The Ritual

Light the candle in the center of your altar and bring your awareness to your Third Eye. Begin to focus on that sense of the you that has traveled far in this life. You have experienced many things. You have accomplished many things. You have also failed at many things and learned from many things. As you allow that awareness of all the successes and the challenges, the highs and the lows, that you have encountered over the many years of your life thus far, take the two cut stalks of wheat and insert the two pieces of wire into their hollow centers, creating two sturdy arms. Cross one stalk over the other at a right angle, reflecting the Hynni of Vision in the four arms that are created. Take the first piece of string from your cauldron. If this string were to represent a core value for you, something that holds your ideals and vision together, what would it be? Use this string to secure the two stalks together in the form of a "X" and snip off any extra with scissors.

Take the first stalk of wheat and lay it across the center "X". Holding it carefully so it does not slide, wrap it around one of the solid arms, then the next, then the third arm, and the fourth. Continue wrapping the wheat stalk around each arm, around and around, until you almost reach the end of the stalk. Take your next stalk of wheat and carefully slide the end into the stalk of the first. If this is difficult, try cutting a bit off the end of the first stalk with your scissors first. Continue to weave, adding stalk after stalk of wheat until you come to the end of the arms. As your "god's eye" begins to take shape, be aware of how your Third Eye is feeling. Be aware of what thoughts are coming to you. Invite an exploration of the beliefs you hold, committing to only allow those beliefs that serve your highest good and highest purpose to be woven into your "god's eye."

When you have woven the arms as full as they can be, reach into your cauldron once more and take out the second piece of string. If this string were to represent a core belief, an energy of self-perception that is informed by your Higher Self, what would it be? Use this string to secure the final stalk to the base. If there is any extra, you can create a loop in order to hang your creation in a place to remind you of your positive core beliefs.

Take all the time you want or need to gaze upon the light of the candle and allow your Third Eye to be filled with the vision and the wisdom of your "god's eye." Use this time to cast coins for an I Ching reading or pull an I Ching card, and read the passage from the associated hexagram to receive a message from the Divine regarding the expression of your True Self in the world and in relationship.

Closure of Ritual

When you are ready to leave this liminal space, bring your conscious awareness back to your breath. Taking one last moment to anchor the connection to your sense of your Essence, using either your breath or a candle snuffer, release the flame of the candle before you. What has been experienced in ritual lives forever in your cells. It need only be called forth from within when you choose.

Take some time to move through the directions once more, thanking the elements for helping to hold space and keep you safe through the ritual. Start again in the North with earth, then move through the East with air, the South with fire (put out the tealight in the cauldron at this point), the West with water, ending with the Below of the material plane and the Above of the cosmic plane. Thank and bid farewell to the deities who have been a part of this ritual with you and know that the wheel may turn around you, but you are—as they are—ever at the center.

Clearing Ritual Space

If you have been using an existing altar, you may decide to keep some items on your altar over the course of the cycle. Your illumined weaving can be put in a window or hang outside as a reminder to use the Essence of your True Self as your compass and guide through your days.

I Ching Deck Recommendations

Aronson, Rosy. *Wisdom Keepers Oracle Deck*. Seal Pup Press, 2015.

O'Brien, Paul. *Visionary I Ching Cards*. Hillsboro, OR: Beyond Words, 2020.

Padma, Me Deva. *Tao Oracle: Illuminated New Approach to the I Ching*. New York: St. Martin's Press, 2002.

Walker, Barbara G. *I Ching of the Goddess*. Beverly, MA: Fair Winds Press, 2001.

I Ching Book Recommendations

Barrett, Hilary. *I Ching*. London: Arcturus Publishing, 2018.

Huang, Taoist Master Alfred. *The Complete I Ching: 10th Anniversary Edition: The Definitive Translation*. Rochester, VT: Inner Traditions, 2010.

Wilhelm, Richard. *The I Ching, or Book of Changes (Bollingen Series XIX)*. Princeton, NJ: Princeton University Press, 1967.

Forty-two

Gaze Upon the Earth with Clarity of Light

The power of Cycle Six is the healing that comes when we know in every cell that the best vision we have of ourselves is the true one. It invites us to be as the child in *The Emperor's New Clothes*, knowing that our ego-free, unhindered vision allows us to see the world as it is, not as we need it to be in order to be compliant. And we have the courage to reflect that to others, projecting the Light of Truth, not the Shadow of Shame, from the laser clarity of our brow chakra. This is not arrogance and righteousness. Not in the least. Truth does not trumpet, it whispers, and vision does not blast, it invites.

You may not always succeed at embodying your best version of Self. There may be times when you do not feel equal to the task. There may be times when the rising tides can feel like tides turning against you and the swells are too high for you to crest. There may be times when a plethora of minutae can seem to continually distract or detract like an army of mosquitoes. In spite of all that, when the "stinkin' thinkin'" has been addressed once and for all, we hold the power to release all those times anytime. Every day, every moment, every breath is a new beginning. We don't need to resort to all-or-nothing thinking, World or Fool, either/or and nothing in between. To gaze upon the world with clarity is to refuse to be polarized into one stance or the other. It is to use both rods and cones. There is darkness in the world. We need to see that. There is unhealthy ego at play in the world. We need to recognize that. But there is also light. There is also beauty. And there is always potential. The empty zero waiting to be filled. In this way, we are the Fool, attaining the World in every moment. When we know the truth of our vision, we have become the Wise Fool. True ego, healthy ego, empowered ego stands still in the center of the World and vibrates with the wisdom of the enlightened Fool.

Key Aspects of Cycle Six[62]

Archetypal Themes	Healing Themes	Indication of Crisis	Healing Practices
Visioning Self Pride; ability; strength	Beliefs; discernment; reaping first fruits and harvests; owning our ability; core negative beliefs	Confused or racing thoughts; difficulty in "turning off the brain"; critical or harsh inner dialogue; difficulty envisioning or planning the future; under- or overactive imagination	Exploration of Core Positive Beliefs; contemplation of the Hermetic Principle of Polarity; activation of Illumined Hynni of Vision
Elemental Reflection	Intuitive Guidance and Tool	Alchemical Reflection	Affirmations
Light	Mythological beasts guides; I Ching	*Distillation* The frequent shift of experience from "as below" to "as above" and back again in order to agitate toward highest potency.	My vision for my life is valid; my vision reflects my highest potential; I am open to receive higher guidance; my beliefs are supportive and encouraging and safe.

62. More information on Key Aspects can be found in *The Great Work: Self-Knowledge and Healing Through the Wheel of the Year* by the author (Llewellyn, 2015).

Part Seven

Cycle Seven
September 20–October 31

From Wounded to Wonder

The Enlightened Hynni of Karma

As Below
Wounded
Alchemical
Coagulation
Inappropriate
behavior
Life purpose

As Above
Wonder
Philosopher's Stone
Effects of gratitude
Higher and sacred
purpose

Synthesis
Giving thanks
Appraisal
Letting go

Forty-three

Mabon and the Higher Self

The Fall Equinox reflects the balanced energies that we have already encountered in spring but with a significant difference. This time of exact balance, when day and night stand equal to each other in that moment of harmony and of tension, contains both the celebration of the Light we have been enjoying and the pull of the Dark that beckons. We stand at the tipping point once more, but this time we are moving toward lengthening nights and shorter days. In the never-ending cycle of life and death, we are moving slowly but surely toward the end of life. This moment of balance is not moving us toward expansion but toward contraction. And though this moment is decidedly one of celebration, specifically for the results of all our hard work, for the abundant harvest we have accumulated, for the riches we have gathered, even if they be more riches of life experiences than produce, there is a bittersweet pang to this celebration.

In this second of what are effectively three harvest festivals in the annual agricultural cycle, we have shifted from the gathering of the grains to the crops of ground and tree, holding the vision of a cornucopia abounding with the root vegetables that will see one through the long, cold winter. *Giving thanks* for the abundance can encompass gratitude to the Divine for the bounty but also recognition for our hard work and the effort we made to maintain, sustain, and ultimately attain all that is necessary for such fullness. There is a lightness to the harvest festival that came before: Lughnasadh and the lightness of the loaf. There is a heaviness to the harvest festival to come: Samhain and the darkness of the cull. In this harvest festival that celebrates such solid sustenance with the balance of light and dark, we are invited to integrate the gifts and the lessons of the full range of our experiences.

This time of year is not just about harvest, though. It is also setting the intention for that which is to come, well over the hump of the dark season. It is the very foundation of common sense that, if one wishes to celebrate a bountiful harvest, one must have planted the seeds to produce it. And, if one wants seeds to plant, then one must have accumulated the seeds in the previous harvest. Mabon sits across the wheel from Ostara and they are mirror reflections to each other. The seeds planted at Ostara are gathered and preserved at Mabon. *Appraisal* is important at this time. What do we keep? What do we release? What is abundant and sustainable? What comes from fear and may be more aligned with a tendency to hoard?

Letting go, the ability to release that which has had its day or that which is given in fullness or that which is infested with a rot that threatens that which remains, is a key ability of harvest. From an inner perspective, it is our strong connection and relationship with our Higher Self that guides us in making determinations about experiences, circumstances, relationships, and lessons in our lives. The Higher Self is that aspect of our Inner Trinity, along with the Inner Child and the Adult or True Self, that holds our sense of purpose and the grand pattern and meaning for our lives. It is the Higher Self that might reflect that, even though there is a huge part of us that loves apples and would love to plant an orchard, we are actually far more knowledgeable about corn, plus we have perfect land and environmental conditions for corn. If we go ahead and plant an apple orchard, we will likely experience wave upon wave of challenge to which the Higher Self usually prompts, "Maybe take another look at corn." But Higher Self would also say, "And don't forget all the things you learned <u>not</u> to do with the apple orchard. That is invaluable information" with exactly that level of kindness, understanding, compassion, and forgiveness.

There is another reflection of letting go that comes with this cycle. In the Development Reflection, this is the time of the final years of life. It is late elderhood, from the 70s up until the moment of death, whenever that moment chooses us. In these late years in life, for many, much of the hard work has been done, although, sadly and tragically, not all can rest in the soft comfort of a setting sun. Regardless of how our last days and years on this Earth unfold, there is an underlying emotional invitation to focus on the sustaining harvest and release that which does not lift us up. The guidance of Ma'at is that we are meant to leave this world as light as how we came into it. That we cannot do if we are weighed down by the heaviness of pain, regret, anger, and shame. If we have not "cleared the fields" on an annual basis, then this time of life is an opportunity to lay down those burdens.

The Core Issue connected with Cycle Seven is having a high tolerance for inappropriate behavior. It is how we stay in situations or relationships that are unhealthy or toxic for us, numbing ourselves to the pain, never fully holding the other as responsible, and not learning from the past. It is akin to preserving the rotten seeds and tossing the full, plump, healthy seeds on the compost. It is akin to working the failing apple trees year after year, becoming weaker and more malnourished each year, rather than listening to that kind but firm voice within that says, "This is not for you." It often stems from wanting to act toward others in that same way and with that same voice our Higher Self speaks to us. We want to respond to others with kindness, understanding, compassion, and forgiveness. We want to access our higher spiritual side and our loving self. The difference is that Higher Self is saying "no" to us in that kind, understanding voice. We are our Higher Self and we are <u>never</u> not in relationship with it. It is with us through thick and thin. It will celebrate with us through the thick and guide us through the thin. When we have high tolerance for the inappropriate behavior of others, we are actually saying "yes." Yes, it is okay to treat me badly. Yes, it is okay to take advantage of me. Yes, it is okay to disrespect me. Excuses, minimizing, turning the other cheek become ways of condoning hurtful or destructive behavior. We are not being kind to the other person. We are being terribly toxic to ourselves. We are not celebrating a rich, nourishing harvest. We are holding on to blight and that will never make for future healthy harvests.

Looking at the patterns in our lives, learning from our lessons, embracing our successes, and moving to true forgiveness for the past is the gift of this season.

In ancient times, the Roman celebrated the *Ludi Romani* in September, originally from the 12th to the 14th, but they later became extended. Seeming almost more aligned with the energies of the "Games of Lugh" than to a harvest festival, there were actually several days after the games that were dedicated to markets and fairs. In China, the *Moon Cake Festival* or *Mid-Autumn Festival* has been long celebrated as the end of the harvest season. Falling on the fifteenth day of the eighth lunar month, this festival can be held any time between August and October. In Korea, it is known as *Chuseok*; in Vietnam as *Tết Trung Thu*; in Japan as *Tsukimi*. *Sukkot* (Jewish) is the weeklong harvest festival, named for the foliage-covered booth that protected the Israelites at the time of exodus from Egypt, giving thanks to God for the protection during their time in the desert. Many countries celebrate Harvest Festivals or Thanksgiving, though there is a wide range of dates. *Bénichon* (Switzerland) is a harvest festival that includes bringing animals down from the pastures high in the Alps. *Erntedankfest* (Germany), which translates as "harvest thanks festival" is often held on the first Sunday after Michaelmas, which puts it generally around the beginning of October. In Canada, *Thanksgiving* is held on the second Monday in October, far earlier than the American Thanksgiving, which is held on the fourth Thursday in November. In the Netherlands, the Harvest Festival is known as *Dankdag voor Gewas en Arbeid* ("Thanksgiving Day for Crops and Labor"). *Dożynki* (Poland) is the ancient harvest festival celebrated at the Fall Equinox. In Belarus, it is known as *Dazhynki;* in the Czech Republic, it is *Dožínky* or *Obžinky*; in the Ukraine, it is known as *Obzhynky*; and in Russia, it is *Obzhynki*. All very similar, both in name, and in intent of celebration.

Mabon, or the Autumnal Equinox, offers us the welcome rest after a long effort, reflecting to us that our hard work has paid off and we can celebrate the resulting abundance.

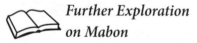 *Further Exploration on Mabon*

Dugan, Ellen. *Autumn Equinox: The Enchantment of Mabon*. Woodbury, MN: Llewellyn, 2005.

Rajchel, Diana. *Mabon: Rituals, Recipes & Lore for the Autumn Equinox*. Woodbury, MN: Llewellyn, 2015.

Forty-four

The Shadow of the Wounded Healer

There is a concept of the Wounded Healer that seems to refract into two distinct and, in many ways, opposing paths. These two reflections start in very similar places, but quickly veer in different directions.

The first reflection of the Wounded Healer comes from the archetypal work of Carl Jung. Inspired by the myth of Chiron, the centaur and healer who becomes incurably wounded by one of Hercules' arrows; and by Asclepius, the first physician and founder of the healing center of Epidaurus, Jung said:

> The analyst must go on learning endlessly …: it is his own hurt that gives the measure of his power to heal. This, and nothing else, is the meaning of the Greek myth of the wounded physician.[63]

There is the understanding in this reflection that, as human beings, we are always in the flux of the healing process, including those who are doing the work of helping or guiding others through that process. We have all had our experiences of pain and spent time hiding our Light in the Shadow. But, as we have found the strength and courage to address that pain, we come to a more compassionate and nuanced understanding for self, including our expectations of what the journey is supposed to look like. In doing so, we develop a deeper appreciation for the struggles of others. The wounds we recognize within ourselves and work toward healing become part of the mechanism at our disposal to become more effective healers.

....

63. Stevens, Anthony. *Jung: A Very Short Introduction.* Oxford, UK: Oxford University Press, 2001 (137).

This is not the case at all for the other path, that of the wounded healer. Rather than emanate from the realm of the archetypes, this reflection is rooted in the shame-based mask of "healer." It tends to present as having all the answers, being the authority, and issuing unsolicited advice. It tends to be attached to the idea of being a healer, especially as knowing what is best for the client, disregarding boundaries and diminishing the client's sense of autonomy. The Wounded Healer listens and fosters empowerment. The wounded healer expounds and fosters dependence. It is a potentially dangerous mask to wear as it is kept in place by the unhealthy ego that needs to be right. As such, it tends to refuse humility, accountability, and, in truth, vulnerability. When, as healers (or teachers and leaders), we are unable to be transparent to the possibility that we do not have all the answers and that we too are prone to error, we may find ourselves backed into the corner of wronging the other in order to ensure we are righting ourselves. In no way is this conducive to supporting the healing (or guiding or leading) process. Shadow is Shadow, no matter at which desk it sits.

As with most things, these energies are not absolutes. There can be degrees and rarely do we find instances of the extreme. Most individuals, healers included, have some awareness of their own issues and learn the tools to ensure that they are not brought into the professional arena. But when this wounded healer subpersonality is found in the extreme, it creates a very toxic dynamic, one that often needs to be healed from itself! This extreme is the *Shadowworker*, who is so blocked and unaware of their own Shadow that it becomes acted out on others. Shame, low self-esteem, and a sense of inadequacy become inflated into control, grandiosity, and boundary violation. In fact, this deeply wounded personality can run the risk of being a predatory healer (or teacher or leader). This is rare but, tragically, not unheard of.

More commonly reflective of the wounded healer is the phenomenon of *Twilightworker*. This individual has good intentions but little self-awareness. Another term for this would be the "codependent healer" who has a high attachment to being seen by the client in a particular positive light as a way to mitigate the uncomfortable feelings of "not being good enough" that lie below the surface. There is a tendency with the Twilightworker to focus on the love and light that emanates from the upper chakras without having done the tough healing work of the lower chakras. There is a truism that says that, unfortunately, we can only take our clients as far as we are willing to go ourselves. If I am afraid to look at my own dark Shadow, I will not be able to recognize the signposts as I walk beside one who is not afraid and who is eager to seek the signposts. The Shadow has an uncanny ability to make itself known, and in the case of the Twilightworker, this often shows up as projection. That which I cannot recognize as needing to be healed in my own Shadow, I will project upon the other as something they need to heal. In truth, that issue may have little to zero relevance to that person's story. My projection of my issues onto the other person can muddy the waters of their own self-awareness and cause a derailment of their own healing process.[64]

The difference between the Shadowworker and the Twilightworker lies in the range of degrees. Both are cases of coming from the energy of the wounded healer. Both are coming from unconsciousness. But the levels of denial and repression in the Shadowworker are far more entrenched, and thus potentially harmful to the client, than the Twilightworker. Beware the arrogance that does not have the capacity to own the error of a misstep. That is a sure directional signal to the Shadowworker.

In the human journey, particularly when looked at through the lens of our soul's healing, this movement from Shadow to Twilight can also be seen as working through one's Life Purpose. "As above, so below," the Hermetic axiom states and, by extension, "as within, so without." What you are working on within yourself as your soul growth is reflected in how your life looks on the outside in relation to the external world. The larger patterns of your life that have been playing out since you first arrived on this Earth are evident in your reactions and responses today in this moment.

The wisdom of Ma'at reflects to us that we are meant to leave this life with our hearts as feather-light as they were when we came into it. It is not possible to journey through this life without picking up some dust and Shadow. That is not an issue. The purpose of life is to learn how to brush the dust off and transmute the Shadow into something immutable. This is the journey from connection with Essence to disconnection with self to the growth back into relationship with Self that comes from

....

64. In clinical terms, this projection of personal Shadow onto a client is referred to as counter-transference and is always problematic if not addressed by the therapist in their own personal healing work. Transference is when the client projects their issues onto the therapist (i.e., "That is just like something my mom would say. You are just like my mom.") and can be quite conducive to the healing process.

addressing the false messaging of shame, and ends with the championing that Wonder Child Within.

When we are so overcome with the shame that the message we hear when we turn our mind within is that we are flawed and unlovable, there is no true image of self. The experience of life in this context is truly that of being lost in the forest, a loss of purpose, a life without a sense of meaning. This is despair. This is depression. This is a terrible place to be. It is the Shadow reflection of every cycle thus far.

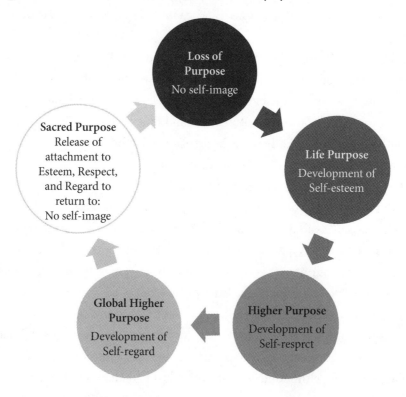

When we start to explore how to find our way out of this dark forest, following the tentative breadcrumbs of a different calling, we move from the aimless meandering of lost purpose to the solid path of Life Purpose. Having the courage to face the fear and the shame that has been with us for so long invites us to see the patterns in the choices we made and the experiences we had. Addressing the self-destruction that comes from an active addiction moves one from the dark forest to the path of Life Purpose. In looking to the patterns, one might see the pain of abandonment that was there for so long. How the addiction tried to cover that pain of abandonment. How that abandonment became amplified and reinforced through the addiction. How the confrontation with and resulting release of the addiction became the springboard to the healing of abandonment. How the healing of abandonment led to the anchoring of positive self-esteem. How the experience of self-esteem changed the inner dynamic and dialogue that impacted on outer relationships. How the transformed relationships resulted in a completely different experience of life. This is powerful Life Purpose stuff!

It is only with the harvest of lived experience that we can begin to gain informed perspective on the patterns that have been there all along. As healers (and teachers and leaders), the more we turn this gaze within, addressing the Shadow wherever it appears, the better we can be of service to those who turn to us for help and guidance.

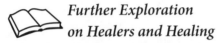 *Further Exploration*
on Healers and Healing

Brennan, Barbara. *Core Light Healing: My Personal Journey and Advanced Healing Concepts for Creating the Life You Long to Live*. Carlsbad, CA: Hay House, 2017.

Lin, Ke-Ming. *Wounded Healers: Tribulations and Triumphs of Pioneering Psychotherapists*. Cambridge: Cambridge University Press, 2020.

Small, Jacquelyn. *Becoming Naturally Therapeutic: A Return to the True Essence of Helping*. New York: Bantam, 1990.

Small, Jacquelyn. *Transformers: The Artists of Self-Creation*. Marina del Rey, CA: Devorss & Co., second edition, 1994.

Forty-five

The Light of the Wonder Healer

When we have managed to navigate a Life Purpose path to come to a place of self-understanding, self-compassion, and clarity, and we begin to move that experience and wisdom out into the world, that is when we will find ourselves solidly in the Jungian arena of the Wounded Healer, the archetype of the healer who strives to be of service even as they continue the lifelong task of addressing the wound within. This is the Lightworker: one who has done and continues to do much inner work, knowing the value of embracing the full experience of being human. The Lightworker recognizes the interplay between the upper and lower chakras, appreciates the importance of balancing higher insight with the wide range of emotions, respects personal boundaries, sees each individual as empowered (or as having access to being empowered, should one choose), and is focused on helping to support an individual process of transformation. Or, as Carl Jung would say, individuation.

In doing the work to reclaim a sense of self that is rooted in esteem and respect, the Lightworker often has much clarity around the particularities of their Higher Purpose. Higher Purpose is the sense that the work we do in the world has meaning. It is the inner work of one's soul as it corresponds to the outer work of one's heart. Higher Purpose gives shape to our lives and clarity to our direction. An appreciation for what our own individual Higher Purpose is cannot be separated from what our Life Purpose is. The more I look to my pain, and the healing of my pain, and the wisdom I gleaned from that process, the more my understanding of my Higher Purpose sharpens, and there is a sureness to walking my path. With Higher Purpose, we have followed those breadcrumbs right out of the dark forest.

When you are learning about your own self, your pain, and your strengths, you are engaged in your own Life Purpose. When you are sharing your hard-won wisdom with others, you are engaged in your Higher Purpose. Often, we find there is a continual process of fine-tuning that occurs while we are engaged in our Higher Purpose. As we do the work of that purpose in the world, so we find that we are continually gaining more and more clarity and depth of insight. More shards of Shadow may be kicked to the surface to be addressed, and that in turn feeds into honing the skills brought to our purpose. When the effect that our work in the world, as informed by our inner journey, starts to ripple out beyond the bounds of what we are even aware of through our own direct connections, we know we are in the realm of Global Higher Purpose. When your story has travelled to those you have not nor ever will meet and is impacting, even in some small way, on planetary evolution, then that is your Global Higher Purpose. With the effects of the internet, this is occurring more and more. What you put out in the world can quickly expand beyond your personal reach. It requires a high degree of self-regard, recognizing the importance of maintaining self-awareness, and a commitment to integrity to be balanced with that responsibility.

This is not necessarily a progressive path. It is not to say that there won't be forays back into the dark forest, but at least we know we have the tools in our backpack to help us to find our way out again. And if, by some circumstance, we lose our backpack full of tools, we know how to follow the sun and read the map of the stars and note the clues in the moss and lichen. We know that, outside of all the tricks, techniques, and tools, it comes right down to the bare bones of presence. Ultimately, it comes down to listening to the unerring directions of Higher Self.

When I come back to "cultivating my garden and hoeing my own row," knowing that, regardless of what I do or say, what I teach or share, how I guide or help, it doesn't really have anything to do with me in the first place, I return to the place of no self-image. Through loss of self to reclaiming of Self, I come to the fullness of experience through Higher Self and recognize that it was always only ever about my relationship to Spirit, however it is that I experience it. Like the tarot Fool's journey, I am no longer defined by the empty zero. Spirit has expanded that circle beyond my farthest vision to even be able to imagine. All I can focus on is honoring the bliss of my own personal dance in the center of the World. In doing so, I embody Sacred Purpose and I have become the Wonderworker: the one who does not differentiate between upper and lower chakras because they correspond to each other; the one who is able to see beauty in chaos and Spirit in material because they each inform each other; and the one who knows that miracles are always present because Spirit is immanent, as well as transcendent. Wonderworkers are the soul-infused activators of transmutation.

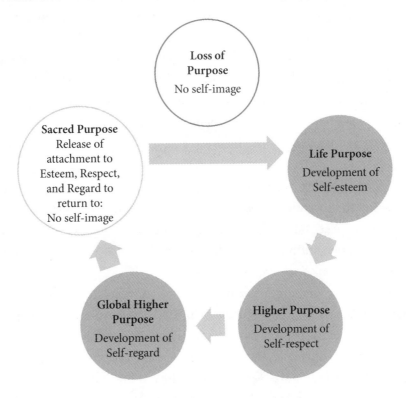

Loss of Purpose
No self-image

Sacred Purpose
Release of attachment to Esteem, Respect, and Regard to return to:
No self-image

Life Purpose
Development of Self-esteem

Global Higher Purpose
Development of Self-regard

Higher Purpose
Development of Self-respect

Inner Workings:
Drafting an Illuminated Contract

As with any dynamic, the more transparency that is brought to expectations and promises, the easier it is to move forward in healthy and co-creative ways. This is as true of our dynamic with Higher Self as it is with any of our human interpersonal relationships. Regardless of whether you are involved in the healing arts or not, you are here for a purpose. The clearer you are on what that purpose is, the more able you are to use its guidance to direct your life's meaning.

Take some time to meditate upon what you have learned about yourself so far in this noble journey. Trace the path from Loss of Purpose—the times when you felt very lost in the dark forest—to where you sit today. Looking back at the time of early spring (Cycle Two), allow yourself to remember and reconnect with what you have learned through your life around your needs and your emotions and how that has shifted and changed with your inner work. *An example might be: Through years of dismissing uncomfortable feelings, I have come to recognize the value of their message.*

Propelling yourself forward in your journey to the time of late spring and the celebration of coming back to life from the brink of barrenness (Cycle Three), allow yourself to remember and reconnect what you have learned through your life about the challenge of defenses and the importance of boundaries. *An example might be: Through years of withdrawing and isolating, I have come to value taking the space I need.*

Moving forward once again to the height of summer and the expression of self that we present to the world (Cycle Five), allow yourself to remember and reconnect with the various faces you have explored, those intended to please others and those reflective of an inner truth. *An example might be: Through years of perfectionism, I have come to respect my dedication to excellence.*

Feeling your feet directly beneath you in the current cycle that celebrates the bountiful harvest of a fully engaged life or process, allow yourself to see how what you have learned, all the triumphs and all the tragedies, not only nourishes your own body and soul with sustenance, but can serve the wider community, even beyond the confines of what you recognize as your community, if that harvest is celebrated with the respect and regard it is due. Bringing all those elements together, think about how what you have harvested in your life brings clarity to moving forward with purpose. Consciously and with lucid purpose, draft an Illuminated Contract with your Higher Self. *An example might be:*

n valuing the information conveyed to me by my emotions, including those uncomfortable feelings, I will integrate those messages into my decisions and actions.

n valuing the physical, emotional, and mental space I need to feel firmly supported, I will risk pushing myself beyond my hesitant comfort zone.

In valuing the opportunity to grow in unimagined ways through courage and vision, I will honor my dedication to excellence.

In this and any other ways that may become evident through my work, I will apply my emotions, my mind, and my spirit to the task of fulfilling my Purpose.

In this and many ways that may become evident through my experiences, Spirit will support and guide my emotions, my mind, and my spirit to the task of embodying my Purpose.

Forty-six

The Bridge Between the Worlds Meditation

Though it has become diffuse in the past decades in its association with the end-of-life journey of a loved pet, the concept of the Rainbow Bridge reaches back hundreds, even thousands, of years. There has always been a sense that there is something that connects the human realm with that of the otherworldly, something that bridges those two realms and allows the passage from one to the other. Norse mythology presents the image of Bifröst, the flaming rainbow bridge, guarded by the all-seeing and all-hearing Heimdall, that connects the realm of the gods, Asgard, with the human realm, Midgard. This image of Heimdall standing guard between the worlds with a bridge of transparent colored light stretched out before him has become far more recognizable in recent years, due to the Marvel Avengers franchise.

It may be the most well-known, particularly in the West, but Bifröst is not the only mythological representation of an otherworldly bridge or one that spans the realms of human and Divine. The Shinto religion offers Ama-No-Ukihashi ("Floating Bridge of Heaven") that connects Takama-Ga-Hare ("High Plain of Heaven"), the realm of the deities, with Earth, the dwelling place of humans. In Zoroastrianism, the Chinvat Bridge ("Bridge of Judgment") is the sifting bridge that all must cross upon dying. How we live in life determines how the bridge will appear to us upon death. If we have lived well, we will be led from the bridge into the House of Song.

This meditation invites you to experience what it is to be filled with gratitude for a life fully lived. The Greeks felt that the purpose of life was to learn how to die well, meaning to know how to let go when it is time to let go. The less we are carrying from the past, the easier it is for us to meet the inevitable moment, whether it is the true end of life or the end of cycle that we continually come up to within our lives. The more we know how to release when the time is right, the more we can open ourselves to the mystery of whatever awaits us beyond the next step.

Meditation

You find yourself once more at the top of the mountain that you have worked so hard to attain. Looking out across the expanse of sky above you, you note how low the sun is in the sky. It is a gorgeous orange orb that seems to be eager to kiss the horizon and you revel in its glory, even as you are aware that the light is fading. This is the time cinematographers call "magic hour," and you can feel the wonder of it coursing through your body, tickling your skin, enlivening your spirit. You have traveled far, and your body may be tired from the journey, but your Spirit is full. You ponder the journey you have made to come to this place, to stand where you stand in this moment. You think about the sacrifices you have made, the release of all that which has weighed you down. Each step you have taken on the path leading up to this place has been a consideration, taking care to remove any stones, circumvent any tree roots, address any obstacles. Each step you have taken on the path leading up to this place has been a revelation, taking time to appreciate the vistas, the flora, the fauna, holding tight to your heart all the gifts received along the way. From this place of great height you can see the lay of the land before you and see where you have come from: the places of triumph and the places of challenge.

As the sun touches the horizon and a burst of oranges and pinks trails across the sky, you notice once more that place directly across the extensive chasm from where you stand, the cave where this whole journey began. Standing here feels like such a mirror, the beginning and the end coming almost full circle. Not quite full. There is that space that holds the end apart from the beginning. As the sun disappears beneath the edge of the horizon line and the soft pastels that trail across the sky start to fade, you turn your mind to what can bridge that chasm. That with all the challenges and obstacles you have met, there has always been a way. You know that this will be no different and, with that thought, that insight, that wisdom, you notice that there is the thinnest ray of glowing violet purple light that seems to shimmer from a place just in front of your feet reaching all the way across to a place near the mouth of the cave.

You shift your thoughts to begin to think about that sense of your Sacred Self, the beliefs you hold, your self-awareness, and what you know with absolute clarity in your mind's eye to be your true vision. As you do, you see a ray of indigo light join that of the purple. You see that there are now two gorgeous glowing rays that join together to bridge where you stand now and the place where you began.

You focus your thoughts on how you present to the world, how you express who you are, how you voice what matters to you, and all that you believe in and all that you hold so dear and, as you do, you see a ray of light blue light flicker into being beside the other two rays.

You think about your heart, what fills your heart, what makes your heart beat, what makes your heart strong, what fills your heart with passion and with courage. As you do, a strand of green light joins the other three. And now there are four rays of multicolored light. You can see that they are creating a bridge—a Rainbow Bridge. You can see that what is being constructed is already fairly substantial, but you know there is more. It does not feel complete.

In thinking about what more is needed to craft this Rainbow Bridge, you begin to think about all you have learned about standing up for yourself and your truth, establishing firm boundaries that are maintained with kindness and yet resoluteness. As you do, you see the shimmer of a yellow ray stretch across the chasm from mountain to cave, alongside the other four rays.

You begin to focus on all the energies and emotions that swirl within you, all the ways in which you have responded to all the experiences you have had. As you become aware of those waves of emotion flowing through you, you see an orange band grow out of the others, all together creating a solid, stable, and yet ethereal arc that stretches across the void.

You know there is one last piece to make it complete and you know this last piece will change everything. It is like listening for the final note that will bring the whole piece to triumphant conclusion. You take a deep breath. You bring your awareness to your body and you think about how this wondrous miracle of a body has carried you through so many, so, so many experiences. It has been with you since the very first moment, and as you send waves of gratitude and appreciation toward this body of yours, you see a glowing stretch of red join the other colors of light, completing the Rainbow Bridge that beckons your feet to take a step.

You hesitate for a moment. You know that to take this step means release. There is nothing of heaviness or regret or shame that can come with you. To step onto the shimmering path of light means that you leave the past in the past and move forward with nothing, absolutely nothing, except the Golden Seed of Self that you hold in your hand. And yet, that feels right to you. You have nourished yourself with the sustenance of all your experiences, the sweet, the savory, and the bitter. And as the last light fades from the sky and the distant landscape disappears from view, all you can see is the rainbow glow at your feet that stretches off into an unknown adventure.

You hold the Seed to your heart. You take a deep breath. You hear the note of your Soul and, in the sweet music it creates, you hear:

I hope for nothing

I fear nothing

I am free.[65]

You take a step.

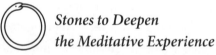 **Stones to Deepen the Meditative Experience**

Petalite has an extremely high vibration that connects us to angelic realms in powerfully protective ways.

Sacred Seven, also known as Super Seven or the Melody Stone, is comprised of seven distinct stones (Amethyst, Clear Quartz, Smokey Quartz, Cacoxenite, Rutile, Goethite, and Lepidochrosite) that opens us to all our senses, bridging groundedness with uplifting expansion.

Tibetan Quartz, which vibrates to the frequency of "om," enhances and amplifies transformation.

....

65. Epitaph on the grave of Nikos Kazantzakis, author of *Last Temptation of Christ* and *Zorba the Greek*

Forty-seven

· ·

The Hermetic Principle
of Correspondence Contemplation

It may be, in a modern context at any rate, the Hermetic Principle of Vibration that garners all the excitement, but truly it is the Hermetic Principle of Correspondence that does much of the heavy lifting, so to speak, in the consciousness of the twenty-first century. Out of all the principles, this is the one that is probably most often quoted or referenced. As the Magician in the tarot knows so well, when one has put the time and dedication into studying all the ways in which the world works and all the ways in which Spirit works, one begins to see the connections where there never seemed to be any before. One starts to see patterns where once there was chaos. One starts to see relevance where previously there was randomness. Once something has been seen and understood in a whole different way, it can be integrated. And perhaps, even more importantly than that, it can be utilized.

The Kybalion presents The Hermetic Principle of Correspondence as:

As above, so below, as below, so above.[66]

These eight small words convey a massive breadth of scope that, when approached with both humility and awe, hold the potential key to open doors to an inkling of Universal truth. They present an encapsulation of the dynamic relationship and interconnectedness of all in the cosmos. Not only that, these eight words convey the

·······························

66. The Three Initiates, "The Kybalion: Chapter II. The Seven Hermetic Principles," www.sacred-texts .com (Yogi Publication Society, 1912), https://www.sacred-texts.com/eso/kyb/kyb04.htm.

dynamic as being harmonious, each part beautifully reflecting the other in perfect balance. This principle shows us that there are connections between the very large and the very small, the Greater and the Lesser, and that there is not incongruence or discord between these aspects. As the planets move, so there are repercussions on the earth or in ourselves. Not pulling against each other, but informing and enhancing each to each. Even within our bodies, reflexology teaches that our foot or our ear has correspondence to the entire body. To massage a tiny spot on the foot or to place acupuncture needles in the tiny spot in the ear is to work toward bringing the corresponding spot in the body into a place of release and balance. The microcosm holds the key to the macrocosm, and vice versa. As William Blake wrote:

> To see a World in a Grain of Sand
> And a Heaven in a Wild Flower
> Hold Infinity in the palm of your hand
> And Eternity in an hour[67]

When we are able to see that which links the very large with the very small, or when we are able to see the underlying, hidden, or indeed, occult, correspondences between seemingly unrelated or disconnected elements, it inspires awe. To the one who can see the true nature of reality, there is no such thing as a miracle and yet, all of existence is a wonder. In magical workings, the Hermetic Principle of Correspondence is key. Those who work magically and symbolically can attest to the power generated when corresponding elements are brought together to amplify work, or the exquisite nuance that can be created when complementary correspondences are introduced. Those who work energetically, particularly in the realm of vibrational healing and medical intuition, can also attest to the vital importance of being able to recognize the patterns that lie beneath the surface of the evident. Attunement to the language of correspondence opens one's ears to the most subtle of messages.

....

67. Blake, William. "Auguries of Innocence." *The Pickering Manuscript*. Whitefish, MT: Kessinger Pub., 2004 (15).

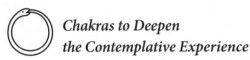

Contemplation

Contemplate how the Enlightened Hynni of Karma reflects the Hermetic Principle of Correspondence: the five-pointed star that brings to mind the perfection of the Vitruvian Man, a reflection of the expression of Spirit on Earth, balancing the four core building blocks or elements of physical existence into the finer perfection of quintessence, the very Essence of Spirit.

Chakras to Deepen the Contemplative Experience

Connect with the **crown chakra** to open yourself to higher consciousness, to the sense of the greater blueprint of your life, the underlying Soul purpose of your time on this Earth. When it is open and connected, this chakra is the Seat of Higher Self, serving as the personal experience of the Divine. It allows us to have a sense of the key archetypes, the key lessons, the deeper meaning and the deeper patterns not just in your own life, but in the unfolding of history and humanity. When blocked, it is driven by ego, the need to be perceived as having the answers, and the feeling that one has an inside track to the direct ear of the Divine.

The higher-vibration chakra that sits in at the very top of the head is the **Fifteenth Chakra of Light Being and Ascension.**[68] Focusing on this chakra enhances our ability to meditate and connect to the wisdom of the higher realms. It allows us to see the connections and correspondences on a very deep level, opening us to perceiving the fabric of the Wyrd or the Tao. There is a high degree of spiritual protection and purification that surrounds the individual who is highly connected to this chakra. Think of how it feels to listen to the Dalai Lama speak and you have a sense of the feeling of this energy.

The Fifteenth Chakra is the doorway to the fifth dimension (or 5D, as it is called in New Age circles), the higher-vibration realm of Light and Love. It is heralded as the New Earth, the reclaiming of Eden, and the attainment of Heaven on Earth. In

....
68. Stone, *Soul Psychology*.

large part, it can be seen as the truth we witness in ourselves, in others, and in the world when we have forever dropped the cloak of shame and see all of existence as a reflection and iteration of the Divine. Some schools of thought believe it is not possible to attain 5D in the context of a human life. Or more specifically, the belief is that if you are able to raise your vibration to such a degree that you are operating in the fifth dimension, then those who are still operating in the vibratory level of the third and fourth dimensions would not be able to see you. Much like the experience of a dog whistle, it is not that you are not energetically present, it is just that the vibration is too high to detect. Just because you can't hear the vibrational note of a dog whistle doesn't mean the dog can't. All you need to do is look at the twitchy ears and cocked head to know there is something going on outside of your ability to hear. Other schools of thought believe that the attainment of 5D in this lifetime is possible, if we are able to consistently release any of the negative or heavy emotions that keep us in a lower vibrational field and engage with the world from beyond the limitations of our five senses. One would be operating at the level of an Ascended Master on the Earth plane, much like the idea of a Bodhisattva.

In the Hynni approach, these dimensions bring together the language of Sage and Alchemist, chakras and Hermetics. The third dimension (culminating in the seventh chakra or the crown chakra) relates to the Great Physical Plane referred to in *The Kybalion*. The fourth dimension (culminating in the Fifteenth Chakra or the Chakra of Light Being and Ascension) relates to the Great Mental Plane. The fifth dimension (culminating in the twenty-second chakra or the chakra in which we merge with the Monad) relates to the Great Spiritual Plane. Each of these great planes has seven smaller sub-planes that correspond to the seven individual chakras.

Third Dimension	Fourth Dimension	Fifth Dimension
The Great Physical Plane	The Great Mental Plane	The Great Spiritual Plane

Root Chakra: *The Plane of Matter (A)*	Ninth Chakra of Joy and Satisfaction: *The Plane of Mineral Mind*	Sixteenth Chakra: I am Pure Spirit: *The Plane of Masters and Adepts*
Sacral Chakra: *The Plane of Matter (B)*	Tenth Chakra of Harmonious Balance: *The Plane of Elemental Mind (A)*	Seventeenth Chakra: I am Utmost Generosity: *The Plane of Angelic Hosts*
Solar Plexus Chakra: *The Plane of Matter (C)*	Eleventh Chakra of Calm Wisdom: *The Plant of Plant Mind*	Eighteenth Chakra: I am Cosmic Connection: *The Plane of Unseen Divinities*
Heart Chakra: *The Plane of Ethereal Substance*	Twelfth Chakra of Samadhi: *The Plane of Elemental Mind (B)*	Nineteenth Chakra: I am Utmost Acceptance
Throat Chakra: *The Plane of Energy (A)*	Thirteenth Chakra of Mediumship: *The Plane of Animal Mind*	Twentieth Chakra: I am Utmost Responsibility
Brow Chakra: *The Plane of Energy (B)*	Fourteenth Chakra of Oneness: *The Plane of Elemental Mind (C)*	Twenty-first Chakra: I am that I am.
Crown Chakra: *The Plane of Energy (C)*	Fifteenth Chakra of Light Being and Ascension: *The Plane of Human Mind*	Twenty-second Chakra: I am One with All

As we already learned with Aristotle's Golden Mean, it is often best to look to the middle path. We can look to the third dimension as being very much reflective of the human experience. Although we can attain wonderful spiritual insights here, particularly through the brow and crown chakras, we are always tending to be working through aspects of our Shadow material. At the other end of the spectrum, there is the fifth dimension, which is very reflective of the spiritual (energetic, vibrational) experience. There is no Shadow here. However, there is also no material existence here either. The middle path is that of the fourth dimension, the one that acknowledges that we can have moments when we reconnect with the bliss of knowing Eden is within us, but that, as long as we are having a human experience in this life, there are going to be those moments when we lose sight of our highest truth. And that is okay. Particularly when we hold the key to the correspondences that can bring us back on track.

Forty-eight

The Golden Gratitude Ritual

At the time of the Fall Equinox when much of the harvest has been gathered and we are able to see the abundant fruits of all our labors, it is a time to give thanks for our blessings. This is not simply having gratitude for all that we appreciate in our lives. It is seeing the whole picture—the good, the bad, and the ugly—and seeing how it all contributed to where you stand at this point in your life. This is the fulfillment of the alchemical journey. It is the attainment of the Philosopher's Stone, which teaches us that the gold lies within. It always has, but it needed all those experiences to really bring it forth and let it shine. This ritual invites you to claim that Philosopher's Stone and mark it with all the qualities within yourself and all the circumstances in your life that you are grateful for today. It is the celebration of a life well-lived, even in the knowledge of all the challenges, obstacles, and pitfalls that may have been encountered along the way.

Symbols to help connect to ritual focus	• A cornucopia • Apples, gourds, seeds • Fall leaves • Statues or photos of those deities that reflect higher wisdom, writing, and knowledge • An image of the Enlightened Hynni of Karma
Optional: Stones from *Bridge Between the Worlds* Meditation	• Petalite • Sacred Seven • Tibetan Quartz
Items needed for ritual activity	• A fresh unused candle (purple, if you want to align with Hynni) • A lighter • A cauldron • A dark-colored palm-sized stone • A gold paint pen • Optional: Candle snuffer • Optional: A preferred form of scrying (crystal, water) or oracle deck

Creating the Altar

Whether on your existing altar or on a surface that can act as altar for this ritual, decorate the space with those elements which bring abundance, hard-won wisdom, and thanksgiving to mind. This could include an image of the Enlightened Hynni of Karma, which reminds the psyche that the Soul always has a guiding star on this human journey, even if sometimes it is obscured by cloud cover.

You may also want to include reflections of the Divine on this sacred space you are creating. This may be statues or photos of the gods and goddesses that are particularly connected to this time. Some possible suggestions are found in the table at the end of chapter 49.

The last things to have on hand are those items that will be used in the ritual working itself. Place these items front and center on the altar so you have ease of access to them. On the left side of your altar, place the stone or crystal and the paint pen. On the right side of your altar, place the cauldron and in front of you, in the center of your altar, place the unlit candle.

When you are done preparing your space, take a moment to feel how the energy you have created affects you. You will want to ensure that there are elements that speak to the general theme of the ritual or the festival itself. This reflects the "Above," the transpersonal or mythic realm. You will also want to ensure that there are elements that represent you on the altar. This reflects the "Below," the realm of the personal. If it feels complete, take some time to prepare yourself for ritual (see Appendix D).

The Ritual

Allow yourself to drop fully into that awareness of being in the place where Cerridwen sits. Note that the cauldron to your right is empty. At this time, nearing the end of this grand seasonal cycle, the work is complete. In Cerridwen's tale, this time of harvest signals the cracking of the cauldron, ensuring no further work can be done. It also represents the revelation of the drops of wisdom, the culmination of the work. It is time to glean the gifts of that labor.

When you are ready to do so, light the candle before you, pick up the stone that lies to your left and, holding it gently in your palm, begin to contemplate all that has brought you to this place in your life. Allow words or simple statements around what you have gained from all your experience to come to you. Each time you grasp hold of a word or statement, write it on your stone with your gold paint pen. You may find that you write them down in a random pattern. You may find a design take shape: spirals, or circles, or rays. You may even choose to write these words in the script gifted by one of the gods: by Odin or Ogma. However it unfolds for you, know that these words of wisdom and gratitude written on this stone are creating a physical manifestation of your Philosopher's Stone. This is the crystallization of your Essence. It is potent. It is wise. And it is never not with you. All you have to do is follow the light of the star within that guides you to where your Essence resides and allow that to fill you until you know the wonder of your life fully and deeply in your cells. Take all the time you need in this moment, gazing at the candle flame, basking in the light of your wisdom. Using your chosen scrying method or oracle deck, invite Divine reflection about your purpose and path at this time.

Closure of Ritual

When you are ready to leave this liminal space, bring your conscious awareness back to your breath. Taking one last moment to anchor the connection to your sense of your Essence, using either your breath or a candle snuffer, release the flame of the candle before you. What has been experienced in ritual lives forever in your cells. It need only be called forth from within when you choose.

Take some time to move through the directions once more, thanking the elements for helping to hold space and keep you safe through the ritual. Start again in the North with earth, then move through the East with air, the South with fire (put out the tealight in the cauldron at this point), the West with water, ending with the Below of the material plane and the Above of the cosmic plane. Thank and bid farewell to the deities who have been a part of this ritual with you and know that the Wheel may turn around you, but you are—as they are—ever at the center.

Clearing Ritual Space

If you have been using an existing altar, you may decide to keep some items, including your Golden Gratitude Philosopher's Stone, on your altar over the course of the cycle.

 *Proxy Scrying Recommendations*

Baron-Reid, Colette. *Postcards from Spirit*. Lifestyles, 2017.

Bernstein, Gabrielle. *The Universe Has Your Back: Transform Fear to Faith Cards*. Carlsbad, CA: Hay House, 2017.

Linn, Denise. *Sacred Destiny Oracle*. Carlsbad, CA: Hay House, 2019.

Virtue, Doreen. *Life Purpose Oracle Cards*. Carlsbad, CA: Hay House, 2011.

Zakroff, Laura Tempest. *Liminal Spirits Oracle*. Woodbury, MN: Llewellyn, 2019.

Forty-nine

Practice Gratitude and Acts of Thankful Appreciation

The power of Cycle Seven is the healing that comes when we know in every cell that our lives have meaning and significance. This is not that some people's lives have meaning. Or that there are certain times in our lives that have meaning. Our lives always are graced with deep meaning that does not just have an impact on those around us, but often has far-reaching impact beyond that of which we can be consciously aware.

Mabon is a festival of thanksgiving. It reminds us to have gratitude for the abundant harvest that is the result of our intention and effort.

All the individual moments that come together, big and small, ecstatic and tragic, precise and directionless, all contribute their distinct and necessary color to the overall vibrancy and nuance of the full pictures that make up our lives. Very often it is not until we are at the end of something that we can see that the twists and turns in the path that have brought us to where we are today were necessary to bring us to this spot. When we are in the thick of our experiences, or in the intensity of our pain, it can be challenging or well-nigh impossible to do anything more than just react to the situation in which we find ourselves, let alone try to find that place within us to feel gratitude. But when we are able to come to a place in which we know, even if we are experiencing pain, even if we are being challenged more than we ever have before, that there is something within us that can rise above even momentarily to gain that higher perspective, we are tapping into a higher truth. It is not about the situation. It is about our recognition of our innate, indestructible Spirit selves. It is about seeing the larger pattern of our Higher Purpose and our Sacred Purpose. It is about identifying our inner strength that is always accessible to us in any situation and in response to any pain. It is that for which we can be grateful. Not for the challenge itself. Not for the pain itself. But for the way in which it invites us to seek out, find, and reveal the very best in ourselves.

We are not defined by what happens to us. We are defined by how we choose to respond to it.

If gratitude is the energy vibration, acts of thankful appreciation are the small ways in which we can put that vibration to work. Even small acts of appreciation can make all the difference in the world. One drop in the ocean still contributes to the ocean. As Aesop said, "No act of kindness, no matter how small, is ever wasted." It is not the size of the gesture that gives it significance. On a spectrum with Shadow at one end and Light at the other, every thankful, kind act brings more of the message of Light into the world. In the US, The Random Acts of Kindness Foundation, established in 1995, has declared February 17 as Random Acts of Kindness Day,[69] but part of the Foundation's mission is to support making kindness the norm, not the exception, envisioning a world in which a friendly word, gesture, or act is just the way in which we relate to each other. What a world that would be!

When we are able to find that place within where we reverberate with gratitude and reflect that gratitude through myriad small acts of appreciation, we are honoring the undeniable meaning of our lives. We are honoring the purpose of our lives. We are honoring the meaning of the lives of others and inviting them to do the same. And thus, we truly are the Wonderworkers of the world, inviting and enacting positive change.

....

69. Though the Foundation began in the US in 1995, Random Acts of Kindness Day was created by Josh de Jong in New Zealand in 2004.

Key Aspects of Cycle Seven[70]

Archetypal Themes	Healing Themes	Indication of Crisis	Healing Practices
Effects of Gratitude on Life Purpose Giving thanks; appraisal; letting go	Higher purpose; thanksgiving; gratitude; making amends; end of life or cycle; final release	Lack of trust that all will work out; resistance to life's lessons; attachment to proof; having one's "head in the clouds"; avoidance of physical or emotional needs	Exploration of life of wonder; contemplation of the Hermetic Principle of Correspondence; activation of Enlightened Hynni of Karma

Elemental Reflection	Intuitive Guidance and Tool	Alchemical Reflection	Affirmations
Thought	Angel guides; scrying	*Coagulation* The attainment of the Philosopher's Stone and the solid, immutable sense of Self	I embrace positive thoughts of myself and my abilities; my thoughts support me in all ways; I am open to seeing the patterns in my life; I am living a life of purpose.

70. More information on Key Aspects can be found in *The Great Work: Self-Knowledge and Healing Through the Wheel of the Year* by the author (Llewellyn, 2015).

Part Eight

Cycle Eight
November 1–December 12

From Despair to Transmutation

The Integrating Hynni of Unity

As Below	**As Above**
Despair	Transmutation
Alchemical Return	As above, so below
Unresolved grief	Healing from loss
Disconnection	Beingness

Synthesis
Death
Protection
Otherworldly connection

Fifty

Samhain and the Zero Point

At the end of the Grand Cycle of the annual agricultural wheel, we find ourselves in the time of Dark. This period from November's start to the Winter Solstice is the darkest time of the year as the days get shorter and the sun's strength gets weaker. There can be a poignancy to this time, a bittersweet melancholy. There is an invitation to allow the beauty and wisdom that is contained in the Dark to seep into our souls, steeping us in the remembrance of that which has always been accessible to us, even in those moments when we were too blinded by the brightness of shiny things to see it. We have a tendency to celebrate the beginnings of things while forgetting that the true beginning always happened in the dark. The spark incubates unseen before it is revealed. This time of year is rarely seen as a new beginning. It is more often seen as the threshold to the Great Beyond.

In ancient times, this was the last of the three harvest festivals, bringing to completion the theme of *Death*. The cutting of the grain, the harvesting of the crops, and finally the culling of the herd to ensure the survival of both tribe and healthy livestock through the long winter months. Death and darkness in such close contact compels attention to *Protection*. Though there is the potential for life in the Dark (as evidenced by the incubating spark of life), there can also be the unpredictable vagaries of the Unseen. At this time when the veil between the worlds is thin, one wants to ensure that one stays on the right side of the veil. But there are loved ones on the other side. There are ancestors, wise beings who also offer visions of beauty and wisdom if we can open ourselves to allowing this *otherworldly connection*, if we can open ourselves to the Great Mystery that there is so much more than that which lies before our eyes.

This festival and celebration of Samhain or Halloween is one of the most-loved celebrations around the world. And yet, its themes speak to some of the deepest fears, anxieties, and issues that touch so many. The fear of death, whether that be fear of death itself or the manner of death, affects most people. We have a fear of the process of letting go, a fear of the unknown, a fear of leaving what we love behind. We have a fear of the pain, or a fear of the process, or a fear of being alone. The Core Issue connected with Cycle Eight is not being able to grieve our past wounds, traumas, and losses. It is the inability to bring our pain out of the past and allow ourselves to be fully present in the now. The inability to grieve our losses can be attached to a belief that our today would look so different, that we might be happier, or more stable, or feel more whole. The inability to grieve our losses can be attributed to an attachment to a love or joy or contentment that we experienced in the past, forgetting that those emotions live in us still. Our emotions are not stuck in the past, though that may be where the situation or relationship remains. The inability to grieve our losses, to heal our wounds, or to soften the grip of our traumas not only keeps us tethered to a past that no longer exists, it stops us from welcoming the beauty of today, and prevents us from incubating the future that awaits us. One of the best things about the celebration of Samhain is how it turns our fears into wonders. And if we can do it in joyous fun-filled recognition of a holiday, we have the inner means to know how to do it in life.

So much of what we experience in the journey around the Wheel of the Year brings to mind where we just came from or where we are heading. We prepare the field in order to be ready to plant the seed. We harvest the crops in order to ensure that we will have food enough to last through the winter. This time of the Dark is like the pause between the inhale and the exhale of a breath. There is nothing really that needs to be done, that needs to be prepared, that needs to be worked. In the pause between the inhale and the exhale, we have access to the Zero Point, the empty pause that is filled with all potential. There is no point but this point and that is the whole point!

This recognition, in so many countries all over the world, of the importance in remembering those who have walked before is truly a testament to our ongoing connection to that which is so much bigger than ourselves. They are a part of our lives as we are a part of theirs, no matter the bridge that separates our worlds.

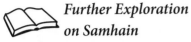 *Further Exploration*
on Samhain

Markale, Jean. *The Pagan Mysteries of Halloween: Celebrating the Dark Half of the Year.* Inner Traditions, 2001.

Rajchel, Diana. *Samhain: Rituals, Recipes & Lore for Halloween.* Woodbury, MN: Llewellyn, 2015.

Rogers, Nicholas. *Halloween: From Pagan Ritual to Party Night.* Oxford: Oxford University Press, 2003.

Skal, David J. *Death Makes a Holiday: A Cultural History of Halloween.* London: Bloomsbury Press, 2002.

Fifty-one

The Shadow Fear of the Dark Specter

When we come right down to it, past even the tangibility of the bones, to the very crux of what keeps us stuck on the Karmic Wheel and prevents us from attaining the World, it is the fear of annihilation. The heart of the matter is that we need to matter. We need to know that we matter; that our existence has a meaning; that our effort has value; and that we will not be reduced to nothing, obliterated, forgotten as if we have never existed.

The Samhain traditions are beautiful in all the ways they honor the ancestors, but is there not something of hopeful solace in the gestures? This is exquisitely illustrated in the movie *Coco*.[71] As long as the ancestors are remembered well, they live on in the Tierra de Muertos. But if they are forgotten, they dissipate into nothingness. They depend on us to remember them so they endure, as one day we will depend on others to remember us.

We fear nothingness. We fear the Void. We fear the despair that is brought upon us by the emptiness. And we fear it because we have lived it.

There is not a person on this planet who has not been filled with the joy of knowing inner perfection and peace only to have it smashed into a million pieces on the rocks of someone else's disregard, dismissal, control, or abuse. The range of what has the potential to move us to a place of inner separation is as expansive as the light spectrum range and anything along that spectrum has the power to cleave our Light

....
71. *Coco*, Pixar (2017).

in two. We feel that separation acutely, within ourselves and with others, and it has the power to drop us into the empty void of shame.

In the pit of the pain of a fractured sense of self, we are shattered. And we become lost in the Dark of that shattering. We do not even know how to look for those pieces again. We don't know how to start to put ourselves back together again. We don't know how to allow the waves of grief for all that has been lost wash over us like waves, slowly, slowly rocking us toward some solid land. We don't trust that we will ever reach solid land again.

Life is loss. The tree knows this, every time a leaf falls. The flower knows this, every time the bloom fades. Everything always ends. Always. But that is never the end of the story. It is only part way through the spin of the wheel and we know this. We know it in our heads, but we are challenged in rooting that knowledge in our bodies in a way that allows ourselves to be rocked by the movement of grief toward the upswing of the wheel that beckons. We become stuck in the fracturing. Like Osiris, parts of our dismembered selves are strewn across the world and we are shocked into inertia.

To get the wheel moving once more, we need to remember. We need to find the courage to sit in the dark, feel what we feel, remember who we truly are, and call our spirits back. We need to Isis ourselves back into animation.

Not all grief is created equal, and it is important to recognize what is healthy and what is unhealthy grief. The function of this process is to support us as we move through loss. It is very much like Isis in her journey around the world to find those parts of her love that were hidden from her. It takes time. It requires attention to discern what piece is still missing. It requires patience to seek high and low, within and without, until that piece is found. And if one finds that it is impossible to find a certain piece, it requires skill and creativity to fashion a replacement.

This is the healing process of soul retrieval. When we encounter those spots within that drop us into despair, or flame us into fury, or drown us in oceans of tears, we know that there is work to be done. Not to keep us in the shame of the experience of separation, but to serve as the indicator light that we are close to finding another lost part! There is something there! We may just have to dig a bit deeper in the sand.

This healing grief is very different than the experience of unhealthy grief. Unhealthy grief is not about seeking wholeness and reclaiming the fractured Self. It is the attachment to a sliver of the past and projecting that sliver into the illusion of the possible future of what could have been. Unhealthy grief is about hanging on to the erroneous belief that our happiness, our safety, our ability to attain the life we want is somehow caught in the past or tied to people from the past. It is not about following the path set by our emotional truth to seek out those parts of ourselves that will bring us back to an experience of wholeness (for, in truth, we are never not whole). Rather, it is about setting us off on wild goose chases that always lead us to dead ends, leaving us feeling helpless and lost. Without being addressed, unhealthy grief can potentially become entrenched into complicated grief, or "persistent complex bereavement disorder" where there is no potential for movement through the grief. We are stuck in the quicksand of despair in the shade of the dark specter.

To look at this another way, if I break my leg, the pain tells me that there is something that needs attention. I need to address what is causing the pain, put some parameters in place to alleviate what is causing the pain, and support that leg during the healing process. I know that the leg will never again be the <u>unbroken</u> leg that it once was, but, with care and attention, it can certainly be a fully functional leg that does everything—or perhaps, almost everything—I need the leg to do. This is healthy grief. If I ignore the pain because the thought of my broken leg is just too much for me to take in, then every step I take as if the leg is <u>not</u> broken is going to cause me such enormous pain that I will be stopped in my tracks. I so want the leg to not be broken that I cannot accept what my body is actively trying to tell me in the present moment. This is unhealthy grief. The resistance is perfectly understandable. We do not like to feel pain. But the axiom "the only way out is through" rings true for a reason. If I continue to validate the illusion rather than listen to what my actual experience is telling me, day after day, week after week, my leg will heal in its own way, without the proper attention and support. But it will be weakened, fragile, susceptible to further trauma. It will never be able to support me truly in the way that I need it to. Likely if I ever need to quickly dash from one place to another, it will seriously hamper me or give out on me or possibly even break again if I step or land on it wrong. There is a high probability that it will constantly ache, even in some small way and I will attribute that pain to the initial break, rather than to the fact that I never allowed the leg to receive the attention it needed in order to be able to heal in the way it needed. This is complicated grief that has layers of pain, beyond even the original loss.

When people say, with the pain glaringly evident in their eyes, "It's not a big deal. What does it matter anyway? The past is the past. What happened when I was a kid has nothing to do with what's going on today," they are lost in the desert with the pieces of their fragmented self calling out to them, unable to hear the distant call through the dark specter that looms over them. This is the path of depression, anxiety, panic, and despair. And it is exactly what leads to the experience of emptiness within that brings us to the Shadow aspect of Cycle One: addiction. This sense of being lost in the desert is rampant in our society. There is a lot of attention being given to addressing issues of mental illness, mental health, and mental wellness. But we are not being supported truly in the way that we need and that will make a significant difference. For one, we are not grieving nor are we even really being supported in acknowledging how important that is. The Canadian Employment Standards Act addresses bereavement leave, stating that employees are allowed up to two days of unpaid leave within a calendar year in response to the death of certain relatives. Let that sink in for a moment. Two days. Unpaid. Per year. And that says nothing of the full range of events and situations that may bring up grief for us, for which there is no accommodation in any Employment Standards Act. We are told that mental health is being treated with the absolute attention it requires and it deserves, when in actual fact we are barely even being given a camel and a water bottle when we are pitched into the desert and told to cross.

Shadow of Cycle Eight: Ungrieved Losses

All ungrieved loss falls within the Shadow work of Cycle Eight; however, a further delineation shows how different losses can align with the energies found on the Wheel of the Year.

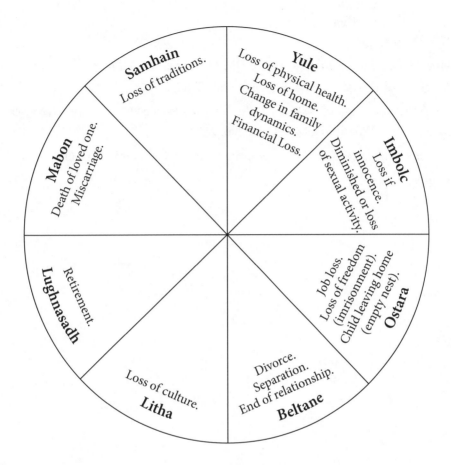

Grief is a natural response to a loss. Rarely have we acknowledged that loss is, was, and always will be, a necessary part of a life's journey. It is impossible to move through life without loss. But it *is* possible to move through life without loss of self. We have all lost much—from the minute to the unfathomable—and rarely have we been given the space to drop into the void and just breathe into the space that may bring us back to new life. Being held and protected while we incubate in that dark space is exactly what calls our soul back. The healing of grief is exactly what is meant by soul retrieval. It *is* soul retrieval. It is nothing less than gathering of the fragmented parts of self and tucking them into a place within our hearts so that they will never ever be lost again.

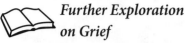 *Further Exploration*
on Grief

Devine, Megan. *It's OK That You're Not OK: Meeting Grief and Loss in a Culture That Doesn't Understand*. Louisville, CO: Sounds True, 2017.

Hughes, Kristoffer. *As the Last Leaf Falls: A Pagan's Perspective on Death, Dying & Bereavement*. Woodbury, MN: Llewellyn, 2020.

Manning, Doug. *Don't Take My Grief Away from Me*. Oklahoma City, OK: In Sight Books, 2011.

Fifty-two

The Lightness of Being

In an article in which he interviewed Roberto Assagioli, psychologist Sam Keen noted that "the Holy of Holies is always empty":[72] a reference to the inner sanctuary of the Tabernacle that was said to house the Ark of the Covenant, which itself was said to house the two stone tablets (or more precisely, the two replacement tablets as the first two were broken) upon which Yahweh had etched the Ten Commandments. This most holy of places to the Hebrew people was only ever to be entered by one person, the high priest, on one day of the year, Yom Kippur, the Day of Atonement. This holy dictum was transgressed in 63 BCE by the Roman general Gnaeus Pompeius Magnus (or Pompey) when he decreed that, as conqueror of Israel and the surrounding territories, he had the victor's right to enter. What he found upon entering was that this sacred place that held the center for an entire people, that was so sacred it could only be accessed once a year by one person, held absolutely nothing.

Or did it?

A Roman general would, of course, be expecting that such a place would hold a priceless treasure. Even outside of the material value of gold or precious stones, Pompey may have considered the stone tablets, outlining as they did the laws of God, to have some immeasurable worth. At least there is something tangible to them. But nothing? Nothing to hang on to, nothing to grasp, nothing to carry back to Rome

....

72. Keen, Sam. "The Golden Mean of Roberto Assagioli." Sam Keen-Thinking Out Loud, December 17, 2009. https://thesamkeen.wordpress.com/interviews-by-sam/interviews -by-sam/the-golden-mean-of-roberto-assagioli/.

in triumph. Nothing of value. This emptiness—this nothingness—must have translated, to a Roman general intent on manifest destiny anyways, as an indication of worthlessness.

But is it?

How do you define the indefinable? How to you put the limitless into a small room? How do you contain that which contains all? The drop is in the ocean. And you certainly can sense the ocean in the drop. But if the ocean is in the drop, that can make for a very damp situation. We can use a trillion words to define and describe the Divine and still we will miss something. The true spirit of Spirit cannot be captured in anything of the tangible, material world. It can only be experienced when we open our hearts to allow that experience to touch us.

Outside of all the moments that make up all the aspects of our lives and who we are, outside of all that static and noise, there is just wholeness. The ultimate "goal" of Alchemy is not the attainment of gold or immortality. It is the Intelligence of the Heart. It turns our worn and battered heart into a heart of gold. It drops us into the timelessness of the love that has always been and will always be. It brings atonement, not through the lens of its definition of making reparation for our sins. Going back to Matthew Fox's statement that "there is no sin, just separation," the Alchemical goal of the Philosopher's Stone and the Intelligence of the Heart is the integration of the absolute knowing of at-one-ment. We have never been, nor can we ever be, separate from the Divine because we are in the Divine and the Divine is in us.

This journey back to Self takes us in numerous directions. One stop along the way is that of transformation. It is very powerful to come to a place where we can recognize that there is choice around the form we present to the world. When we have spent so much of our lives being shaped and defined by the words, expectations, and reactions of others, to come to a place in which we choose our own cloak is powerful indeed. Transformation implies changing from the ground up and from the outside in. The caterpillar transforms into a butterfly and that is an awesome, powerful process to undergo. But there is a bit of an assumption that we would rather be butterflies than caterpillars. There is a niggling sense of progression toward the perfection of a lesser way of being to a preferred way of being. And that approach will always hold the potential to slide back into an experience of separation.

To see ourselves as Divine and to entertain the possibility that, if we are looking for the Holy of Holies, it is within us. That we ourselves are the sacred space that holds the potential for atonement, releasing forever the idea that we can ever be separate. This is transmutation. It is to change something so completely, down to cellular, DNA level that it can never go back to being anything other than what it is. To transmute means to make immutable. It implies changing from Source down and from the inside out, being filled with Light. Transmutation is when the caterpillar and the butterfly both know, forever and without question, that they are one and the same. That there is something of the caterpillar that is always there, even in butterflyness. And there is something of the butterfly that is always there, even when the outer appearance is caterpillar.

We need to go through transformation. We learn important things about who we are and who we are not through that process. Everything we learned about our strengths (who we are and who we are not) and our boundaries (how to make a stand for who we are and reject that which we are not) in Cycle Three is an absolute necessity on the journey. The diamond Hynni of Esteem needs to be the needle of the compass that points our way. Transmutation takes that diamond and spins it so fast, raising its vibration so high, that it becomes a stunning container that is the three-dimensional diamond Hynni of Unity.

Resting in the center of all that you have been and all that you will be, in your blood and your bones, in your heart and your soul, in the fabric of your being and the essence of all you do, you know the absolute, immutable truth.

You were never broken.

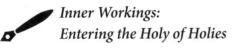

Inner Workings:
Entering the Holy of Holies

Just be. . . .

Fifty-three

Resting in the Cosmic Egg Meditation

In the space between that from which we have come and that toward which we are going, there is a gap. It is the zero point between the inhale and the exhale. It is the pause between the upswing and the downturn. The interlude. The plateau. The respite. It is the grace that holds us as we ready to journey forth once more. We all know this grace, although we spend much time running from it.

In mythology, there are many iterations of the moment that precedes creation. In Greek Orphic tradition, it is the Orphic Egg or the World Egg. This archetypal incubator held the primordial hermaphrodite who, through being the container of equal and balanced energies, became the progenitor of all things. This Orphic Egg was often pictured as encircled by the serpent, the symbol of transformation. In Eastern Vedic tradition, creation is preceded by the Golden Womb which breaks open to reveal two halves, Heaven and Earth. A very similar duality is reflected in the far more modern Finnish epic, *Kalevala*.

an egg's lower half
became mother earth below,
an egg's upper half
became heaven above[73]

In the seasonal cycle, we come to this place of stillness before the Grand Cycle begins once more, time and time again. We are constantly being invited to explore how to begin again. We enter into life from a place of wholeness, then, like Humpty

---

73. Lönnrot and Bosley, *The Kalevala an Epic Poem after Oral Tradition*, 7.

Dumpty, we take a tumble and shatter. As we go through the many trials and triumphs of the journey on the "earth below," we are able to transform. Unlike that tragic egg, we are able to put things somewhat back together again, but there is always a bit of a tell, a hairline sliver, a golden kintsugi thread. The difference is that we do have a key to finding our way to wholeness once again. From the dismemberment of the fall, we hold the key to remembrance. In this time of darkness and stillness, when we rest fully in the "sky above," we have access to that key. We are able to transmute.

This meditation invites you to fully release everything that has brought you to this moment and allow yourself to drop into being fully enwrapped by the support of the All. Be as if in the Golden Womb and drift into the awareness of all you are and all you will be.

Meditation

Close your eyes. Focus on your breath. Slow your breath down and allow yourself to be fully aware of each inhale and each exhale. Allow yourself to be fully aware of the space between, and know that you yourself are in a space between, a place that is both familiar and a place that you have never been before. It is full dark. The sun is but a distant memory in this place of darkness, this place between the space in your breath.

You are in a void, but not in a way that feels empty to you. It feels filled to the brim. You are aware there is a place you have come from. You can feel the Rainbow Bridge that you stepped onto, stretching out behind you; it leads back to that place of so many experiences, so many challenges, so many adventures. There were times when you soared. There were times when you stumbled. You are aware of so much abundance of all that you experienced that lies just out of reach, stretching back along the Rainbow Bridge.

And shifting your focus, you are aware that there is a reflective abundance that awaits you further along the Rainbow Bridge. You don't quite have the shape of it yet, but there is a definite energy to it. You can almost grasp the sense of that energy, almost sense the shape and impetus of it.

As you breathe in this place of darkness, being aware of all that you have come from, and being aware of all that you are moving to, and being aware of the arc beneath your feet, you know that you have always been supported. You see the ribbons of light start to shift and move. The multi-colors start to snake around you, enwrapping you until you are cocooned in a rainbow, enfolded in light. Each inhale anchors the sense of safety. Each exhale solidifies the sense of security. You are so warm, held, protected in this place and you feel the final coming together of all your fragmented parts. Anything that was kept at a distant or any shard that had fallen by the wayside, here in this cocoon of light they all reunite, reforming into the resonance of you, remembering the full harmonics of your song. And this prism of light that surrounds you, as you return to wholeness, as you regain your holy self, each distinct color reverberates back to white light, shell white, egg white. The whole, holy Self that is you is encircled by the white light of the Cosmic Egg and you know, you know who you are: the Golden Seed of Self that you have carried for so long. You are one and the same. First Matter and Philosopher's Stone. Alpha, omega, and every step in between. There is just you and that is All.

Breathe into this place. Breathe into this knowing. Whole and holy.

In the fullness of the eternity that is that breath, you become aware of an energy outside the shell that enfolds you. You know this energy. It is strong. It is sure. It is protective. You have met this energy before, many, many times.

You feel the gentlest of bumps as something lands on the Cosmic Egg that holds you. You feel the nudges and turns as it feels like something wraps itself around and around your current home, your egg-shaped nest. You know with everything that you are and to the depth of your being that your dragon has found you. Your dragon is protecting you. Your dragon is nesting you. Your egg is encircled in strong, dragon energy and you are safe for as long as you need to be here. Just breathing into this space, knowing that when the time is right and in the fullness of time, you will emerge.

And the journey will begin.

Once again.

 *Stone to Deepen
the Meditative Experience*

Lemurian Seed Crystal, said to have originated in the ancient civilization of Mu and called intuition in crystal form, carries the encoded wisdom of Lemuria that is accessed during meditation, and helps our minds with rapid and high-level assimilation.

Fifty-four

. . . .

The Hermetic Principle of Mentalism Contemplation

As we come to the final Sage teaching at the end of a long journey, we actually find ourselves at the very first of all the Hermetic Principles. The Hermetic Principle of Mentalism is addressed in several chapters in *The Kybalion*. It can be encapsulated by a few statements.

THE ALL IS MIND; the Universe is Mental.[74]
The Infinite Mind of THE ALL is the womb of the Universes.[75]

This principle provides the underpinning for the entire alchemical process, which illustrates what is required to move us from THE ALL to the All, from the Above to the Below, from One Mind to all things, from the immaterial to the manifest. It reflects a Platonic perspective of higher reality that indicates that all we know on this plane of physical reality is a dim dilution of the truth. That is not to say that it doesn't contain an aspect or degree of the whole truth, but, as with the archetypes, it is impossible to truly understand their full breadth of scope while we are living a human life. I can understand and name distinct qualities of "mother" through the experience of my mother, but that is only going to be a sliver of the qualities of MOTHER. To truly

....

74. The Three Initiates, "The Kybalion: Chapter II. The Seven Hermetic Principles," www.sacred-texts .com (Yogi Publication Society, 1912), https://www.sacred-texts.com/eso/kyb/kyb04.htm.

75. —-, "The Kybalion: Chapter V. The Mental Universe," www.sacred-texts.com (Yogi Publication Society, 1912), https://www.sacred-texts.com/eso/kyb/kyb07.htm.

touch the energy of MOTHER, we would have to have a complete understanding of all mothers for all people for all parts of the world for all of the time frames of all of existence. If we miss even one person's experience of mother, then we have missed MOTHER.

From our limited human understanding, it is impossible to access the full measure of the truth of existence. Science has been trying for thousands of years, and recent discoveries of the Higgs boson may be bringing us closer to proving what Alchemy and Hermetics have also been saying for thousands of years. Science has known about particles and subatomic particles since the Golden Age of Greek Philosophy. In the fifth century BCE, Leucippus and his student Democritus came up with the concept of the primary indivisible building block of reality and called it the atom. Through the centuries, science has expanded the range of particles that we know about, but what was not known was what informed how the particles moved and what gave them mass. In order to understand how particles have mass, the Higgs field was proposed, but seemed impossible to prove.

Imagine that you have a baseball, a tennis ball, and a foam ball that you drop into a seemingly empty jar. All these balls are about the same size, but as you watch you see that the baseball seems to plummet to the bottom of the jar. The tennis ball moves fairly quickly toward to bottom. The foam ball takes its time. You know there is a reason they move so differently, but there is nothing specific that you can see that creates that cause.

Imagine now that you decide this jar is not empty, but is, in fact, filled with a kind of invisible molasses that would account for why these three balls respond so differently. It would help to bring understanding to the behavior. It would actually indicate that each of these three balls has a different mass that causes them to move differently through this substance. The only problem is, because your molasses is invisible, it can't be proven. This is kind of what happened to particles. In order to explain why they acted the way they did, the Higgs field was determined to be real. It had to be! The only problem was it was impossible to prove—until the Large Hadron Collider at CERN. It was proposed that, if the Higgs field did indeed exist, there would have to be a "force-carrier." If you could find the carrier, you can prove the existence of the field. I may not be able to see the molasses, but if I can feel the stickiness, I know it's there. On March 14, 2013, CERN announced that it indeed discovered the "carrier," called the Higgs boson, which ultimately proved the existence of the Higgs field.[76] Or, in other words, it proved that there is indeed a fabric of reality. There is an ALL and we know this because we have seen, unequivocally, the behavior of the All.

> While All is in THE ALL, it is equally true that THE ALL
> is in ALL. To him that understands this truth hath come
> great knowledge.[77]

The implications have yet to be determined. Science has not yet fully explored this realm and there are other intriguing questions that beckon. But when this fairly recent discovery is filtered through the lens of the personal, what we have is a presentation of reality that is akin to the question, "In the middle of the night, with the lights off, and no one is around to see you, who are you?" When I strip away all the balls I can finally feel the molasses. When I take away all the particles, I can finally enter the experience of the Higgs field. When I strip away the different reflections of the All, I can finally start to know THE ALL that I have always carried within. I can start to get to the absolute truth of what it is. Who I am may be in part the role I play in this situation or in that situation, but the truth of who I am is so much greater than any of the roles I play in any of those situations. It is present in all those different roles, although it is not any of those different roles.

One of the things I have heard more than once in my work is "that was the time when I was not on my path." The Hermetic Principle of Mentalism says that is impossible. Your Essence, your Truth, your Purpose is always with you. It is imbedded into every single cell. You can no more not be on your path in every moment than you can be separated from your DNA as you live and breathe. There is no such thing as fragmentation, and soul retrieval is nothing more than re-membering that you are always whole. This may not be our experience. But it _is_ the truth. You are always part of THE ALL.

....

76. Achintya Rao, "The Higgs Boson: What Makes It Special?" CERN, May 20, 2020, https://home .cern/news/series/lhc-physics-ten/higgs-boson-what-makes-it-special.

77. The Three Initiates, "The Kybalion: Chapter VII. "'The All'" in All," www.sacred-texts.com (Yogi Publication Society, 1912), https://www.sacred-texts.com/eso/kyb/kyb09.htm.

Contemplation

Contemplate how the Integrated Hynni of Unity reflects the Hermetic Principle of Mentalism: that there is just One Thing in spite of all the different facets, and who I am is the truth that lies in the center, refracting out in a multitude of ways.

Chakras to Deepen
the Contemplative Experience

Connect with the **soul star chakra** to open yourself to Unity Consciousness. This chakra is the portal to higher realms, whether from the third dimension to the fourth or from the fourth dimension to the fifth. It is the doorway through which we are able to step into realms that we previously had not thought possible, inviting us to expand our consciousness and see beyond the limitations of what we thought was true.

This chakra connects us to Unity Consciousness. It is through the soul star chakra that we have the opportunity to experience the web of interconnection between all beings. Carl Jung introduced the concept of the collective unconscious that lies at a deeper level in our unconscious than even our personal memories and experiences. The collective unconscious is the storehouse of memory for humankind. It informs our personal unconscious even if we don't have direct access to its contents. The collective unconscious can be seen as reflected through the Earth Star chakra, the portal to the vibrational memory of all of history encoded into the earth itself, the stones, the elements, and nature. The soul star chakra can be seen as the collective superconscious, holding the best potential for humankind, recognizing that we are all one. We are all reflections of Spirit in action, whether we know that or not, align with that or not, working actively for it or actively against it. We are all part of THE ALL and it is through the soul star chakra that we are able to open ourselves to that tangible experience and explore its implications in the here and now of our lives.

Fifty-five

Embraced by the Dark Ritual

At the threshold to the darkest time of the year, there is nothing to be done except breathe into the invitation to rest, listen to the heartbeat of the cosmos, open yourself to the gathering energies, and await the Light.

Symbols to help connect to ritual focus	• Items that help connect to your ancestors, such as photographs or heirloom objects. • Skulls and calaveras (sugar skulls) • Jack-o-lanterns, carved gourds • Statues or photos of psychopomps or those deities that reflect, inhabit, or preside over the otherworld • An image of the Integrating Hynni of Unity
Optional: Stones from Resting in the Cosmic Egg Meditation	• Lemurian Seed Crystal
Items needed for ritual activity	• A fresh unused candle (gold, if you want to align with Hynni) • A lighter • A cauldron • Optional: Candle snuffer • Optional: Oracle deck

Creating the Altar

Whether on your existing altar or on a surface that can act as altar for this ritual, decorate with those elements which reflect the final release, the Great Mystery, and the interconnection of all. This could include an image of the Integrating Hynni of Unity. It is helpful to incorporate symbols associated with the many traditions around the world which honor the profound mystery, the time of transition into the unknown. You may also want to include reflections of the Divine on this sacred space you are creating. This may be statues or photos of the gods and goddesses that are particularly connected to this time. Place the gold candle on your altar and, if you have already done the ritual for Cycle Seven, you can also include your Philosopher's Stone as well.

There are no supplies needed for this ritual. Nothing that is needed other than a comfortable place in which to curl, a favorite chair, or a pile of cushions on the floor. When you are ready, take some time to prepare yourself for ritual (see Appendix D).

The Ritual

Light the gold candle and set the intention to embrace the stillness of the dark and journey wherever it is you are guided to go. Move as close as you can into a fetal position in your chair or on the cushions. You may want to cover yourself with blankets in order to feel completely enveloped and safe. If you have your Philosopher's Stone or a Lemurian Seed Crystal, you may choose to hold the one, the other, or both in your hands.

As you begin to focus solely on your breath, you realize you no longer sit in the place where Cerridwen sits. You are lying in her cauldron, taking your final journey before reemerging into the Light. Imagine that, in this deeply silent space, you hear the faint thrumming rhythm of a drumbeat. This is the sound of her heart, the heart of the mother, the mother of Awen, the mother of All. Allow this faint heartbeat to take you on a journey. There is nothing you need to do. Just allow yourself to be carried along—beat by beat by beat—until the journey comes to its natural close.

Ever so slowly, allow yourself to uncurl. Slowly stretch as you "emerge from the cauldron" and see the golden flame that has held the space while you journeyed. Take some time to gaze into that flame and take this time to open your heart to receive a message from Spirit from the deck you have chosen to work with for the ritual.

Closure of Ritual

Bring your conscious awareness back to your breath. As you focus on the breath moving in and out of your body, pay attention to how your body feels in this moment. This is your natural rhythm. Your unique energy. The flow of your Spirit. The pulse of your Soul. Remember this!

Taking one last moment to anchor the connection to this Soul remembrance, using either your breath or a candle snuffer, release the flame of the gold candle on your altar. What has been experienced in ritual lives forever in your cells. It need only be called forth from within when you choose.

Take some time to move through the directions once more, thanking the elements for helping to hold space and keep you safe through the ritual. Start again in the North with earth, then move through the East with air, the South with fire (put out the tealight in the cauldron at this point), the West with water, ending with the Below of the material plane and the Above of the cosmic plane. Thank and bid farewell to the deities who have been a part of this ritual with you and know that the wheel may turn around you, but you are—as they are—ever at the center.

Clearing Ritual Space

If you have been using an existing altar, you may decide to keep some items, most especially photos of or heirloom objects from your ancestors, on your altar over the course of the cycle.

 Proxy Scrying Recommendations

Campbell, Rebecca (author) and Danielle Noel (illustrator). *The Starseed Oracle*. Carlsbad, CA: Hay House, 2020.

Hart, Francene. *Sacred Geometry Cards for the Visionary Path*. Inner Traditions, 2008.

Krans, Kim. *The Wild Unknown Archetypes Deck and Guidebook* by Kim Krans. San Francisco: HarperOne, 2019.

Listrani, Fabio. *Santa Muerte Oracle*. Woodbury, MN: Llewellyn, 2018.

Fifty-six

We Are All Part of the All

As a drop is to the ocean, we are one with the Divine. And, if this is true for us, it must be true for all. That we are all part of THE ALL.

This is beautiful in theory, but so very challenging, and even painful, when we see wrongs in the world. When we see injustice and inequity, oppression and violation, discrimination and abuse. When we see those who are acting out of Shadow, and control, and righteousness, not only is it almost impossible to see that we are all part of THE ALL, but sometimes we do not <u>want</u> to see it. When you see someone act in a way that offends everything you know in your core being about what is precious and valuable, you do not want to see what connects you to that person. It can be traumatic to even entertain the possibility of commonality. It has always been thus. We see the other as separate because to do anything else would put our own souls at risk of deeper trauma.

To know that the Divine is in all does not mean that everyone is always being informed from a place of Light. We may all be part of THE ALL, but we also exist in the human realm, which offers the experience of separation and limit. To honor Unity Consciousness means that we can come from a place of love. We can access the Intelligence of the Heart. We can respect the Holy of the Holies. And we can still know when we have to draw a line in the sand.

Key Aspects of Cycle Eight[78]

Archetypal Themes	Healing Themes	Indication of Crisis	Healing Practices
Healing from Loss Death; protection; otherworldly connection	Interconnection of all; void; the in-between; holism; bardo; rest	Isolation from humanity; debilitating fear of death; challenge in resolving ancestral legacy issues; inability to live in the moment; past-life bleed-through	Exploration of Transmutation; contemplation of the Hermetic Principle of Mentalism; activation of Integrating Hynni of Unity

Elemental Reflection	Intuitive Guidance and Tool	Alchemical Reflection	Affirmations
Energy	Spirit guides (ancestors); channeling	*Return* The attainment of the Philosopher's Stone and the solid, immutable sense of Self.	I always have been and always will be; my Energy flows with ease; I am part of all that is; the purity of my Essence makes a positive difference to all; I cherish the beauty of all humanity.

....

78. More information on Key Aspects can be found in *The Great Work: Self-Knowledge and Healing Through the Wheel of the Year* by the author (Llewellyn, 2015).

Part Nine
The Noble Art in Practice

Hynni Energy Healing for Practitioners

Fifty-seven

Session Considerations and Ethics

Whenever one considers entering into a healing dynamic, there are certain parameters and criteria, particularly from a practitioner perspective, that one must observe in order to ensure that ethics and standards are being observed. There is a sacred trust between practitioner and client that needs to be acknowledged in all its implications. Ego—unhealthy, that is—needs to be checked at the door, for certainly ambition, control, and attachment to being right have no place in a healing dynamic that holds empowerment as a central guiding principle. The Hynni energy approach sees the practitioner-client dynamic as being on equal footing. The practitioner does not know more than the client. The practitioner may simply have gathered a few more techniques than the client. Ultimately it is the client who knows what is best for themselves, and so powerful things happen when the practitioner invites the client to be an equal partner in the session. The following parameters can serve as checks and balances to address any potential unhealthy ego issues, uphold the sacred trust, and create the most positive healing experience for both practitioner and client.

Scope of Practice

It is highly advised that you not do anything that is outside of your scope of practice, or that falls within the category of a "controlled act" or regulated profession. Hynni is energy healing, recognizing the vibrational nature of energy that includes the physical, emotional, and mental bodies as part of the continuum. We may listen to what the body or the emotions have to say, but this is not a medical practitioner session nor a psychotherapy session. It is listening for where the energy is stuck and gently inviting the

Hynni energy to release the block. An interdisciplinary approach is often very effective. Encouraging the client to seek medical advice or psychotherapeutic support, particularly if the block seems sticky and pernicious, is the best rule of thumb when it comes to maintaining an ethical approach to scope of practice.

Client-Centered versus Practitioner Intuition

As will be seen in the following chapter, Hynni energy sessions invite the active participation of the client in the session process. Though there is a format or script that is followed as a guideline to the shape of the session, where the session goes is going to be directed more by the client than the practitioner. The simplest example of this would be the Guidance Reflection part of the session. It is highly likely that the practitioner might receive some information guidance or see a particular guide show up, but in a Hynni session this information is <u>not</u> shared with the client. The focus is on encouraging the client to connect to a guide on their own and then to help the client to discern the message or the affirmation that is being given from whatever or whoever does show up. This is not to suggest that the practitioner intuition is not bang on. But to focus on highlighting what comes up for the client rather than what comes up for the practitioner cultivates the far greater experience of empowerment for the client. When the need to be right or to reflect the practitioner's connection to intuition trumps the client's experience of growth and self-awareness, it is a skewed compass that is directing the session. This may result in skewed ethics.

Metaphor versus Diagnosis

On that same front, it is not the role of the practitioner to diagnose. To do so most definitely falls outside scope of practice. When we are working with energy and energy healing, best practice is to stay in the realm of metaphor. If, while I am activating the Hynni of Synthesis over the client's heart, I become aware of a dark energy over the heart chakra, I will not go immediately to a place of assuming the person has heart disease, or a broken heart, or an entity attachment. To assume any of those is diagnostic and putting more weight on the practitioner's intuition than the client-centered experience. Instead, the first thing to do would be to say: "I am sensing a dark energy over your heart. Does that mean anything to you? Is there anything that might be weighing on your heart at this time?" If the client says that there is nothing that would be causing anything as far as they know, use the session to explore deeper, if the client is open to doing that. If you have a strong inner nudge that perhaps something medical or deeply emotional might be going on, gently and without alarming the client, recommend a check-in with a specialist or professional. Making sure your feet are solidly in the land of metaphor ensures that you are not slipping into slidey ethics.

Client Will and Choice

Closely connected to a client-centered approach is the issue of client will and choice. Nothing is more important than this. Anything that is in this book can be used in a Hynni session, not just these session scripts. The Inner Workings, the guided visualization meditations, even the Hermetic principle contemplations, all offer different ways to explore Universal energy and archetypal themes. But the choice is always up to the client. Explicit consent is always necessary. It is helpful for the practitioner to state the intent of the approach or the focus of the session before beginning. This can be as simple as: "To explore active and passive energies within, how about a meditation to connect with Grandfather Sun and Grandmother Moon?" or "In alignment with the energies of the Summer Solstice, would you like to do a Hynni session to explore your throat chakra and the Hynni of Expression?" This tells the client right from the start that the reins of the session lie in the client's hands. This is the most powerful way to establish and maintain trust with a client.

Conversational versus Silent

In direct relation to the previous several points, Hynni sessions involve a lot of dialogue. It tends to be a very different experience for the client than receiving a more traditional energy healing session. Because the focus is on connecting the client to the wisdom within, it is necessary for the practitioner to ask questions that will draw the client's attention to their own inner experience. It can be helpful to advise the client of this right at the start. It is not uncommon for a client to say after being asked a question, "Am I supposed to answer that out loud?" Of course, if the client is uncomfortable sharing, silence is fine, but the response to that question would be, "Absolutely, if that feels comfortable for you."

Suggestion versus Direction

Another aspect to consider when it comes to being client-centered is how to introduce themes or avenues of exploration without being controlling or directive. Everything in the session is invitational. Scripts can be tossed out in a second if the client has sniffed out a fertile path for exploration. It can be helpful to remember that a Hynni session holds that sacred purpose of providing the client with the opportunity to reacquaint oneself with Self. The practitioner can—and must—pay attention to the breadcrumbs along the way, but ultimately it is the client's Higher Self that is dropping them. Paying attention to how one asks questions as a practitioner can make all the difference between a vibrant, lush, fruitful session and a controlled, controlling one. An example of a suggestive question would be: "What are the particular strengths of this Bird Guide who has shown up?" An example of a directive question would be: "How does this Bird Guide make you feel strong?" The first question is open-ended and can be responded to with a wide range of possible strengths. The second question contains the presumption that the Bird Guide makes the client feel strong when maybe it doesn't. It could be that the strength of the Bird Guide is in the way it makes the client feel quiet, soft, and contemplative. Language is very important. There are subtle ways that we can consciously or unconsciously nudge people toward a specific way of answering questions. From an ethics perspective, to ensure that the client's experience is as clear and unmuddied as possible, asking open-ended, non-directive questions keeps the focus client-centered.

The Importance of Role-Modeling Self-Determination and Empowerment

The Cycle Five axiom is Walk Your Talk. It almost goes without saying that the process of individuation and self-actualization is an ongoing, lifetime process. But, as was indicated previously, there is also the understanding that, when we are serving as the guide in the exploration of the Dark Forest, we can only take our client as far as we have been willing to go ourselves. If you want to hold safe space in a dynamic of sacred trust in a process of exploration for the client that ultimately holds empowerment, enlightenment, and engagement as points to aim the compass, then those will need to be points that are within the experience and understanding of the practitioner. As a practitioner, it is helpful to go through the Personal Reflections questions and Hynni meditations in *The Great Work: Self-Knowledge and Healing Through the Wheel of the Year* to bring some clarity within one's own process to each of the cycles. We do the work contained within the framework of our Life Purpose before we start to bring it out into the world through our Higher Purpose. In that way, we really <u>do</u> walk our talk.

 Further Exploration on Ethics

Feinstein, David. *Ethics Handbook for Energy Healing Practitioners*. Fulton, CA: Energy Psychology Press, 2011.

Light, Heidi. *Ethics in Energy Medicine: Boundaries and Guidelines for Intuitive and Energetic Practices*. Berkeley, CA: North Atlantic Books, 2018.

Fifty-eight

Pre-Session Assessment

Regardless of whether it is the first session with a client or the hundredth, the practitioner will want to take a few minutes to check in with the client to determine which cycle would be the best to focus on in the session. There are several easy ways to do this, and the practitioner can use one method or a combination of several.

Seasonal Assessment

Look to the cycle that is reflected in nature and use that as the guide to which cycle to work on and which Hynni to activate and amplify.

Energy Scanning

With the client on the bodywork table or sitting in a chair, activate your palm chakras and do a quick scan of the chakras from root to soul star. Pay attention to any shifts in energy as you scan. Heat, cold, static, or heaviness can all be possible indications that there is a block in the chakra around which these are experienced. This would indicate which chakra needs focus and the Hynni session would be around the cycle associated with that chakra.

Pendulum

Rather than using their hands to scan, the practitioner can use a pendulum to determine which chakras are blocked or could benefit from some energy work. Again, moving from the root chakra up to the soul star chakra, hold the pendulum steady in place. (Note that for the root chakra it works best to hold the pendulum down by the knees.) A clockwise swing indicates the chakra is open and flowing. A counter-clockwise swing would indicate a block and that the cycle associated with this chakra would be a good candidate for a session.

Chakra Stones

It is easy enough to create a full set of chakra stones. The simplest and most readily accessible stones to put together for a set would be: Bloodstone (root), Carnelian (sacral), Citrine (solar plexus), Rose Quartz (heart), Aquamarine (throat), Lapis Lazuli (brow), Amethyst (crown), and clear Quartz (soul star). But you can play with what stones resonate with you the most, or craft a set using the high-vibration stones of the new consciousness that are introduced before each cycle meditation. For the purpose of a Hynni session, assessment is as easy as having the client pull one of the stones from a bag.

Chumpi Stones

These alabaster pieces are part of the tradition of a line of Andean shamans and come in sets of either twelve or seven. For Hynni assessment, it is best to work with a set of seven. Associated with seven sacred mountains and aligned with the seven chakras, these are excellent indicators of which chakra, and thus cycle, needs attention. To account for the possibility that at times it will be the soul star chakra (Cycle Eight) that requires the focus, I have taken the liberty of adding a specially charged stone into my set and have found that it works very well with the Andean stones. As with chakra stones assessment, this technique is also as easy as having the client pull one of the chumpi stones from a bag. The number of nodes on the stone indicate which chakra is requesting energy work.

Prescriptions

The table found at the end of each final cycle chapter includes Indication of Crisis, a list of five circumstances that could indicate a benefit to focusing on that particular cycle. These can be used as a checklist before each session to give a quick indication of which cycles may benefit from energy healing. If there are several that show up, chat with the client to determine which one to focus on in the current session. Other cycles can be addressed in future sessions.

Indications for Cycle One

[ ] A sudden, unexpected loss or change of life circumstance

[ ] Feeling isolated or disconnected from the world or other people

[ ] Fear around new directions in life

[ ] A persistent sense of being "ungrounded"

[ ] Being triggered by spending time with your family

Indications for Cycle Two

[ ] Overwhelmed by emotions

[ ] An inability to identify or experience emotions

[ ] Excessive or extreme reactions to current situations

[ ] Difficulty in relationships with others

[ ] Discomfort or shame regarding sexuality

Indications for Cycle Three

[ ] A shaky sense of self-esteem

[ ] Inflated guilt over little incidences

[ ] Challenges or uncertainty while in the company of others

[ ] Feeling not in control of one's own life or choices

[ ] An inability to establish healthy boundaries

Indications for Cycle Four

[ ] A lack of passion for activities and ventures

[ ] Resentment toward others

[ ] Unhealthy relationship dynamics

[ ] Lack of compassion or empathy for others

[ ] Burnout (particularly as relates to healthcare workers and healers)

Indications for Cycle Five

[ ] Difficulty sharing your thoughts and beliefs

[ ] Repressed creativity

[ ] A sense that what you say doesn't matter

[ ] An excessive need to communicate

[ ] A depleted sense of will or belief in the efficacy of your choices

Indications for Cycle Six

[ ] Confused or racing thoughts

[ ] Difficulty in "turning off the brain"

[ ] Critical or harsh inner dialogue

[ ] Difficulty envisioning or planning the future

[ ] Under- or overactive imagination

Indications for Cycle Seven

[ ] Lack of trust that all will work out

[ ] Resistance to life's lessons

[ ] Attachment to proof

[ ] Having one's "head in the clouds"

[ ] Avoidance of physical or emotional needs

Indications for Cycle Eight

[ ] Isolation from humanity

[ ] Debilitating fear of death

[ ] Challenge in resolving ancestral legacy issues

[ ] Inability to live in the moment

[ ] Past-life bleed-through

Pre-Session Chat

If it is possible, it is always the best option to take some time to chat with the client before the start of the energy work. Engaging active listening and tuning one's ears to "cycle language" can be very helpful in determining what would be the best focus in session.

Questions to help prompt a sense of which cycle to work with:

1. Do you feel you are gearing up to something or gearing down from something?
   (Gearing up would be Cycles 1, 2, 3, 4. Gearing down would be Cycles 5, 6, 7, 8.)

2. Do you feel called to action or does it feel like a period of rest for you?
   (Action would be Cycles 2, 3, 4, 6, 7. Period of rest would be Cycles 1, 5, 8.)

3. Does your process feel more externally or internally focused at this time?
   (External would be Cycles 2, 4, 5, 6, 8. Internal would be Cycles 1, 3, 7.)

Self-Actualization Survey

The last method for determining which cycle to work with is the Self-Actualization Survey. This is best to do once a year. In *The Great Work: Self-Knowledge and Healing Through the Wheel of the Year*, this survey is presented on December 20 as a moment of pause between Grand Cycles. In a session context, this would be helpful to give to the client to fill out in order to get a sense of which cycles may be best to focus on for the next several sessions, or which cycles will likely continue to crop up as issues over the course of a year. It takes some time to go through, so you might prefer to give it to your client to fill out before coming to the session.

The Self-Actualization Survey as Hynni Indicator

Respond to each statement below according to a scale from 0 to 5. Allow your response to come from your first, intuitive sense of where you are at today. Mark down the number according to the range below in the space provided beside each statement.

0	1	2	3	4	5
Never	Rarely	Sometimes	Often	Frequently	Always

1. I respond to new situations enthusiastically. _____

2. I balance my physical, emotional, intellectual, and spiritual needs. _____

3. I am comfortable with confrontation. _____

4. I eat properly and nutritiously. _____

5. I respond to my hurt with gentleness. _____

6. I have creative outlets. _____

7. I have compassion toward others. _____

8. I feel secure. _____

9. I notice and work with synchronicity. _____

10. I listen to my anger and communicate its message appropriately. _____

11. I am reconciled to the knowledge that my life will come to an end. _____

12. I know how to discern between safe and unsafe people. _____

13. I speak my truth with integrity. _____

14. I allow experiences of awe and wonder. _____

15. I am comfortable with solitude. _____

16. I embrace my sexuality. _____

17. I recognize there are mysteries I cannot know in this life. _____

18. I take ownership for my decisions. _____

19. I am confident in my ability to plan and manifest. _____

20. I know my worth and value. _____

21. I own my choices. _____

22. I know I am more than my job. _____

23. I release that which no longer serves me. _____

24. I have a supportive network of friends. _____

25. I honor the teachings of my elders, my heritage, and my ancestors. _____

26. I know my path is not everyone's path. _____

27. I am open to love. _____

28. I listen to my intuition. _____

29. I communicate to others whether they are able to hear me or not. _____

30. I recognize my fear is information to be explored, rather than an absolute message to stop. _____

31. I am actively fulfilling what I feel to be my purpose in this life. _____

32. I grow from all my relationships. _____

33. I embrace the full range of my emotions. _____

34. I establish appropriate boundaries and know how to say no. _____

35. I take time to connect with the Divine. _____

36. I celebrate my accomplishments. _____

37. I know what strengths I contain within that will carry me through any of life's challenges. _____

38. I am open to the transcendent. _____

39. I know my expression in the world is important. _____

40. My connection to the world and to others is important to me. _____

Transcribe the number response you have assigned to each statement onto the following Table. For example, if you responded with a 4 (frequently) to statement 1 and 2 (sometimes) to statement 2, put 4 in the box for Cycle 1 and 2 in the box for Cycle 6. When all have been transcribed, tally up the numbers in each cycle box to get that cycle's total.

Key to Cycle Associations

Cycle 1	Cycle 2
1. _____	5. _____
4. _____	10. _____
8. _____	24. _____
12. _____	30. _____
20. _____ Cycle total _____	33. _____ Cycle total _____
Cycle 3	**Cycle 4**
3. _____	7. _____
15. _____	16. _____
22. _____	27. _____
34. _____	32. _____
37. _____ Cycle total _____	40. _____ Cycle total _____
Cycle 5	**Cycle 6**
6. _____	2. _____
13. _____	18. _____
21. _____	19. _____
29. _____	28. _____
39. _____ Cycle total _____	36. _____ Cycle total _____
Cycle 7	**Cycle 8**
9. _____	11. _____
14. _____	17. _____
23. _____	25. _____
31. _____	26. _____
35. _____ Cycle total _____	38. _____ Cycle total _____

Cycle with the lowest total: _____

This is the cycle that could benefit from Hynni energy healing as well as ongoing attention post-session.

Cycles with the next lowest totals: _____, _____

These are the cycles that could benefit from some attention, inquiry, and processing, perhaps in later sessions.

Cycle with the highest total: _____

This is the cycle that provides strength, support, and insight to the client, although there may be benefit to exploring whether there is any spiritual bypassing at play.

Fifty-nine

Scripts for Hynni Energy Healing Sessions

Following are sample scripts for each of the cycles that can be used by practitioners for Hynni energy healing sessions. The entry into each session follows these same steps:

1. Center yourself, call in your own guides, and connect with client by placing your hands gently on their shoulders, waiting for the "click" that indicates that you are in sync.

2. Relax client with head connection. Slip your hands under the client's head, fitting your fingers under the groove right at the base of the cranium. Pulling ever so gently to allow a stretch down the spine, very slowly angle your hands first one direction then the other in order to rock your client's head from side to side. This loosens any tension in the neck and helps drop your client deeper into the session. After a few moments, return the client's head to the center position and slide your hands out from beneath the head.

3. Center client with solar plexus connection. Move from the head to the solar plexus, making sure you never lose connection with the client. This may mean keeping one hand gently resting on the client's head as you place the other hand on the solar plexus and then bringing the first hand to join the second. Ask the client to breathe into the place beneath your hands, paying attention to the rise and fall of the torso.

From here you can move into the main body of the session, which differs with each cycle. Note that with small adaptations, these sessions can be done with the client in a chair rather than on a bodywork table or via distance session. With a distance session, ask the client to visualize the Hynni symbol as you imagine that the client is lying in front of you and allow your hands to attune to the client's energy field in the etheric space before you.

Cycle One: The Solid Hynni of Grounding

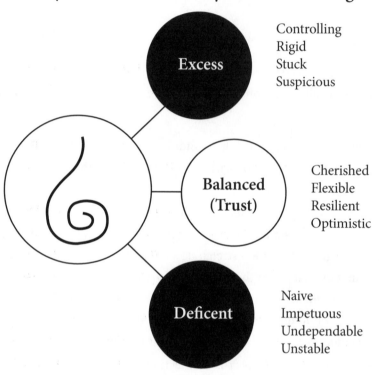

At times when one is feeling that the ground beneath one's feet is tenuous at best, it is important to consciously tether oneself to that which is going to provide continued encouragement and positive direction. When all else in our lives seems to be up for grabs, particularly if we have gone through great loss, sometimes it is the one thing that is unquestionably foundational that provides the keystone for us to start to rebuild.

If the client has indicated any of the following circumstances, a session to activate the Solid Hynni of Grounding would be appropriate:

- Going through a time of upheaval
- Depleted energy levels
- A time of uncertainty following a loss (including giving up an addiction or unhealthy habit)
- Realization of disconnection with Essence
- Feeling lost and alone

Working with the Solid Hynni of Grounding encourages the client to find or craft the reassuring ground beneath their feet. It conveys the sense of calm within the chaos that reminds the client that there can be a sense of direction, even in the dark, and that the Earth can support us both physically and energetically.

Before starting the session, convey to your client that you will be focusing on activating the energies of Cycle One to which the client is already connected. These energies are innate within us, although sometimes we do not consciously acknowledge them. The intent of this session is to reawaken the connection with the Divine Child within. Ask for permission from the client to touch shoulders, head, solar plexus, and feet <u>only</u>. If express permission is not given, you must hold your hands above those parts of the body at the required times.

Cycle One Session

1–3. See start of this chapter.

4. Say the following (or your own adaptation of the following) to guide your client into the working of the session.

  Begin to become aware of your body. This body that has carried you through so many experiences. It has been with you from the beginning and will be with you to the very end. Others may come and go, but you can be certain that your body is a constant. It is yours and it is a miracle. As you breathe, become acutely aware of the movement of your body. The rise and fall of your torso. The sensation of your diaphragm inflating like a balloon. Imagine that each breath is filling you with health and vitality. Become

aware of the blood coursing through your system, nourishing you. Become
aware of all the pathways and mechanisms that go on in your body at every
moment without any conscious thought from you. The messages from your
brain. The communication to the nerves and muscles. Breathe into each
area of your body and truly experience it for the wonder that it is.

5. Lifting your hands from the client's body and raising them above the torso, activate the Solid Hynni of Grounding. (For distance sessions, ask the client to also visualize the Hynni symbol.) Visualize waves of golden light sending the energy of the Hynni toward the client's body. If it feels that your hands want to move this energy around the client's body, do so. Continue to move your hands and send the energy of the Solid Hynni of Grounding as you dialogue with your client through sections 6–9.

6. Ask client to remember a time of upheaval and how that felt in the body. This could be a current situation. Where is it felt in the body? How does it feel in the body? What descriptive words fit with the sensation? Is this a familiar sensation? If familiar, when was the earliest time in their life that the client experienced this sensation? Explore the felt-sense of discomfort in the body.

7. Ask the client to recall how they dealt with upheaval. If there was an earlier remembrance of this sensation, focus on how discomfort was handled then. How were they supported through the process? If they did not feel supported, how did the client react in order to come through the situation? What role or "false self" was taken on for survival or acceptance? What self-soothing habits were born? Invite the client to engage the Shadow challenge of Cycle One: the ways in which they felt abandoned and the ways they tried to keep themself safe.

8. Amplifying the energy of the Solid Hynni of Grounding symbol, invite the client to visualize the Infant or Toddler Child Within, encouraging the client to see the situation through the eyes of that Inner Being. Ask the client to be open to hearing what the Inner Infant or the Inner Toddler needed in the past situation and how that may relate to what the Inner Infant or the Inner Toddler needs in the current situation. *This is a simple shift but can be very profound for the client.*

9. Releasing the connection to both the situation and the Inner Child, bring the client's attention back to their breath and ask the client to invite in an animal teacher or guide. If there was an animal—one that walks, trots, hops, or slithers upon the Earth– that would best address the situation or the needs of the Inner Child, which animal would that be? When one appears, ask the client to connect more deeply with that animal. What are the particular qualities and strengths of this animal? How do those qualities or strengths relate to the situation? How might embodying those qualities allow for a different approach to handling the situation? In what ways does this animal offer solid support and guidance? Invite the client to craft a supportive message or affirmation from the animal guide. This should be short enough to be easily remembered and in the present tense.

10. Moving back to the client's head, place your left hand underneath on the nape of the neck and hold your right hand above the client's brow chakra. Repeat the client's animal guide affirmation three times out loud so the client can hear. If the client has had difficulty crafting an affirmation, any one of the following can be used.

I am safe and secure.
My body is strong and healthy.
I know how to take care of myself.
I create a solid foundation upon which to build.
I am comfortable with change.

11. As you are imbuing the client with the energy of the affirmation, invite the client to focus once more on their breath but this time visualizing it as the color "red," breathing a rich, vibrant red into each and every cell in their body.

12. Release your hands from the neck and brow. Begin to "sweep" down the client's whole body with hands slightly above the body, unruffling and smoothing the energy field and bringing any excess energy down toward the feet. After a final sweep, when it feels that the entire energy field is balanced, place your hands firmly on the top of your client's feet.

13. Give client a few minutes to come back into the present time and space. When client has opened their eyes and is ready to sit up, you may choose to have client pick a rune for a final message and guidance. If you are working with stone runes, you will likely need to provide interpretation for the client. If you are using one of many rune oracle decks, invite the client to interpret what the image holds for them as a message.

14. Give client a glass of water. Take some time to process the experience, encouraging client to identify a significant takeaway that will be helpful post-session.

Entry into Session Cycle One	• Connect with client (1) • Relax client (2–3) • Guide client into session focus (4) • Activate Solid Hynni of Grounding (5)
Exploration of Blocks and Shadow	• Invite client to explore sense of upheaval/discomfort (6) • Psychological Reflection: Explore Shadow challenge of cycle: trust/abandonment (7) • Development Reflection: Connect to Inner Infant or Toddler (8)
Invitation to Shift into Light and Essence	• Guidance Reflection: Connect with animal guide (9) • Affirmation (10) • Energetic Reflection: Color breathwork (11)
Exit from Session	• Aura sweep and ground (12) • Optional Intuitive Reflection: Runes (13) • Debrief session (14)
What client can do post-session to continue to connect with cycle energies	• Breathwork, conscious breathing

Cycle Two: The Loving Hynni of Ebb and Flow

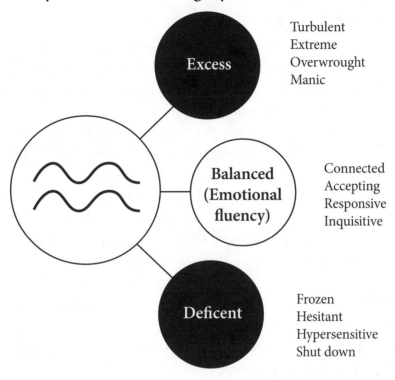

Excess

Turbulent
Extreme
Overwrought
Manic

Balanced
(Emotional
fluency)

Connected
Accepting
Responsive
Inquisitive

Deficent

Frozen
Hesitant
Hypersensitive
Shut down

The presence of emotions is a constant in our lives. As much as we may try to disconnect ourselves from them, we cannot except to our detriment. Even a slow leak can cause enormous damage if it is not addressed. Emotions can wreak havoc on the balance in our lives if we choose to push aside the ones that make us uncomfortable. When instead we open ourselves to their valuable wisdom, the subtext at play is the message that our needs are important, our experience is valid, and our worth is celebrated.

If the client has indicated any of the following circumstances, a session to activate the Loving Hynni of Ebb and Flow would be appropriate:

- Overwhelmed by emotions
- An inability to identify or experience emotions
- Excessive or extreme reactions to current situations

- Difficulty in relationships with others
- Discomfort or shame regarding sexuality

Working with the Loving Hynni of Ebb and Flow encourages the client to find a way of connection to inner equilibrium, even if circumstances that surround the client are in a place of upheaval. It invites surrender to the movement of waves, experiencing them as rocking rather than turbulent.

Before starting the session, convey to your client that you will be focusing on activating the energies of Cycle Two to which the client is already connected. These energies are innate within us, although sometimes we do not consciously acknowledge them. The intent of this session is to embrace the wisdom of connecting to our lush, inner emotional life. Ask for permission from the client to touch shoulders, head, solar plexus, and feet <u>only</u>. If express permission is not given, you must hold your hands above those parts of the body at the required times.

Cycle Two Session

1–3. See start of this chapter

4. Say the following (or your own adaptation of the following) to guide your client into the working of the session.

> *Begin to become aware of your body. Of the movement of breath through your body. Of the flow of energy through your body. Be aware of the blood coursing through your entire system and the pathways that allow it to reach every single part of you. See the blood that flows as vital and healthy, nourishing and strengthening you. Gradually expand your awareness to encompass the earth. Reach out with a sense of flow to the streams, rivers, lakes and oceans. Allow yourself to be taken on a journey from the littlest brook to the most magnificent waterfall, above ground and the hidden subterranean passageways. You are a drop and yet you are part of the whole network of waterways that brings nourishment to all forms of life.*

5. Lifting your hands from the client's body and raising them above the torso, activate the Loving Hynni of Ebb and Flow. (For distance sessions, ask the client to also visualize the Hynni symbol.) Visualize waves of golden light send-

ing the energy of the Hynni toward the client's body. If it feels that your hands want to move this energy around the client's body, do so. Continue to move your hands and send the energy of the Loving Hynni of Ebb and Flow as you dialogue with your client through sections 6–10.

6. Ask client to connect to a time when they put someone else's needs ahead of their own. This could be a current situation. What is the main emotion that comes up as the client reflects on the situation? Where is it felt in the body? How does it feel in the body? What descriptive words fit with the sensation? How does it feel that the emotion is moving? Does it feel stuck or flowing? Does it feel like a gentle stream or a wild tsunami wave?

7. Ask client to explore how they respond to this emotional energy. Does it feel comfortable or uncomfortable? Is this an emotional energy that the client is able to embrace or is there an impulse to turn away from it? If the impulse is to turn away, what would invite the client to greet this emotion, no matter how uncomfortable, and be willing to hear its message?

8. Guide client to explore the energy and message of the emotion. What is it about the situation that makes the client feel this emotion? If the emotion was a person what would they say to the client? What would the message be? How does this message speak to the client's needs?

9. Amplifying the energy of the Loving Hynni of Ebb and Flow symbol, invite the client to visualize the Preschool Child Within, encouraging the client to appreciate the innate instinctive sense that this Inner Being brings to all experiences. Ask the client to be open to holding space to support and validate this emotional perspective. *This is a simple shift but can be very profound for the client.*

10. Releasing the connection to the Inner Child and any emotions that have been activated, bring the client's attention back to their breath and ask client to invite in an aquatic animal teacher or guide. If there was an animal—one that moves through the earth's waters or both water and land—that would best address the situation, which animal would that be? When one appears, ask the client to connect more deeply with that animal. What are the particular qualities and strengths of this animal? How do those qualities or strengths relate

to the situation or emotion? How might embodying those qualities allow for a different acceptance of the emotional energy of the situation? Invite the client to craft a supportive message or affirmation from the animal guide. This should be short enough to be easily remembered and in the present tense.

11. Moving back to the client's head, place your left hand underneath on the nape of the neck and hold your right hand above the client's brow chakra. Repeat the client's animal guide affirmation three times out loud so the client can hear. If the client has had difficulty crafting an affirmation, any one of the following can be used.

I go with the flow.
I release with ease.
I move through my life with fluidity.
My emotions run clear.
My emotions help to guide my healthy choices.
I am able to share my feelings with others.
I am cleansed by the blessings that surround me.

12. As you are imbuing the client with the energy of the affirmation, invite the client to focus once more on their breath but this time visualizing it as the color "orange," breathing a bright, fresh orange into each and every cell in their body

13. Release your hands from the neck and brow. Begin to "sweep" down the client's whole body with hands slightly above the body, unruffling and smoothing the energy field and bringing any excess energy down toward the feet. After a final sweep, when it feels that the entire energy field is balanced, place your hands firmly on the top of your client's feet.

14. Give client a few minutes to come back into the present time and space. When client has opened their eyes and is ready to sit up, you may choose to have client drink a cup of loose-leaf tea and look for symbols in the leaves that provide a final message and guidance, taking some time to process the experience,

allowing client to express their experience of the session and the significant takeaway that will be helpful post-session. If you choose not to use tea leaves as intuitive guidance, be sure to give the client a glass of water to ground and bring him or her fully back into the body as you debrief what came up for the client in the session.

Entry into Session Cycle Two	• Connect with client (1) • Relax client (2–3) • Guide client into session focus (4) • Activate Loving Hynni of Ebb and Flow (5)
Exploration of Blocks and Shadow	• Psychological Reflection: Explore Shadow challenge of cycle: feelings/codependency (6) • Invite client to explore emotions of situation (7–8) • Development Reflection: Connect to Inner Preschool Child (9)
Invitation to Shift into Light and Essence	• Guidance Reflection: Connect with aquatic guide (10) • Affirmation (11) • Energetic Reflection: Color breathwork (12)
Exit from Session	• Aura sweep and ground (13) • Optional Intuitive Reflection: Tea leaf reading (14) • Debrief session (14)
What client can do post-session to continue to connect with cycle energies	• Drumming

Cycle Three: The Centering Hynni of Esteem

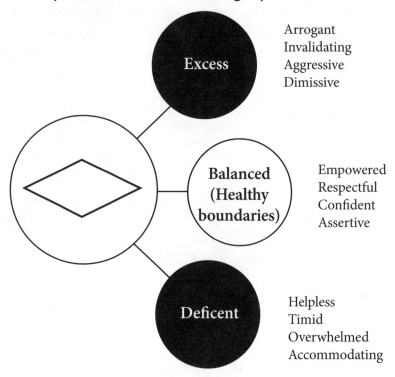

Excess
Arrogant
Invalidating
Aggressive
Dimissive

Balanced (Healthy boundaries)
Empowered
Respectful
Confident
Assertive

Deficent
Helpless
Timid
Overwhelmed
Accommodating

Knowing who we are and valuing who we are, as separate and unique from everyone else in our lives, is an absolute imperative if we want to instill a solid sense of self-esteem within and hope to establish healthy relationships in the future. The recognition of strong and appropriate boundaries, the courage to honor and protect those boundaries, and the care to ensure the internal dialogue is supportive and encouraging are all aspects of coming back to life.

If the client has indicated any of the following circumstances, a session to activate the Centering Hynni of Esteem would be appropriate:

- A shaky sense of self-esteem
- Inflated guilt over little incidences
- Challenges or uncertainty while in the company of others

- Feeling not in control of one's own life and choices
- An inability to establish healthy boundaries

Working with the Centering Hynni of Esteem encourages the client to have a definitive sense of that which is self and that which is not self, exploring the qualities that can be claimed as self and releasing those qualities that have been imposed by others. This Hynni symbol represents the Seed of Self that is to be planted and cultivated in order to manifest to rich harvest of self-fulfillment.

Before starting the session, convey to your client that you will be focusing on activating the energies of Cycle Three to which the client is already connected. These energies are innate within us, although sometimes we do not consciously acknowledge them. The intent of this session is to reconnect the client with the True Self and the commitment to putting that self in the center of one's life. Ask for permission from the client to touch shoulders, head, solar plexus, and feet <u>only</u>. If express permission is not given, you must hold your hands above those parts of the body at the required times.

Cycle Three Session

1–3. See start of this chapter

4. Say the following (or your own adaptation of the following) to guide your client into the working of the session.

> *Bring your awareness to the center of your torso. What does it feel like in that space in your body? How much tension do you generally hold there? As you breathe, allow yourself to become aware of what the tension may be trying to tell you about what is going on in your life at this time. Or what it may be telling you about your feelings about yourself and your ability to manoeuvre through life's challenges. Be aware, as you breathe, of the movement of air. Connect with the sense of openness and freedom that comes with the movement of the air currents. Of freshness and clarity and direction. Allow the movement of air to clear out anything of density, weight and heaviness in your solar plexus.*

5. Lifting your hands from the client's body and raising them above the torso, activate the Centering Hynni of Esteem. (For distance sessions, ask the client to also visualize the Hynni symbol.) Visualize waves of golden light sending the energy of the Hynni toward the client's body. If it feels that your hands want to move this energy around the client's body, do so. Continue to move your hands and send the energy of the Centering Hynni of Esteem as you dialogue with your client through sections 6–10.

6. Ask client to connect to an inner sense of self and all that is contained within that delineation. If there is anything that feels "not of the self," anything that feels like it is someone else's overlay (parent, partner, peer), visualize that as being released and set outside the client's energy field. Guide client to imagine opening the windows within and allowing a fresh breeze to clear out all the old, stagnant thoughts, beliefs, and identifications that no longer fit.

7. In the space that remains, ask client to explore the voice of the Inner Critic. What has been internalized as the voice of self that does not come from an encouraging, supportive place? What are the messages that tend to undermine the sense of self? If possible, explore the source of these negative messages (parents, teachers) and where they actually belong in the "not of the self" category.

8. Guide client to explore what unconscious reactions or defenses come into play in an internal effort to appease the Inner Critic or to escape from its harsh messaging. Isolation and withdrawal? People-pleasing or perfectionism? In what ways does the client shift away from the authentic sense of self in order to feel accepted by that inner voice?

9. Amplifying the energy of the Centering Hynni of Esteem symbol, invite the client to visualize the School Age Child Within, encouraging him or her to appreciate energy, vitality, willingness to engage in life that this Inner Child brings. Ask the client to be open to prioritizing this Inner Being, protecting him or her from any reflection that carries the taint of shame. *This is a simple shift but can be very profound for the client.*

10. Bring client's attention back to their breath and ask client to invite in a bird guide. If there was a creature—one that soars through the air or is winged but

land-bound—that would best address the situation, which creature would that be? When one appears, ask the client to connect more deeply with that bird guide. What are its particular qualities and strengths? How do those qualities or strengths relate to the situation or emotion? How might embodying those qualities allow for a different acceptance of the client's True Self? Invite the client to craft a supportive message or affirmation from the animal guide. This should be short enough to be easily remembered and in the present tense.

11. Moving back to the client's head, place your left hand underneath on the nape of the neck and hold your right hand above the client's brow chakra. Repeat the client's bird guide affirmation three times out loud so the client can hear. If the client has had difficulty crafting an affirmation, any one of the following can be used.

> *I am open to a fresh perspective.*
> *I experience freedom in my life.*
> *I am comfortable saying "no."*
> *I am responsible for my own feelings and experiences.*
> *I am important and valuable.*

12. As you are imbuing the client with the energy of the affirmation, invite the client to focus once more on their breath but this time visualizing it as the color "yellow," breathing a strong, empowered sunshine yellow into each and every cell in their body

13. Release your hands from the neck and brow. Begin to "sweep" down the client's whole body with hands slightly above the body, unruffling and smoothing the energy field and bringing any excess energy down toward the feet. After a final sweep, when it feels that the entire energy field is balanced, place your hands firmly on the top of your client's feet.

14. Give client a few minutes to come back into the present time and space. When client has opened their eyes and is ready to sit up, you may choose to have client pick an oracle card from one of your favorite or preferred decks for a final message and guidance. Invite the client to interpret what the image holds for him/her as a message.

15. Give client a glass of water and take some time to process the experience, allowing client to express their experience of the session and the significant takeaway that will be helpful post-session.

Entry into Session Cycle Three	• Connect with client (1) • Relax client (2–3) • Guide client into session focus (4) • Activate Centered Hynni of Esteem (5)
Exploration of Blocks and Shadow	• Psychological Reflection: Explore Shadow challenge of cycle: identity/boundaries (6) • Invite client to explore Inner Critic (7–8) • Development Reflection: Connect to Inner School Age Child (9)
Invitation to Shift into Light and Essence	• Guidance Reflection: Connect with bird guide (10) • Affirmation (11) • Energetic Reflection: Color breathwork (12)
Exit from Session	• Aura sweep and ground (13) • Optional Intuitive Reflection: Oracle (14) • Debrief session (15)
What client can do post-session to continue to connect with cycle energies	• Toning, chanting, singing

Cycle Four: The Bridging Hynni of Synthesis

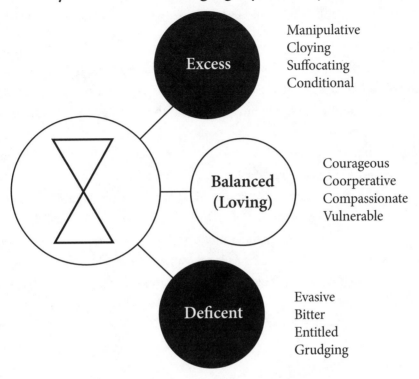

Excess: Manipulative, Cloying, Suffocating, Conditional

Balanced (Loving): Courageous, Coorperative, Compassionate, Vulnerable

Deficent: Evasive, Bitter, Entitled, Grudging

When we have the time and space to focus on ourselves and be accountable to ourselves, it is relatively simple and straightforward to be healthy and balanced in our life and our responses to situations. The challenge comes when we are faced with other people who have their own issues, perspectives, needs, and biases. When we have done the work of the self, it is important to pay attention to the work of interpersonal dynamics.

If the client has indicated any of the following circumstances, a session to activate the Bridging Hynni of Synthesis would be appropriate:

- A lack of passion for activities and ventures
- Resentment toward others
- Unhealthy relationship dynamics

- Lack of compassion or empathy for others
- Burnout (particularly as relates to healthcare workers and healers)

Working with the Bridging Hynni of Synthesis explores how solidly we have integrated the strength we came to in Cycle Three. It takes the Seed of Self and brings it into direct relation with the other. This Hynni symbol represents the meeting place of opposites—spirit and matter, self and other—and the touch point that can bring life to both.

Before starting the session, convey to your client that you will be focusing on activating the energies of Cycle Four to which the client is already connected. These energies are innate within us, although sometimes we do not consciously acknowledge them. The intent of this session is to help the client's awareness of how they operate in relationship, whether familial, romantic, friendship, or work. Ask for permission from the client to touch shoulders, head, solar plexus, and feet <u>only</u>. If express permission is not given, you must hold your hands above those parts of the body at the required times.

Cycle Four Session

1–3. See start of this chapter

4. Say the following (or your own adaptation of the following) to guide your client into the working of the session.

> *Bring your awareness to the center of your chest, specifically around your heart center. Feel the attention focused there as a soothing, loving hug, reminding you that you are important and loved. That you are truly the center of your own universe. As you breathe into that part of your body, allow yourself to expand so that you are aware of the ground beneath you and the sky above you. Feel yourself as connected with all that supports your foundation—with the energy that pulses through the earth, feeding and nourishing you. Feel yourself connected with all that inspires you— with the highest energy of the cosmos. You are human and you are spirit. You are your feelings and you are your intellect. You are the force of pure emotion and the cool gaze of reason. You walk your path alone but in the company of others. The interplay of opposing poles comes together in the*

heart. Not at odds, but each validating the other, making them both greater than they are separately.

5. Lifting your hands from the client's body and raising them above the torso, activate the Bridging Hynni of Synthesis. (For distance sessions, ask the client to also visualize the Hynni symbol.) Visualize waves of golden light sending the energy of the Hynni toward the client's body. If it feels that your hands want to move this energy around the client's body, do so. Continue to move your hands and send the energy of the Bridging Hynni of Synthesis as you dialogue with your client through sections 6–10.

6. Ask client to connect to a significant relationship, one that may feel out of balance or experiencing a wobble in the dance at the moment, imagining that dynamic playing out and paying attention to what may be contributing to the imbalance.

7. Invite the client to imagine the relationship dynamic as the Hynni symbol, with the client represented by one of the triangles and the other person represented by the other. Are the triangles equal in size? Do they meet at the point or does one triangle cut into the space of the other? Have the client see the relationship reflected in the Hynni symbol and explore what that may mean.

8. Now invite the client to shift the symbol as they are seeing it into the true Bridging Hynni of Synthesis. What would need to happen to balance those triangles and have them not encroach on each other?

9. Amplifying the energy of the Bridging Hynni of Synthesis symbol, invite the client to visualize the Adolescent Child, connecting to an endless energy to engage, to experience situations and relationships with the full force of Being. Ask the client to be open to embracing this Inner Being, knowing that that level of passion for life can carry with it a risk—the risk to be hurt, the risk to make a mistake, the risk to be vulnerable—but that with the wisdom gleaned from past experiences, this is a risk worth taking. *This is a simple shift but can be very profound for the client.*

10. Bring client's attention back to their breath and ask client to invite in a wee guide. If there was a creature—one of the wee ones that flourish in the warm, summer months—that would best reflect the energy of the Heart in this moment, which

creature would that be? When one appears, ask the client to connect more deeply with that wee guide. What are its particular qualities and strengths? How do those qualities or strengths relate to the client? How might embodying those qualities allow for a different acceptance of the client's True Self? Invite the client to craft a supportive message or affirmation from this guide. This should be short enough to be easily remembered and in the present tense.

11. Moving back to the client's head, place your left hand underneath on the nape of the neck and hold your right hand above the client's brow chakra. Repeat the client's wee guide affirmation three times out loud so the client can hear. If the client has had difficulty crafting an affirmation, any one of the following can be used.

I embrace my human nature and my Spirit.
I treat myself with care and respect.
I am open to love.
I am inspired and inspiring.
I bring passion to my ventures and endeavors.

12. As you are imbuing the client with the energy of the affirmation, invite the client to focus once more on their breath but this time visualizing it as the color "green," like the taste of chlorophyll or the smell of fresh-cut grass, seeping into each and every cell in their body

13. Release your hands from the neck and brow. Begin to "sweep" down the client's whole body with hands slightly above the body, unruffling and smoothing the energy field and bringing any excess energy down toward the feet. After a final sweep, when it feels that the entire energy field is balanced, place your hands firmly on the top of your client's feet.

14. Give client a few minutes to come back into the present time and space. When client has opened their eyes and is ready to sit up, you may choose to have client pick an ogham card for a final message and guidance. Invite the client to interpret what the image holds for him/her as a message.

15. Give client a glass of water and take some time to process the experience, allowing client to express their experience of the session and the significant takeaway that will be helpful post-session.

Entry into Session Cycle Four	• Connect with client (1) • Relax client (2–3) • Guide client into session focus (4) • Activate Bridging Hynni of Synthesis (5)
Exploration of Blocks and Shadow	• Psychological Reflection: Explore Shadow challenge of cycle: giving and receiving love (6) • Invite client to explore shifted relationship dynamic (7–8) • Development Reflection: Connect to Inner Adolescent (9)
Invitation to Shift into Light and Essence	• Guidance Reflection: Connect with wee guide (10) • Affirmation (11) • Energetic Reflection: Color breathwork (12)
Exit from Session	• Aura sweep and ground (13) • Optional Intuitive Reflection: Ogham (14) • Debrief session (15)
What client can do post-session to continue to connect with cycle energies	• Dancing

Cycle Five: The Clear Hynni of Expression

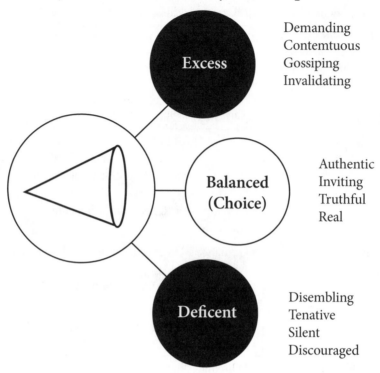

Excess

Demanding
Contemtuous
Gossiping
Invalidating

Balanced (Choice)

Authentic
Inviting
Truthful
Real

Deficent

Disembling
Tenative
Silent
Discouraged

How we express ourselves in the world is vitally important to continue to solidify and anchor an empowered sense of Self. This has naught to do with how others perceive us and everything to do with the inner relationship. The more we dissemble who we are, the more we disassemble who we are. The more we try to present as other than who we are, the more we internalize the message that there is something wrong with us and the more we sabotage all the fruitful work done so far to establish positive self-esteem and self-regard.

If the client has indicated any of the following circumstances, a session to activate the Clear Hynni of Expression would be appropriate:

- Difficulty sharing thoughts and beliefs
- Repressed creativity

- A sense that what they say doesn't matter
- An excessive need to communicate
- A depleted sense of will or belief in the efficacy of one's choices

Working with the Clear Hynni of Expression gives the opportunity to release fears around sharing the truth of Self to others. It takes the Seed of Self that was claimed in Cycle Three, brought into healthy dynamic with other in Cycle Four, and introduces that glorious Self to the world. The Hynni symbol represents the confident sharing of one's true voice and the amplification of that voice for all to hear through all methods and means of communication and creative expression.

Cycle Five Session

1–3. See start of this chapter

4. Say the following (or your own adaptation of the following) to guide your client into the working of the session.

   Begin to sense what the energy feels like in your throat—if it feels like it is moving and flowing or if it is blocked and stuck. Be aware of this energy as carrying that which is deep within you to the external world. It can either act as a megaphone, amplifying and expanding your message for all to hear, or it can act as a clamp shutting down the flow of all your expressions and actions.

5. Lifting your hands from the client's body and raising them above the torso, activate the Clear Hynni of Expression. (For distance sessions, ask the client to also visualize the Hynni symbol.) Visualize waves of golden light sending the energy of the Hynni toward the client's body. If it feels that your hands want to move this energy around the client's body, do so. Continue to move your hands and send the energy of the Clear Hynni of Expression as you dialogue with your client through sections 6–9.

6. Ask client to connect to the sense of their expression in the world: the choices made, the conversations engaged in, the creativity explored. Say the following (or your personal adaptation) in order to bring your client deeper into connection

with the energy of the throat chakra expression, asking your client to be aware of what comes up within as you say the words.

> *As you focus on your throat, feel your voice becoming clear. You are the soft nudge of a whisper. You are the joyful shout from the rooftops. You are the monologue heard by many ears, the dance of dialogue and the melody of vibrant discussion. You are filled with messages that support the integrity and importance of your voice. You are seen and heard. Whether others agree and acknowledge or not, your voice is significant.*

7. Ask client to explore anything that comes up in relation to voice and choice. How effective does the client feel their voice is? How valid their opinions? How secure in their choices? How visible or invisible does the client feel and in which situations or dynamics? Allow client to explore and expand on any feelings of minimizing or dismissing the validity of their voice or the potency of their choice.

8. Amplifying the energy of the Clear Hynni of Expression symbol, invite the client to visualize themselves as a young Adult, being aware of the impulse to sometimes wear a mask to fit in, but being aware of the choice to be oneself, to operate with authenticity and integrity. This is the time in our lives when we start to step out on our own and make the choices that are going to build our own life's foundation. Have the client connect to the person that walked through the world as an early Adult. *This is a simple shift but can be very profound for the client.*

9. Bring client's attention back to their breath and ask client to invite in an elemental guide. If there was a creature of the Elements—Gnome or Dwarf, Undine or Mermaid, Sylph or Faery, Salamander—that would best reflect the client's voice at this time, which creature would that be? When one appears, ask the client to connect more deeply with that elemental. Which element does it reflect? What are some of the myths and lore connected to this elemental? What are its particular qualities that are evident from its tales and how do those qualities or strengths relate to the client? How might embody-

ing those qualities allow for a different amplification of voice and choice, truth and integrity, creativity and expression for the client? Invite the client to craft a supportive message or affirmation from this guide. This should be short enough to be easily remembered and in the present tense.

10. Moving back to the client's head, place your left hand underneath on the nape of the neck and hold your right hand above the client's brow chakra. Repeat the client's elemental guide affirmation three times out loud so the client can hear. If the client has had difficulty crafting an affirmation, any one of the following can be used.

> *My choices are informed by my Essence.*
> *My core self is pure and unchanging.*
> *I am balanced in all areas of my life.*
> *I communicate clearly and effectively.*
> *What I say matters.*
> *I express openly and safely.*

11. As you are imbuing the client with the energy of the affirmation, invite the client to focus once more on their breath but this time visualizing it as the color "light blue," seeping into each and every cell in their body

12. Release your hands from the neck and brow. Begin to "sweep" down the client's whole body with hands slightly above the body, unruffling and smoothing the energy field and bringing any excess energy down toward the feet. After a final sweep, when it feels that the entire energy field is balanced, place your hands firmly on the top of your client's feet.

13. Give client a few minutes to come back into the present time and space. When client has opened their eyes and is ready to sit up, you may choose to have client pick a tarot card for a final message and guidance. Invite the client to interpret what the image holds for him/her as a message.

14. Give client a glass of water and take some time to process the experience, allowing client to express their experience of the session and the significant takeaway that will be helpful post-session.

Entry into Session Cycle Five	• Connect with client (1) • Relax client (2–3) • Guide client into session focus (4) • Activate Clear Hynni of Expression (5)
Exploration of Blocks and Shadow	• Psychological Reflection: Explore Shadow challenge of cycle: seen and heard (6–7) • Development Reflection: Connect to early Adult (8)
Invitation to Shift into Light and Essence	• Guidance Reflection: Connect with elemental guide (9) • Affirmation (10) • Energetic Reflection: Color breathwork (11)
Exit from Session	• Aura sweep and ground (12) • Optional Intuitive Reflection: Tarot (13) • Debrief session (14)
What client can do post-session to continue to connect with cycle energies	• Journaling

Cycle Six: The Illumined Hynni of Vision

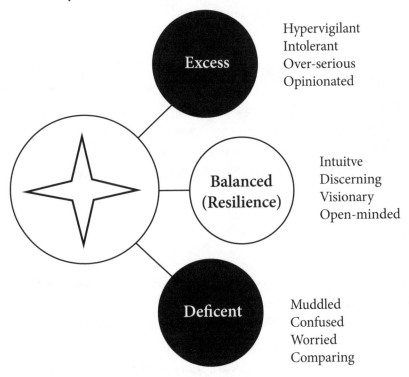

Excess — Hypervigilant / Intolerant / Over-serious / Opinionated

Balanced (Resilience) — Intuitve / Discerning / Visionary / Open-minded

Deficent — Muddled / Confused / Worried / Comparing

It is one thing to have clearly identified a sense of Self, clearing out the pain of the past in order to land fully in the present. It is another to be able to turn that laser gaze on the horizon of the future and know that we have all that is required to ensure that future will at some point become the manifest now. It requires the innocent optimism of the Inner Child and the confident ability of the Inner Adult to actualize the inspired vision of the Higher Self. That is not always as straightforward a path as it seems.

If the client has indicated any of the following circumstances, a session to activate the Illumined Hynni of Vision would be appropriate:

- Confused or racing thoughts
- Difficulty in "turning off the brain"
- Critical or harsh inner dialogue

- Difficulty envisioning or planning the future
- Under- or overactive imagination

Working with the Illumined Hynni of Vision clears the sight regardless of the direction of the gaze. The Hynni symbol represents the need for us to always have the courage to bring clarity and truth to both the past and the future (the Below and all that has brought us to today, including our deepest pain; and the Above and all that inspires us to the future, including our most precious dreams), but that those temporal perspectives need also to bring the internal and external dynamics into consideration. At any given point in my life, I need to know how it reaches out to affect and be affected by a multiplicity of factors.

Cycle Six Session

1–3. See start of this chapter

4. Say the following (or your own adaptation of the following) to guide your client into the working of the session.

   Bring your awareness to the space in the center of your forehead just above your brows. Begin to sense what the energy feels like in this place. Be very gentle as you focus on this area. If it begins to ache or if you feel pressure, allow your focus to be diffused. Expand your attention to your brow as part of your entire body, feeling a connection to the earth through your feet. Allow your perception to expand, casting light in dark areas and reaching the furthest corners. From this place, you may choose to focus on a particular situation that has been causing challenge. With your mind's eye, allow the situation to play out in its familiar way. The way you have been seeing it. The way that is causing the challenge.

5. Lifting your hands from the client's body and raising them above the torso, activate the Illumined Hynni of Vision. (For distance sessions, ask the client to also visualize the Hynni symbol.) Visualize waves of golden light sending the energy of the Hynni toward the client's body. If it feels that your hands want to move this energy around the client's body, do so. Continue to move your

hands and send the energy of the Ilumined Hynni of Vision as you dialogue with your client through sections 6–9.

6. Ask the client to think of a current situation that is being experienced as confusing or complicated, allowing the client to explore what seems to be causing a shadow over clarity of vision with respect to this situation. Invite the client to specifically focus on any restricting words or critical thoughts that come up that may contribute to feeling cynical or pessimistic. Is there a sense of this particular situation (including the words and thoughts) that feels similar to an earlier time in the client's life?

7. Guide the client to explore the restricting words and critical thoughts that have come up. How do these contribute to a limiting self-perception? What words and thoughts would be supportive and expansive in this situation? What phrase or belief would allow for the client's vision to become focused and clear? What would contribute to a sense of resilience in the ability to overcome and move on from this situation?

8. Amplifying the energy of the Illumined Hynni of Vision symbol, invite the client to visualize themselves as an older Adult. This may be in the client's actual future or it may already be in the client's past. What is being accessed here is that aspect of self that has weathered a certain range of experience and come out the wiser for it.

9. Bring client's attention back to their breath and ask client to invite in a mythological beast as a guide. If there was a creature that would best support the client in shifting the situation or more accurately, shifting their perception of the situation, which creature would that be? When one appears, ask the client to connect more deeply with that creature. What are the particular qualities and strengths of this mythological beast? If it is one of those creatures made up of several different animals (such as a flying horse) what are the individual qualities that come together in even more powerful ways? How do those qualities or strengths relate to the situation? How might embodying those qualities allow for a different approach to handling the situation? Invite the client to craft a supportive message or affirmation from this guide. This should be short enough to be easily remembered and in the present tense.

10. Moving back to the client's head, place your left hand underneath on the nape of the neck and hold your right hand above the client's brow chakra. Repeat the client's mythological beast guide affirmation three times out loud so the client can hear. If the client has had difficulty crafting an affirmation, any one of the following can be used.

My vision for my life is valid.
My vision reflects my highest potential.
I am open to receive higher guidance.
My beliefs are supportive and encouraging.
I see clearly from the highest perspective.

11. As you are imbuing the client with the energy of the affirmation, invite the client to focus once more on their breath, but this time visualizing it as the color "indigo," seeping into each and every cell in their body.

12. Release your hands from the neck and brow. Begin to "sweep" down the client's whole body with hands slightly above the body, unruffling and smoothing the energy field and bringing any excess energy down toward the feet. After a final sweep, when it feels that the entire energy field is balanced, place your hands firmly on the top of your client's feet.

13. Give client a few minutes to come back into the present time and space. When client has opened their eyes and is ready to sit up, you may choose to have client pick an I Ching card for a final message and guidance. Invite the client to interpret what the image holds for them as a message. If you are particularly inspired, you can take the time to do an actual I Ching reading, with the tossing of three coins six times to determine the hexagram and using an I Ching book to relay the message.

14. Give client a glass of water and take some time to process the experience, allowing client to express their experience of the session and the significant takeaway that will be helpful post-session.

Entry into Session Cycle Six	• Connect with client (1) • Relax client (2–3) • Guide client into session focus (4) • Activate Illumined Hynni of Vision (5)
Exploration of Blocks and Shadow	• Psychological Reflection: Explore Shadow challenge of cycle: all-or-nothing thinking (6–7) • Development Reflection: Connect to older Adult (8)
Invitation to Shift into Light and Essence	• Guidance Reflection: Connect with mythological beast guide (9) • Affirmation (10) • Energetic Reflection: Color breathwork (11)
Exit from Session	• Aura sweep and ground (12) • Optional Intuitive Reflection: I Ching (13) • Debrief session (14)
What client can do post-session to continue to connect with cycle energies	• Scrapbooking, mindmapping, creating a Vision Board

Cycle Seven: The Enlightened Hynni of Karma

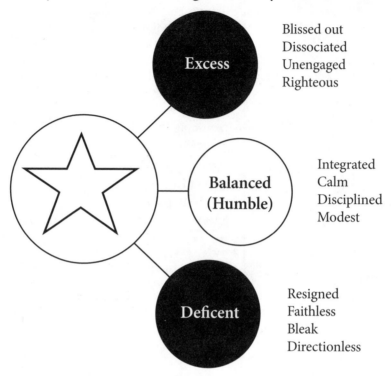

Excess
Blissed out
Dissociated
Unengaged
Righteous

**Balanced
(Humble)**
Integrated
Calm
Disciplined
Modest

Deficent
Resigned
Faithless
Bleak
Directionless

One of the challenges in the healing journey is the inability to be fully present enough to be able to address what needs to be shifted or changed. There can be a tendency to be so caught up in the past that there isn't the discernment to recognize that we are no longer trapped in the disempowering circumstances of the past anymore. We can actually take a breath and make a different choice. But, interestingly, the other main challenge that presents in the healing journey is the complete opposite condition. It is the inability to step out of the attachment to the present long enough to be able to see how intimately and intricately linked it is to events from the past. It is this inability to see connections that can often keep the client stuck in old patterns.

If the client has indicated any of the following circumstances, a session to activate the Enlightened Hynni of Karma would be appropriate:

- Lack of trust that all will work out
- Resistance to life's lessons
- Attachment to proof
- Having one's "head in the clouds"
- Avoidance of physical or emotional needs

Working with the Enlightened Hynni of Karma opens us to recognize and integrate the patterns and lessons that weave meaning into all the moments of our lives, Enfolding the input and experiences from many different areas and filtering them all through the lens of our Higher Self, the Hynni symbol represents the polestar that acts as True North on the compass of our life's journey.

Cycle Seven Session

1–3. See start of this chapter

4. Say the following (or your own adaptation of the following) to guide your client into the working of the session.

   Bring your awareness to the space right at the top of your head. Begin to sense what the energy feels like in this place. Feel the energy flowing through your body to this spot and up through the top of your head, connecting you to the entire Universe and feel the energy from the Universe flowing back into you from this place. As your breath moves in and out of your body, so does the energy of All flow in and out of your crown chakra

5. Lifting your hands from the client's body and raising them above the torso, activate the Enlightened Hynni of Karma. (For distance sessions, ask the client to also visualize the Hynni symbol.) Visualize waves of golden light sending the energy of the Hynni toward the client's body. If it feels that your hands want to move this energy around the client's body, do so. Continue to move your hands and send the energy of the Enlightened Hynni of Karma as you dialogue with your client through sections 6–9.

6. Ask client to connect to the sense of their purpose in the world, including all the experiences which have provided a deepening of learning, a balancing of energies or karma, and a greater awareness of wonder and magic in the world.

Connect with your Higher Self, experiencing the unconditional love and strong guidance that your Higher Self offers you, consistently and always. This is the aspect of self that truly knows you are Divine and that you have much to offer the world. It is the Higher Self that reflects the best of us in our worst moments and the strength of us in our most fearful moments. Higher Self is the keeper of the blueprint of our lives, guiding us to see the vision and plan for our lives and supporting us in continuing the effort to manifest that plan, in spite of (or as a response to) life's circumstances. Higher Self helps us to remember that everything unfolds in its own good time. It is the babelfish of Wyrd, communicating to us that nothing is by accident. Every cause has an effect and every effect is motivated by a cause. Everything is connected. We are connected to it all and we are a wonder in the world, bringing our own manner of magic into the world

7. Guide the client to explore the sensations, feelings, and images that arise from connecting with Higher Self. If there are any hints of Shadow or the deeply unconscious messages of "not being good enough," of self being untethered from higher reflection, guide the client to just note them, note where they may be coming from, note if the voice is familiar, and note how Higher Self responds to the Shadow voice. If the Higher Self connection is clear of any negative or Shadow static, invite the client to simply spend time connecting and communing with this energy, becoming intimately familiar with its resonance in the whole of Self.

8. Amplifying the energy of the Enlightened Hynni of Karma symbol, invite the client to visualize themselves as a much, much older Adult. Explore that sense of being near the end of life, the completion of the journey. With that Higher Self communion, invite the client to explore what it might feel like to be near end of life. How would they want to feel about the life that has been led? Are there any regrets? What would have to shift in order to release those regrets?

9. Bring client's attention back to their breath and, with an open heart and open mind, ask the client to invite an archangel or companion angel. Feel the energy of this otherworldly being as a reflection of the Divine. What support or guidance does this angel bring to you? What words or messages? What encourage-

ments or praise? Invite the client to craft a supportive message or affirmation from this guide. This should be short enough to be easily remembered and in the present tense.

10. Moving back to the client's head, place your left hand underneath on the nape of the neck and hold your right hand above the client's brow chakra. Repeat the client's angel guide affirmation three times out loud so the client can hear. If the client has had difficulty crafting an affirmation, any one of the following can be used.

I embrace positive thoughts of myself and my abilities.
My thoughts support me in all ways.
I choose positivity.
I co-create with my Higher Self.
I am open to seeing the patterns and lessons in my life.
I am living a life of purpose.
Every experience I have is touched by Spirit.

11. As you are imbuing the client with the energy of the affirmation, invite the client to focus once more on their breath but this time visualizing it as the color "purple," seeping into each and every cell in their body.

12. Release your hands from the neck and brow. Begin to "sweep" down the client's whole body with hands slightly above the body, unruffling and smoothing the energy field and bringing any excess energy down toward the feet. After a final sweep, when it feels that the entire energy field is balanced, place your hands firmly on the top of your client's feet.

13. Give client a few minutes to come back into the present time and space. When client has opened their eyes and is ready to sit up, you may choose to have client pick an oracle card for a final message and guidance.[79] Invite the client to interpret what the image holds for them as a message.

....
79. The Intuitive Reflection for Cycle Seven is scrying, which is too difficult to do in the context of a session, but there are several great oracle decks that capture the essence of this cycle and that are appropriate to use instead.

14. Give client a glass of water and take some time to process the experience, allowing client to express their experience of the session and the significant takeaway that will be helpful post-session.

Entry into Session Cycle Seven	• Connect with client (1) • Relax client (2–3) • Guide client into session focus (4) • Activate Enlightened Hynni of Karma (5)
Exploration of Blocks and Shadow	• Psychological Reflection: Explore Shadow challenge of cycle: Woundedness (6–7) • Development Reflection: Connect to Inner Elder (8)
Invitation to Shift into Light and Essence	• Guidance Reflection: Connect with angel guide (9) • Affirmation (10) • Energetic Reflection: Color breathwork (11)
Exit from Session	• Aura sweep and ground (12) • Optional Intuitive Reflection: Oracle (13) • Debrief session (14)
What client can do post-session to continue to connect with cycle energies	• Yoga

Cycle Eight: The Integrating Hynni of Unity

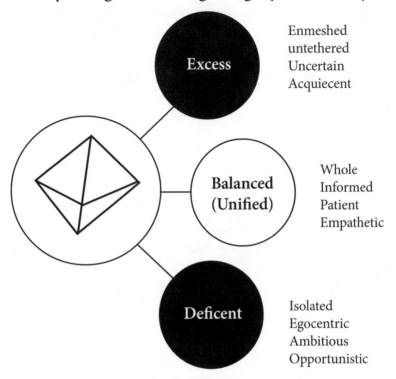

Excess

Enmeshed
untethered
Uncertain
Acquiecent

**Balanced
(Unified)**

Whole
Informed
Patient
Empathetic

Deficent

Isolated
Egocentric
Ambitious
Opportunistic

There comes a time when sometimes the greatest work we can do is no work at all. The greatest action we can take is inaction. The greatest step toward healing we can make is the realization that we have always been nothing less than completely whole. There are many times and many seasons in which we can roll up our sleeves and get down to the nitty gritty. This is the one time that for certain we can keep those sleeves rolled down and just allow the moment to unfold as it will.

If the client has indicated any of the following circumstances, a session to activate the Integrating Hynni of Unity would be appropriate:

- Isolated from humanity
- Debilitating fear of death
- Challenge in resolving ancestral legacy issues
- Inability to live in the moment
- Past-life bleed-through

Working with the Enlightened Hynni of Unity opens us up to appreciating that not everything is about moving toward something, achieving something, or resolving something. It supports us in being able to let go, to know that we have let go, and that to rest in the beingness of no-thing-ness is to activate the Divine Within. We have always been whole and holy.

Cycle Eight Session

1–3. See start of this chapter

4. Say the following (or your own adaptation of the following) to guide your client into the working of the session.

    Bring your awareness to the space about a foot above the top of your head connecting you to your soul star chakra. Visualize a funnel reaching upward from this place, expanding as it reaches higher, opening you to the energy of the cosmos.

5. Lifting your hands from the client's body and raising them above the torso, activate the Integrating Hynni of Unity. (For distance sessions, ask the client to also visualize the Hynni symbol.) Visualize waves of golden light sending the energy of the Hynni toward the client's body. If it feels that your hands want to move this energy around the client's body, do so. Continue to move your hands and send the energy of the Integrating Hynni of Unity as you dialogue with your client through sections 6–8.

6. Ask client to connect to the sense of all that was, all that has been, all that is, and all that will be.

    Visualize a web reaching outward from this place, connecting you to every being on Earth through this energetic network. This wonderful web of interconnection pulses and glows. Be aware of how the energy flows along this web. Be aware of how shifts in you echo out from your place on the web, weaving through all the places of intersection. If you are aware of any spots in which the energy seems dim or blocked, send the energy of love to that place. Allow yourself to be fully in a place of receptivity and experience. Imagine that a stream of Divine gold light is pouring down and filling every aspect of your being with compassion and wisdom. From this place you are connected to all that was and all that will be. From this place you have access to anything you need to know. You need only use your consciousness as your light to find your direction.

7. Amplifying the energy of the Integrating Hynni of Unity symbol, invite the client to rest in this place of no time and no space, of all time and all space. There isn't anything that needs to be explored or processed or understood. Allow this to be a time of incubation, drawing in all the energy that is necessary for the next part of the journey.

8. Bring client's attention back to their breath and, with an open heart and open mind, ask the client to invite a spirit guide, asking that only a guide of the highest vibration and purest intention come in this space. Guide the client to explore how this spirit guide feels. Does the energy in the room feel different? Is the energy of this spirit guide a familiar one—of perhaps a loved one or ancestor? What support or guidance does this guide bring to you? What words or messages? What encouragements or praise? Invite the client to craft a supportive message or affirmation from this guide. This should be short enough to be easily remembered and in the present tense.

9. Moving back to the client's head, place your left hand underneath on the nape of the neck and hold your right hand above the client's brow chakra. Repeat the client's spirit guide affirmation three times out loud so the client can hear. If the client has had difficulty crafting an affirmation, any one of the following can be used.

I always have been and always will be.
My Energy flows with ease.
I am part of all that is.
The purity of my Essence makes a positive difference to all.
I cherish the beauty of all humanity.

10. As you are imbuing the client with the energy of the affirmation, invite the client to focus once more on their breath but this time visualizing it as the color "gold," seeping into each and every cell in their body.

11. Release your hands from the neck and brow. Begin to "sweep" down the client's whole body with hands slightly above the body, unruffling and smoothing the energy field and bringing any excess energy down toward the feet. After a final sweep, when it feels that the entire energy field is balanced, place your hands firmly on the top of your client's feet.

12. Give client a few minutes to come back into the present time and space. When client has opened their eyes and is ready to sit up, you may choose to have client pick an oracle card for a final message and guidance.[80] Invite the client to interpret what the image holds for them as a message.

13. Give client a glass of water and take some time to process the experience, allowing client to express their experience of the session and the significant takeaway that will be helpful post-session.

Entry into Session Cycle Eight	• Connect with client (1) • Relax client (2–3) • Guide client into session focus (4) • Activate Integrating Hynni of Unity (5)
Exploration of Blocks and Shadow	• Psychological Reflection: Explore Shadow challenge of cycle: Inability to just be (6) • Development Reflection: Beingness (7)
Invitation to Shift into Light and Essence	• Guidance Reflection: Connect with spirit guide (8) • Affirmation (9) • Energetic Reflection: Color breathwork (10)
Exit from Session	• Aura sweep and ground (11) • Optional Intuitive Reflection: Oracle (12) • Debrief session (13)
What client can do post-session to continue to connect with cycle energies	• Hynni (living fully in each moment, being informed by physical, emotional, mental, and spiritual selves, knowing one's life as heroic)

....

80. The Intuitive Reflection for Cycle Eight is channeling, which is too difficult to do in the context of a session, but there are several great oracle decks that capture the essence of this cycle that are appropriate to use instead.

Sixty

· ·

Hynni Harmonics

Moving through the Grand Cycle as a progression through the spokes on the Wheel of the Year allows one to drop deeply into each cycle and explore the themes, lessons, and gifts with much focus and clarity. But the beautiful thing about working with cycles is that the non-linear approach allows for the perspective of multiple lenses through diverse and complex dynamics. There is the energy of the cycle in which one is working, but there are relationships to other cycles in different contexts, far easier to see as dynamics in and around a circle than it is to see when the process is presented in a straight line.

"As Above" contemplation chapters elaborate on the Energetic Reflection in each cycle. One of the ways of working with and balancing the chakras is vibrationally through sound. If each cycle relates to a note on a major scale, then the Grand Cycle moves through each of the seven notes on the scale from Cycle One to Cycle Seven, resolving itself back to the beginning at a higher octave (literally the "eighth note") in Cycle Eight. Each of these notes is like the archetypal theme of the cycle. In much the same way as playing two notes together gives us a more nuanced experience of each of the individual notes, exploring each cycle in relation to one or more of the other cycles informs our understanding of both in wondrous new ways.

Working with the cycles bringing the interplay of Hynni harmonics into the equation is like moving from listening to a monophonic sound on a transistor radio to surround sound digital radio with Bose speakers. The information was always there, but now you can pick up a fuller range of subtleties. Now it can start to make the hair on your arms stand up through sheer awe at the gorgeous symmetry and patterning that has always been there.

Resonant Reflections

Resonant Reflections looks at the relationship of the cycles that sit across from each other on the Wheel of the Year. They are the mirror reflections that have a commonality of energy but seen from the opposite perspective. Brought together, these two cycles dialogue with each as Yin and Yang, offering a beautiful completion each to each.

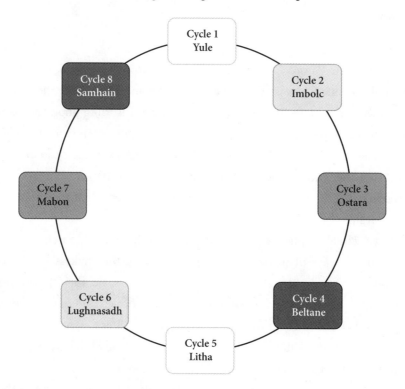

Cycles One and Five both speak to the relationship with *hope*. Yule, with the Birth of the Divine Child, brings the Light of hope to a whole new process of growth and expansion. Litha, to a large degree, sees the fulfillment of that hope. Though there is still work to be done, most of the uphill climb has been accomplished.

Cycles Two and Six both speak to the need for *preparation*. Imbolc, with the clearing of the fields to receive the seed, puts its energy behind preparation that is holding a vision and hope for what may be with diligence and dedication. Lughnasadh, with the beginning of the harvest in sight, puts its energy behind preparing to bring home the fulfillment of the vision that has transpired due to diligence, attention, sacrifice, and hard work.

Cycles Three and Seven both speak to *celebration of life*. Ostara, with its theme of resurrection and renewal, celebrates that life that is to come along with the recognition of the strength that has brought us to the place where we can actually step into that life. Mabon, with its theme of thanksgiving and gratitude, celebrates the life that was. Especially seen through the lens of the Developmental Reflection, this cycle relates to the 70s and beyond, the last phase of our life before we enter into the Great Mystery. The celebration of the life that was is a strong theme for this cycle on many fronts.

Cycles Four and Eight both speak to the *relationship between the human and Spirit realms*. Beltane, with the maypole dance, speaks to the fusion of Spirit and human, brought together in the passionate expression of life's unity. Samhain, with its strong connection to the otherworldly realms and the Void, speaks to the dissolution of the fusion of Spirit and human. There is a different sort of unity that is experienced through Cycle Eight.

To begin to get a sense of the truth that lies in the center between two poles, explore the resonance of one cycle with its partner across the wheel. Much like the phenomenon one finds with Tibetan singing bowls, when you strike these two notes together, you very often find that there is a subtle, yet very profound overtone that becomes discernible. It is this overtone that lies in the space between the two cycles that brings one to a greater truth that informs each individual cycle.

Cycle Chords

Similar to playing a chord on an instrument, Cycle Chords looks at the information that comes to us when we combine three or more cycles together. As the Resonant Reflections looked at the relationship between cycles in light of their archetypal themes, it is helpful to look at the Cycle Chords from the perspective of the Hermetic Principles. There are seven traditional Hermetic Principles and, in Hynni, I have included a "silent" eighth principle, which is that of Universal Law itself. The principles themselves fall naturally into two categories. There are those principles that seem to refer to the nature of movement. They are the active principles and are ever changing. Then there are those principles that refer to the nature of relationship. They are the static principles. They don't indicate any sort of change or movement within themselves, but they show the way to facilitate change through the understanding of relationship.

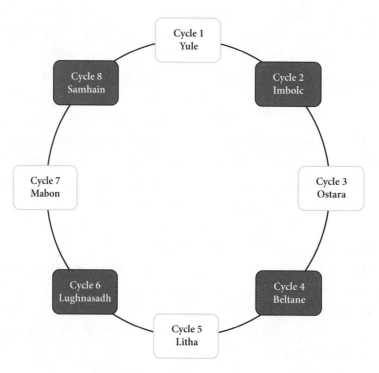

Looking at the chord that is created with the foundation of Hermetics and the concept of *Universal Law* itself in Cycle One (Yule), we have the three Principles of Relationship: the Hermetic Principle of Cause and Effect (Ostara, Cycle 3, Law 6); the Hermetic Principle of Polarity (Litha, Cycle 5, Law 4); and the Hermetic Principle of Correspondence (Mabon, Cycle 7, Law 2). These are the principles of the solstices and the equinoxes. They are tethered to the relationship of the Above to the Below. There is a sense of immutability with these three, that cannot be negotiated or compromised. They are anchored in solidity and provide the solid parameters to be able to understand what contributes to the activation of change. In their different ways, each of these cycles teaches us how to stand in the center of our beings, observing the dynamic created with that which lies beyond us. To explore these four cycles together brings a deeper understanding of the nature of relationship and how to anchor ourselves in the immutable Self, even as we experience change.

Looking at the chord that is created with the first Hermetic Principle of Mentalism in Cycle Eight (Samhain), we have the three Principles of Movement: The Hermetic Principle of Gender (Imbolc, Cycle 2, Law 7); the Hermetic Principle of Rhythm (Beltane, Cycle 4, Law 5), and the Hermetic Principle of Vibration (Lughnasadh, Cycle 6, Law 3). These are the principles of the cross quarter days and there can tend to be a bit more fluidity to the timing of their celebration, particularly considering that the determining factor for dates is more regionally influenced, rather than influenced by considerations that are informed by nature or the cosmos. There is a sense of mutability with these three principles. They are always in motion and flux, ever shifting, changing, and morphing. Even the Principles of Mentalism, which seems immoveable in its all-encompassing scope, describes the interplay between the All and THE ALL, implying the movement from one to the other. In their different ways, each of these cycles teaches us how to be comfortable with finding our place in the ever-shifting flow of being. To explore these four cycles together brings a deeper familiarity with the nature of change, helping us to not only feel more comfortable with a fluid, non-static, non-binary approach to existence, but to recognize that such fluidity is ultimately necessary for the healthy continuance of life.

Energetic Chopsticks

The third approach to exploring the relationship between the cycles is inspired by the piano piece known as "Chopsticks." Composed by Euphemia Allen under the pseudonym Arthur de Lulli in 1877 when she was just sixteen years old, the piece was originally called "The Celebrated Chop Waltz" as a reference to it being playing with hands held upright and parallel to each other, striking at the piano keys as if one were chopping them. It is a variation of "Resonant Reflections" as it brings two cycles into relationship with each other to explore how each is informed and enhanced by an understanding and appreciation of the other. Taking the chakra associations of the cycles into consideration first and foremost, this approach starts with the cycles aligned with the two chakras that bookend the seven chakras found in the physical body (root and crown). Like the musical piece, starting with those two outer energies, Energetic Chopsticks progresses in from the outer edges, to the next two chakras or cycles (sacral and brow) and the next two (solar plexus and throat) until the "hands" meet in the middle at the cycle aligned with the heart chakra.

Bringing the cycles into relationship in this way seems to reflect the highest degree of polarization. As such, this approach has the potential to highlight the darkest corners and most hidden nuggets in each of the cycles.

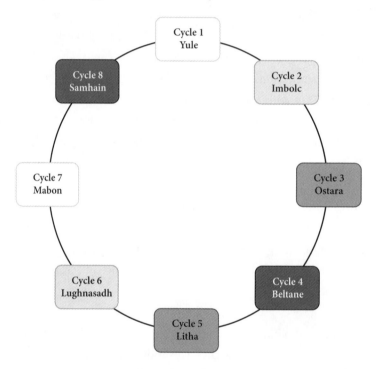

Cycles One and Seven are aligned with the two chakras within the energy of the human body that are unidirectional. The root chakra (Cycle One) sits at the base of the spine and opens downward toward the earth. The crown chakra (Cycle Seven) sits at the top of the head and opens upward toward the cosmos. As such, both these cycles (Yule and Mabon) have the potential to teach us about our relationship to Spirit and the ways in which we are nourished by energies that are always there to support us.

Cycles Two and Six are aligned with the two chakras that reflect the extreme difference between emotion and reason. The sacral chakra (Cycle Two) is the seat of our emotional energy. It invites us to honor the wisdom of the full range of our emotions. The brow chakra (Cycle Six) is the seat of our mental energy. It invites us to exercise discernment with the application of reason. For too long, we have been taught that reason trumps emotion. This dynamic shows just how interconnected and interdependent they actually are.

Cycles Three and Five are aligned with the two chakras that represent our relationship to identity. The solar plexus chakra (Cycle Three) is the seat of the self. It is here that we anchor into the knowledge of who we are. The throat chakra (Cycle Five) is the impetus of expression. What is expressed through the throat is informed by what is experienced in the solar plexus, informed by either the wisdom of Essence or the slime of shame.

Having played the "notes" of root and crown together, sacral and brow together, solar plexus and throat together, the "hands" are ultimately brought together in the heart chakra, the chakra that unites Spirit and Matter, which is aligned with Cycle Four, the cycle that weaves Spirit and Earth together. And when we strike that singular note in the heart chakra, it creates an overtone in Cycle Eight, aligned with the soul star chakra of Unity Consciousness. This last tone and overtone invites us to experience the deep soul sense that whether we exist in the physical realms or the non-physical realms, Spirit and Matter are ultimately reflections of exactly the same thing.

More often than not, when preparing for a Hynni energy session, the focus is on activating the current cycle in the Grand Cycle or, after an initial chat with the client, what internal cycle they might benefit from exploring. Regardless of whether the deciding factor is more external (seasonal) or internal (personal), what is being decided is which <u>one</u> cycle is to be the focus of the session. It is not very often that a Hynni practitioner will encounter the circumstance of more than one cycle calling for attention and focus, but when it does, looking at Hynni Harmonics can bring a deeper level of understanding to what some of the themes and patterns being worked through by the client might be. And this in turn will help to bring a greater clarity of focus to the session itself. It is yet another technique in the healing toolbox.

Three candles that illuminate every darkness:
Truth, Nature, and Knowledge
~ Celtic Triad

Conclusion

The Sweet Song of the Self

I began *The Great Work* with the sentence: *We are living in changing times*. Since I first wrote those words several years ago, it has felt that there have been significant changes in the world—and not necessarily for the better. I would now say we are living in chaotic and discordant times. Such times—like the Void, the Bardo, the Unknown—can be met with fear, oppression, and the need to control. Or they can be met with strength and patience, understanding and courage. Such times are uncomfortable, at times devastating, but they do have the potential to move us through the void of uncertainty into the birth of new possibility, inviting us to revive, to come back to full life. They do have the potential to be the excruciating labor pains of a future we can dare to dream possible. They do hold the discordant notes that can very well resolve into harmony. As long as we have resolve to maintain our integrity through the process. As long as we have the fortitude to see the transmutation through to conclusion. As long as we have the faith to hold on to the future of a positive, possible future.

After being stirred and stirred, Cerridwen's cauldron releases the three drops of wisdom that are the culmination of so much attention, dedication, and work. And, having done so, almost as though overcome with the effort itself, the cauldron cracks, releasing the remaining toxic sludge to the earth.

We need the wisdom of those three drops. We need the inspiration of Awen to bring wonder to life and vision to our direction, transmuting the experiences of our lives into a solid core of self-esteem, self-respect, and self-regarding, and releasing the toxicity of negative inner messages forever. That is not to say that there won't ever be a tough day, an uncertain moment, or a painful exchange. Those happen. It is a part of life. But having partaken of Cerridwen's drops and cracked Arianrhod's cosmic, karmic wheel, we do not lose the rhythm of our own movement through our lives. We do not lose the thread of the melody of our own song. We weave the challenges we encounter into the dance and the song, never forgetting the truth of who we are, never letting the sludge entrap again.

We need the people who have the courage to transmute their own Shadows into resilient, impenetrable Light to be on the forefront of the change that needs to come. It is those who dare to challenge the Dark within, chase shame from the inner core, and who choose to walk through the world with humility, kindness, and grace who have the strength in their hands and soul to do the work of Awen on Earth.

As I began *The Great Work* with the sentence, "We are living in changing times" so I end *The Noble Art* with a vision of transmuted times. May the sun be setting on the hegemony of Shadow, shame, and separation and make way for the dawn of the Age of Truth, Nature, and Knowledge. We, the beloved Earth beneath our feet, and the wondrous Stars above our heads, deserve nothing less that that.

Appendix A:
Chart of Cycle Correspondences

OPTIONAL ELEMENTS TO HELP DEEPEN EXPERIENCE OF SESSION				
Cycle	Instruments	Essential Oils	Third Dimension Chakra Stones	Fourth Dimension Chakra Stones
Cycle One: Roots and Foundations	Rattle Shaker Frame drum (heartbeat)	Cedarwood Cypress Patchouli Vetiver	Bloodstone Garnet Hematite Lodestone Smoky Quartz	Black Moon-stone Geothite Shungite Vatican Stone Vesuvianite
Cycle Two: Gifts from the Inner Child	Ocean drum Spring drum Rainstick Rain gourd	Bergamot Neroli Sweet orange Ylang-ylang	Carnelian Goldstone Orange Calcite	Fire Opal Merlinite Mystic Septarian Shattuckite
Cycle Three: Nurturing Empower-ment and Self-Esteem	Whistle Bird whistle Voice Djembe drum (warrior beat)	Black pepper Fennel Ginger Grapefruit Lemon	Citrine Yellow Topaz Golden Beryl Golden Cat's Eye	Chrysanthe-mum Stone Healerite Rhodizite
Cycle Four: Union and Partnerships	Tongue drum Kalimba Bells	Geranium Jasmine Lime Palmarosa Rosewood	Green Jade Rose Quartz Pink Tourmaline	K2 Morganite Nirvana Quartz Prairie Tanzinite Star Ruby

OPTIONAL ELEMENTS TO HELP DEEPEN EXPERIENCE OF SESSION				
Cycle	Instruments	Essential Oils	Third Dimension Chakra Stones	Fourth Dimension Chakra Stones
Cycle Five: Shining Our Truth and Creativity	Tibetan singing bowl	Basil Chamomile Lemongrass Peppermint	Aquamarine Turquoise Chaldecony Blue Kyanite	Purpurite Stone of Solidarity Tiffany Stone
Cycle Six: Visioning Self	Tuning forks	Clary sage Rosemary Sandalwood	Lapis Lazuli, Sodalite Blue Moonstone	Ametrine Atlantisite Auralite Quantum Quattro
Cycle Seven: Effects of Gratitude on Life Purpose	Crystal singing bowl	Frankincense Lavender Myrrh Sage	Quartz Amethyst Flourite Lepidolite Charoite	Petalite Sacred Seven Tibetan Quartz
Cycle Eight: Healing from Loss	Silence	Unscented	Herkimer Diamond	Lemurian Seed Crystal

Appendix B:
Cheat Sheets for Hynni Energy Healing Sessions

HYNNI ENERGY HEALING—CYCLE FOCUS AND GUIDANCE			
Cycle 1 (Yule): Earth Roots and Foundations	Exploring Family of Origin: Place within tribe, Victory of order over chaos, Rebirth of the Light	Animal Guide	Runes; Breathing
Cycle 2 (Imbolc): Water Gifts from the Inner Child	Exploring Feelings: Love, Purification, New beginning	Aquatic Guide	Tea Leaf Reading; Drumming
Cycle 3 (Ostara): Air Nurturing Empowerment and Self-esteem	Exploring Self-esteem: Renewal, Resurrection, Preparation	Bird Guide	Oracle; Toning, Chanting, Singing
Cycle 4 (Beltane): Fire Union and Partnerships	Exploring Relationships: Union, Passion, Synthesis	Wee Guide	Ogham; Dancing
Cycle 5 (Litha): Aether Shining Our Truth and Creativity	Exploring Voice and Choice: Accomplishment, Acknowledgment, Gathering strength	Elementals	Tarot; Journaling

HYNNI ENERGY HEALING—CYCLE FOCUS AND GUIDANCE			
Cycle 6 (Lughnasadh): Light Visioning Self	Exploring Beliefs: Pride, Ability, Strength	Mythological Beasts Guide	1 Ching; Scrapbooking, Mindmapping, Vision board
Cycle 7 (Mabon): Thought Effects of Gratitude on Life Purpose	Exploring Higher Purpose: Giving thanks, Appraisal, Letting go	Angel Guide	Scrying (not in session); Yoga
Cycle 8 (Samhain): Energy Healing from Loss	Exploring Unity Consciousness: Death, Protection, Other-worldly protection	Spirit (Ancestor) Guide	Channeling (not in session); Hynni

HYNNI ENERGY HEALING—INDICATORS OF BLOCKS AND AFFIRMATIONS		
CYCLE 1: Dec 21–Jan 31 Birth of Wonder Child Solid Hynni of Grounding	A sudden, unexpected loss or change of life circumstance Feeling isolated or disconnected from the world or other people Fear around new directions in life A persistent sense of being "ungrounded" Being triggered by spending time with family	I am safe and secure I am safe in the world with others I honor and meet the needs of my body I know how to take care of myself I am grounded

HYNNI ENERGY HEALING—INDICATORS OF BLOCKS AND AFFIRMATIONS		
CYCLE 2: **Feb 1–Mar 14** Purification Through Light Loving Hynni of Ebb & Flow	Overwhelmed by emotions An inability to identify or experience emotions Excessive or extreme reactions to current situations Difficulty in relationships with others Discomfort or shame regarding sexuality	I go with the flow I release with ease My emotions run clear I am able to share my feelings with others I am cleansed by blessings that surround me
CYCLE 3: **Mar 22–May 2** Celebration of Life Centring Hynni of Esteem	A shaky sense of self-esteem Confused or conflicted thoughts Challenges or uncertainty while in the company of others Feeling not in control of one's own life or choices An inability to establish healthy boundaries	I am open to a fresh perspective I experience freedom in my life I am comfortable saying "no" I am responsible for my own feelings I am important and valuable
CYCLE 4: **May 3–Jun 13** Synthesis of Spirit and Matter Bridging Hynni of Synthesis	A lack of passion for activities and ventures Resentment toward others Unhealthy relationship dynamics Lack of compassion or empathy for others Burnout (particularly as it relates to healthcare workers/healers)	I embrace my human nature and my spirit I treat myself with care and respect I am open to love I am inspired and inspiring I bring passion to my ventures/ endeavors

HYNNI ENERGY HEALING—INDICATORS OF BLOCKS AND AFFIRMATIONS		
CYCLE 5: **Jun 21–Aug 1** Celebration of Effort Clear Hynni of Expression	Difficulty sharing your thoughts and beliefs Repressed creativity A sense that what you say doesn't matter An excessive need to communicate A depleted sense of will or belief in the efficacy of your choices	My choices are informed by my Essence My core self is pure and unchanging I am balanced in all areas of my life I communicate clearly and effectively What I say matters
CYCLE 6: **Aug 2–Sept 12** Reaping First Harvests Illuminated Hynni of Vision	Confused or racing thoughts Difficulty in "turning off the brain" Critical or harsh inner dialogue Difficulty envisioning or planning the future Under- or overactive imagination	My vision reflects my highest potential. I embrace the paradox of my human-spirit nature. I see clearly from the highest perspective. My vision for my life is valid I am open to receive higher guidance My beliefs are supportive and encouraging
CYCLE 7: **Sept 20–Oct 31** Thanksgivings Enlightened Hynni of Karma	Lack of trust that all will work out Resistance to life's lessons Attachment to proof Having one's "head in the clouds" Avoidance of physical or emotional needs	I embrace positive thoughts of myself My thoughts support me in all ways I choose positivity I am living a life of purpose I am open to seeing life patterns/ lessons I co-create with my Higher Self

HYNNI ENERGY HEALING—INDICATORS OF BLOCKS AND AFFIRMATIONS		

CYCLE 8:
Nov 1–Dec 12
Entering the Mystery
Integrated Hynni of Unity
 	
	Isolation from humanity
	Debilitating fear of death
	Challenge in resolving ances-
	    tral legacy issues
	Inability to live in the
	    moment
	Past-life bleed-through
		I have always been and always
		    will be
		My Energy flows with ease
		I am part of all that is
		I cherish the beauty of all
		    humanity
		The purity of my Essence makes a
		    positive difference to all

Appendix C:
Sample Hynni Practitioner Session Notes Sheet

Client: _____ Date: _____

Cycle being worked on: _____

Session working *(what came up for client in main body of session?):*

_____

_____

_____

_____

_____

_____

_____

_____

Guidance reflection *(what was the message from the animal, angel, or ancestor?):*

_____

_____

_____

_____

_____

_____

_____

Intuitive reflection *(did you have client pull card from the cycle's oracle method?)*:

_____
_____
_____
_____
_____
_____
_____
_____

Practitioner's thoughts on session:

_____
_____
_____
_____
_____
_____
_____
_____

Practitioner's thoughts on client's takeaway from session:

_____
_____
_____
_____
_____
_____
_____
_____

Appendix D:
Ritual Preparation

Once you have prepared your altar, you will want to take some time to ready yourself for ritual. Hold the intent of letting go of any mundane concerns or thoughts that may interfere with your ability to step fully into the ritual experience. Some people like to have a cleansing bath or shower. Using a fizzy if taking a bath or adding a few drops of essential oil to the tub to scent the steam of a shower can amplify the cleansing experience.

Similarly, you will want to take some time to cleanse the space around your altar itself. Sweeping with a besom or broom not only cleans the physical space but, when done with intention, it also cleanses the energetic space. Some people like to use sage or smudge, but there are many herbs that can be burned to clear space. If you have scent sensitivities, use sound (toning, chanting, singing bowls) or intention (visualize white light moving through the space dispelling anything of heaviness). If you are doing ritual outside, you may want to walk a perimeter—holding the intention of creating a boundary—that delineates your safe ritual space from mundane surroundings. Or visualize a bubble of white light around the space you are using for ritual. There can be an element of creating an energetic "cloak of invisibility" in these two techniques that can also be handy.

Having prepared the space within and out for the reception of the Divine, take some time to position yourself in this space. With each of four breaths, bring your awareness fully to each of the four directions that surround you and the elements that are aligned with them. Breathe into North and the element of earth. Breathe into East and the element of air. Breathe into South and the element of fire. Breathe into West and the element of water.

With each of the next two breaths, bring your awareness fully into the "Below" and the "Above." Breathe into the Below and feel the unwavering foundation of the earthbound material plane. If appropriate to your location, take a moment also to acknowledge the ancestral Indigenous peoples of the place where you are with a land acknowledgement statement. Breathe into the Above and expand into the limitless breadth of the cosmic plane. With your next breath, find the place in the very center in which all these directions, including above and below, come together. Breathe into this center and the element of Aether or Spirit. If you have placed deity statues on your altar, take a moment at this point to acknowledge their Divine presence in this space.

Take several more deep breaths and know that you yourself are also at the center of this sacred space. You too hold this space of the very hub of the Universe. You are the meeting place of Spirit above, Matter below, and the Magic that surrounds. You are the place where Cerridwen sits. And with the awareness of yourself at this sacred center holding space with the Divine, you are ready to begin the ritual.

Appendix E
Steps for a Three-Armed Brigid's Cross
(Cycle Two Ritual)

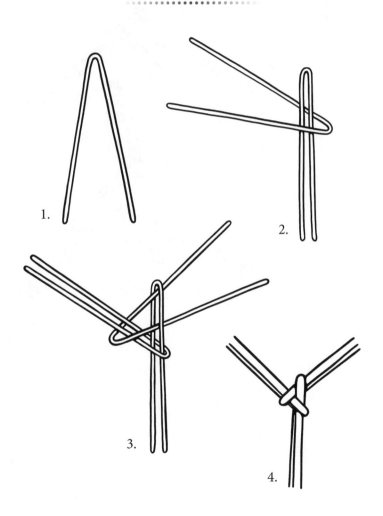

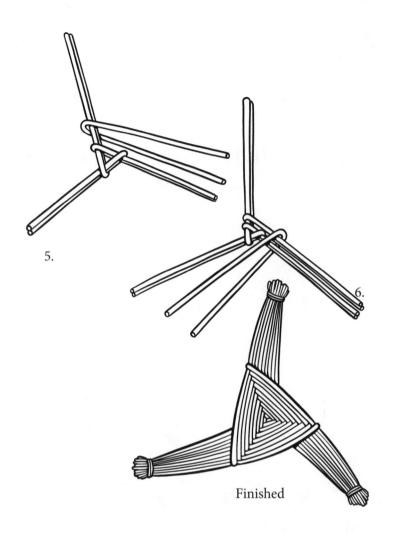

5.

6.

Finished

Appendix F
Steps for Branch Weaving
(Cycle Four Ritual)

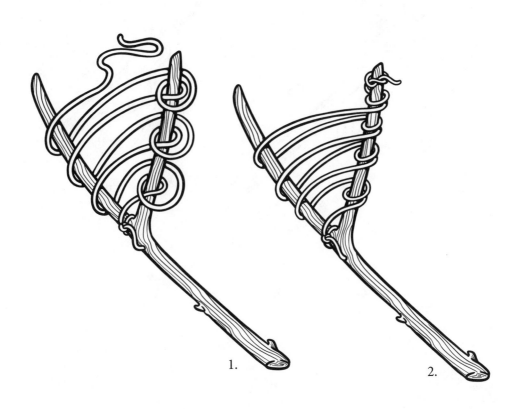

1.

2.

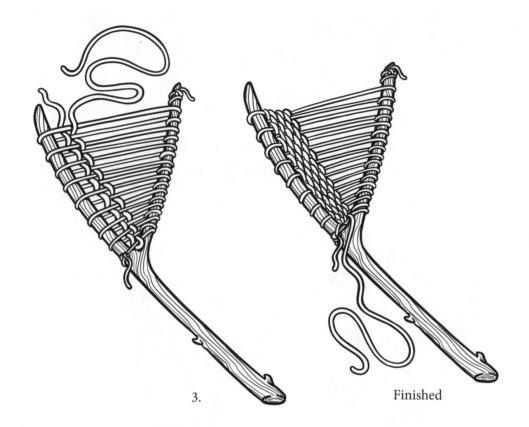

3.   Finished

Appendix G
Steps for God's Eye Weaving
(Cycle Six Ritual)

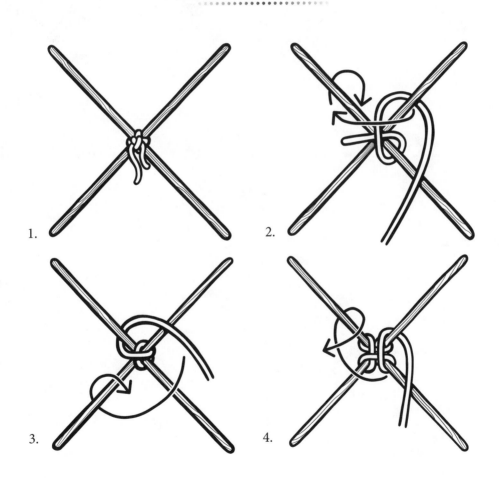

1.

2.

3.

4.

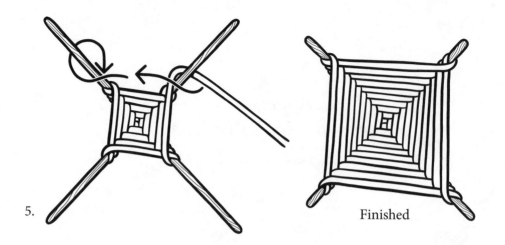

5.

Finished

Bibliography

Antony, Martin M., and Richard P. Swinson. *When Perfect Isn't Good Enough: Strategies for Coping with Perfectionism*. Oakland, CA: New Harbinger Publications, 2009.

Barrett, Hilary. *I Ching: Walking Your Path, Creating Your Future*. London, UK: Arcturus Publishing LTD, 2018.

Bartlett, Robert C., and Susan D. Collins. *Aristotle's Nicomachean Ethics*. Chicago, IL: University of Chicago Press, 2012.

Bates, Brian. *The Way of Wyrd: Tales of an Anglo-Saxon Sorcerer*. London, UK: Hay House, 2005.

Blake, Deborah. *Midsummer: Rituals, Recipes, & Lore for Litha*. Woodbury, MN: Llewellyn Publications, 2015.

Blavatsky, H. P. *The Complete Works of H.P. Blavatsky: Isis Unveiled; a Master-Key to the Mysteries of Ancient and Modern Science and Theology*. Pasadena, CA: Theosophical University Press, 1988.

Brackett, Marc. *Permission to Feel: The Power of Emotional Intelligence to Achieve Well-Being and Success*. New York, NY: Celadon Books, 2020.

Bradford, Michael. *The Healing Energy of Your Hands*. Freedom, CA: Crossing Press, 1995.

Brennan, Barbara. *Core Light Healing: My Personal Journey and Advanced Healing Concepts for Creating the Life You Long to Live*. Carlsbad, CA: Hay House, 2017.

Burgo, Joseph. *Why Did I Do That? Psychological Defense Mechanisms and the Hidden Ways They Shape Our Lives*. Chapel Hill, NC: New Rise Press, 2012.

Campbell, Joseph, *The Hero with a Thousand Faces.*, 3rd ed. Novato, CA: New World Library, 2008.

Carson, Rick. *Taming Your Gremlin: A Surprisingly Simple Method for Getting Out of Your Own Way*. Revised edition. New York, NY: William Morrow, 2003.

Chambers, John. *The Metaphysical World of Isaac Newton: Alchemy, Prophecy, and the Search for Lost Knowledge*. Rochester, VT: Destiny Books, 2018.

Cicero, Chic, Sandra Tabatha Cicero, and Israel Regardie. *Gold: Israel Regardie's Lost Book of Alchemy*. Woodbury, MN: Llewellyn Publications, 2015.

Connor, Kerri. *Ostara: Rituals, Recipes, & Lore for the Spring Equinox*. Woodbury, MN: Llewellyn Publications, 2015

D'Aoust, Maja and Adam Parfrey. *The Secret Source: The Law of Attraction Is One of Seven Ancient Hermetic Laws—Here Are the Other Six*. Port Townsend, WA: Process Media, 2007

Dale, Cyndi, and Richard Wehrman. *The Subtle Body: An Encyclopedia of Your Energetic Anatomy*. Boulder, CO: Sounds True, 2009.

Demartini, John F. *Values Factor: The Secret to Creating an Inspired and Fulfilling Life*. New York, NY: Berkley, 2013.

Devine, Megan. *It's Ok That You're Not Ok: Meeting Grief and Loss in a Culture That Doesn't Understand*. Boulder, CO: Sounds True, 2017.

Dugan, Ellen. *Autumn Equinox: The Enchantment of Mabon*. Woodbury, MN: Llewellyn Publications, 2005.

Eden, Donna, David Feinstein, Brooks Garten, and Cindy Cohn. *Energy Medicine: Balancing Your Body's Energies for Optimal Health, Joy, and Vitality*. Expanded edition. New York, NY: Tarcher Perigree, 2008.

Feinstein, David. *Ethics Handbook for Energy Healing Practitioners*. Fulton, CA: Energy Psychology Press, 2011.

Foote, Jeffrey, Carrie Wilkens, Nicole Kosanke, and Stephanie Higgs. *Beyond Addiction: How Science and Kindness Help People Change*. Reprinted. New York, NY: Scribner, 2014.

Gerber, Richard. *Vibrational Medicine: The #1 Handbook of Subtle-Energy Therapies.* Rochester, VT: Bear & Co., 2001.

Greenspan, Miriam. *Healing through the Dark Emotions: The Wisdom of Grief, Fear, and Despair.* Reprint edition. Boulder, CO: Shambhala, 2004.

Harner, Michael J. *The Way of the Shaman.* San Francisco, CA: HarperOne, 1990.

Hauck, Dennis William. *The Emerald Tablet: Alchemy for Personal Transformation.* New York, NY: Penguin Compass, 1999.

Huang, Taoist Master Alfred. *The Complete I Ching: The Definitive Translation.* Rochester, VT: Inner Traditions, 2010.

Hughes, Kristoffer. *As the Last Leaf Falls: A Pagan's Perspective on Death, Dying & Bereavement.* Woodbury, MN: Llewellyn Publications, 2020.

Ingerman, Sandra, and Hank Wesselbank. *Awakening to the Spirit World: The Shamanic Path of Direct Revelation.* Boulder, CO: Sounds True, Inc., 2010.

Jung, C. G. *Collected Works of C.G. Jung, Volume 6: Psychological Types.* Princeton, NJ: Princeton University Press, 2014.

———. *Memories, Dream, Reflections.* New York, NY: Vintage Books, 1965.

Jung, C. G., and Sonu Shamdasani. *The Red Book = Liber Novus.* New York, NY: W.W. Norton, 2012.

Light, Heidi. *Ethics in Energy Medicine: Boundaries and Guidelines for Intuitive and Energetic Practices.* Berkeley, CA: North Atlantic Books, 2018.

Lin, Keh-Ming. *Wounded Healers: Tribulations and Triumphs of Pioneering Psychotherapists.* Cambridge, UK: Cambridge University Press, 2020.

Lönnrot Elias, and Keith Bosley. *The Kalevala: An Epic Poem after Oral Tradition.* Oxford, UK: Oxford University Press, 2008.

Malkin, Craig. *Rethinking Narcissism: The Bad-and Surprising Good-about Feeling Special.* New York, NY: HarperWave, 2015.

Mankey, Jason. *Llewellyn's Little Book of Yule.* Woodbury, MN: Llewellyn Publications. 2020

Manning, Doug. *Don't Take My Grief Away from Me.* 3rd edition. Hereford, TX: InSight Books, 2011.

Marquis, Melanie. *Beltane: Rituals, Recipes, & Lore for May Day*. Woodbury, MN: Llewellyn Publications, 2015.

———. *Lughnasadh: Rituals, Recipes & Lore for Lammas*. Woodbury, MN: Llewellyn Publications, 2015.

Markale, Jean. *The Pagan Mysteries of Halloween: Celebrating the Dark Half of the Year*. Rochester, VT: Inner Traditions, 2001.

Maslow, A. H. *Motivation and Personality*. New York, NY: Harper & Row, 1954.

———. *The Farther Reaches of Human Nature*. Fourth printing. New York, NY: Viking, 1973.

Maté, Gabor. *In the Realm of Hungry Ghosts: Close Encounters with Addiction*. Berkeley, CA: North Atlantic Books, 2010.

Matthews, Caitlín, and John Matthews. *Walkers between the Worlds: The Western Mysteries from Shaman to Magus*. Rochester, VT: Inner Traditions International, 2004.

May, Gerald G. *Addiction & Grace: Love and Spirituality in the Healing of Addiction*. San Francisco, CA: Harper San Francisco, 1988.

Neal, Carl F. *Imbolc: Rituals, Recipes & Lore for Brigid's Day*. Woodbury, MN: Llewellyn Publications, 2015.

Ogilvy, Guy. *The Great Wizards of Antiquity: The Dawn of Western Magic and Alchemy*. Woodbury, MN: Llewellyn Publications, 2019.

Pesznecker, Susan Moonwriter. *Yule: Rituals, Recipes & Lore for the Winter Solstice*. Woodbury, MN: Llewellyn Publications, 2015.

Potter-Efron, Ronald T., and Patricia S. Potter-Efron. *Letting Go of Shame: Understanding How Shame Affects Your Life*. Center City, MN: Hazelden, 1989.

Prechtel, Martín. *Secrets of the Talking Jaguar: Memoirs from the Living Heart of a Mayan Village*. New York, NY: Tarcher Perigree, 1999.

Raedisch, Linda. *Night of the Witches: Folklore, Traditions & Recipes for Celebrating Walpurgis Night*. Woodbury, MN: Llewellyn Publications, 2011.

———. *The Old Magic of Christmas: Yuletide Traditions for the Darkest Days of the Year*. Woodbury, MN: Llewellyn Publications, 2013.

Rajchel, Diana. *Mabon—Rituals, Recipes and Lore for the Autumn Equinox*. Woodbury, MN: Llewellyn Publications, 2015.

Rajchel, Diana. *Samhain: Rituals, Recipes & Lore for Halloween*. Woodbury, MN: Llewellyn Publications, 2015.

Rogers, Barb. *Twenty-Five Words: How the Serenity Prayer Can Save Your Life*. San Francisco, CA: Red Wheel/Weiser, 2005.

Rogers, Nicholas. *Halloween: From Pagan Ritual to Party Night*. Oxford, UK: Oxford University Press, 2003

Rowan, John. *Subpersonalities: The People Inside Us*. London, UK: Routledge, 1990.

Skal, David J. *Death Makes a Holiday: A Cultural History of Halloween*. Living Sacrifice Book. Co, 2005.

Simon, Sidney B., Leland W. Howe, and Howard Kirschenbaum. *Values Clarification*. Revised ed. Boston, MA: Grand Central Publishing, 2009.

Small, Jacquelyn. *Awakening in Time: The Journey from Codependence to Co-Creation*. Austin, TX: Eupsychian Press, 2000.

Small, Jacquelyn. *Becoming Naturally Therapeutic: a Return to the True Essence of Helping*. New York, NY: Bantam, 1990.

Small, Jacquelyn. *Transformers: The Artists of Self-Creation*. Marina del Rey, CA: DeVorss Publications, 1994.

Smith, Tiffany Watt. *The Book of Human Emotions: An Encyclopedia of Feeling from Anger to Wanderlust*. London, UK: Profile Books, 2015.

Stone, Joshua David. *Soul Psychology: How to Clear Negative Emotions and Spiritualize Your Life*. New York: Ballantine Wellspring, Ballantine Pub. Group, 1999

Temple, Della. *Tame Your Inner Critic: Find Peace & Contentment to Live Your Life on Purpose*. Lyons, CO: Button Rock Press, 2019.

The Three Initiates. *The Kybalion*. New York, NY: Jeremy P. Tarcher/Penguin, 2008.

Underland-Rosow, Vicki. *Shame: Spiritual Suicide*. Shorewood, MN: Waterford Publications, 1995.

Villoldo, Alberto. *The Illumination Process: A Shamanic Guide to Transforming Toxic Emotions into Wisdom, Power, and Grace*. Carlsbad, CA: Hay House, 2017.

Weatherstone, Lunaea. *Tending Brigid's Flame: Awaken to the Celtic Goddess of the Hearth, Temple, and Forge.* Woodbury, MN: Llewellyn Publications, 2015.

Weber, Courtney. *Brigid: History, Mystery, and Magick of the Celtic Goddess.* San Francisco, CA: Red Wheel/Weiser, 2015.

Whitfield, Charles L. *Boundaries and Relationships: Knowing, Protecting, and Enjoying the Self.* Deerfield Beach, FL: Health Communications, Inc., 2010.

———. *Co-Dependence: Healing the Human Condition: The New Paradigm for Helping Professionals and People in Recovery.* Deerfield Beach, FL: Health Communications, Inc, 1991

———. *Not Crazy: You May Not Be Mentally Ill* Atlanta, GA: Muse House Press, 2011

———. *Wisdom to Know the Difference: Core Issues in Relationships, Recovery and Living.* Atlanta, GA: Muse House Press, 2012.

Wilhelm, Richard, and Cary F. Baynes. *The I Ching; or Book of Changes (Bollingen Series XIX).* Princeton, NJ: Princeton University Press, 1967.

Wilkinson, James John Garth, *The Book of Edda Called Völuspá: A Study in Its Scriptural and Spiritual Correspondences*, Facsimile reproduction (1897; repr., Whitefish, MT: Kessinger Publishing, 2009).

Williamson, Marianne. *A Return to Love.* New York, NY: Harper Collins, 1993.

To Write to the Author

If you wish to contact the author or would like more information about this book, please write to the author in care of Llewellyn Worldwide Ltd. and we will forward your request. Both the author and the publisher appreciate hearing from you and learning of your enjoyment of this book and how it has helped you. Llewellyn Worldwide Ltd. cannot guarantee that every letter written to the author can be answered, but all will be forwarded. Please write to:

Tiffany Lazic
℅ Llewellyn Worldwide
2143 Wooddale Drive
Woodbury, MN 55125-2989
Please enclose a self-addressed stamped envelope for reply,
or $1.00 to cover costs. If outside the U.S.A., enclose
an international postal reply coupon.

Many of Llewellyn's authors have websites with additional information and resources. For more information, please visit our website at http://www.llewellyn.com.

Notes

Notes

Notes